John C. Wolfe is the former Chief Speechwriter to former New York Governor George E. Pataki. He has worked as an advertising copywriter, a magazine editor and the Senior Writer for the *Monroe County Executive* in Rochester. He was Pataki's Chief Speechwriter for nearly ten years. He spent the remaining two years of Pataki's tenure as Senior Writer to the SUNY Chancellor in Albany. In 2007, he retreated to the Adirondacks and worked as a Zoning Officer in Chestertown, New York. His writing was limited to a series of published op-eds in several newspapers, including the *New York Times, the Baltimore Sun* and the *Times of Israel*. He began writing about his battle with alcoholism in 2014.

Names in this story have been changed in certain circumstances, but other than that, it's pure, easily-authenticated non-fiction.

A DAY OF CLARITY

John C. Wolfe

A DAY OF CLARITY

Vanguard Press

VANGUARD PAPERBACK

© Copyright 2023
John C. Wolfe

The right of John C. Wolfe to be identified as author of
this work has been asserted by them in accordance with the
Copyright, Designs and Patents Act 1988.

All Rights Reserved

No reproduction, copy or transmission of this publication
may be made without written permission.
No paragraph of this publication may be reproduced,
copied or transmitted save with the written permission of the publisher,
or in accordance with the provisions
of the Copyright Act 1956 (as amended).

Any person who commits any unauthorised act in relation to
this publication may be liable to criminal
prosecution and civil claims for damages.

A CIP catalogue record for this title is
available from the British Library.

ISBN 978 1 80016 613 4

*Vanguard Press is an imprint of
Pegasus Elliot Mackenzie Publishers Ltd.*
www.pegasuspublishers.com

First Published in 2023

**Vanguard Press
Sheraton House Castle Park
Cambridge England**

Printed & Bound in Great Britain

Dedicated to the truest hero in this story, my mother, Terry McConnell.

Chapter One

The Family Strain

"YOUR THEORY IS ABOUT TO BE TESTED," said Charles as we approached a group of about ten NYPD officers huddled at the corner. At the last bodega, I had bought two forty-ouncers to drink for our long walk from East 39th street to Lower Manhattan.

Charles, a sergeant with the New York State Police, said it was illegal to walk down the street with an open container of alcohol. I said it was perfectly legal if the container was in a brown bag. Both of us were drunk enough to let the police decide who was right.

It was after eleven o'clock at night and dead quiet. Aside from the police and National Guardsmen, Third Avenue was deserted.

Earlier that day, more than three thousand people had been killed when two planes flew into the World Trade Center. That was' why Charles and I had decided to get drunk and walk from our hotel in Midtown back to Ground Zero, where we had spent our entire miserable day.

Beers in hand, we strolled right past the small crowd of cops. A few of them even said, "Hi" and "What's up?"

That's the only 9/11 story I've ever felt comfortable sharing. I wasn't traumatized by what I saw at Ground Zero on September eleventh. But for over a decade, I've turned away from the subject entirely. I don't know why, and I've never cared. Recently, though, I've thought long and hard about it and studied the whole issue right down to its boring, selfish, unspectacular truth.

I don't like talking about September eleventh for the same reason I don't like talking about a lot of other things that happened when I was drinking. It's the same reason I don't like talking to blind people about the color red. I just don't know what to say or where to start.

When the subject comes up, I just block it out. Today I know why.

It has everything to do with alcohol and nothing to do with 9/11.

ABOUT TWENTY-SEVEN YEARS EARLIER, as a sophomore at Springfield College, I was in my dorm room getting ready for a wrestling tournament. I weighed in with the rest of the wrestling team then came back to my room looking for something to eat and wound up drinking with my friends instead. At first, I didn't think having one beer would affect my ability to wrestle. But one beer turned into five, then five turned into a pint of Southern Comfort and a wager. The bet was that I could get drunk and still win my next match against a very good wrestler from West Point who had already beaten me twice.

I walked out feeling more confident than ever. He was wearing a hard-shell face mask to protect a broken nose. As soon as the whistle blew, I went at him more aggressively than I usually would, trying to stand him up straight, tie up his arms and set him up for a Greco-Roman-style throw. It was a cocky and reckless tactic to use against a good wrestler and it pissed off the coaches in both of our corners — not to mention his entire team and most of the crowd.

My antagonistic, alcohol-inspired attack startled him enough to throw off his game and I wound up scoring a two-point takedown in the first twenty seconds — something I was rarely able to do against him. I wasn't drunk per se, but with a pint of liquor and five beers in my system, I was inebriated enough to throw all caution to the wind. I took him down again in the middle of the first period, but at the start of the next period, I began to feel the energy draining from my body. I was still winning 4–2.

I held my lead until the middle of the second period, when he started on top. I stood up twice, trying to escape, but both times he brought me back down to the mat — hard. I was out of breath and my arms were burning with lactic acid. I tried another escape and he brought me down again. I complained to the referee that he should be warned for stalling. The ref brushed it off. The next time we were on the mat, I threw a hard elbow straight to his face, right where his nose would have been without the mask.

His coaches, his teammates and most of the crowd went berserk. I was disqualified and escorted to the locker room. I left that night thinking

I had won. In a way, I had. I used to get really worked up and nervous before certain matches. Thanks to the beer and Southern Comfort, that didn't happen this time.

They say everyone has bad moments. I liked the concept of bombarding those moments out of my life with lots of beer and one or two shots of vodka. From the beginning, my drinking habits were different from everyone else's. They drank Thursday through Sunday. I drank Thursday through Sunday too, but I also drank Monday through Wednesday. They did most of their drinking in bars; I drank in the dorm. They drank to get laid; I drank to get drunk.

I honestly couldn't understand how my friends could stop drinking on Sunday and not touch another drop of alcohol until Thursday. Getting drunk put them in such a good mood on the weekend, so why not do it every day?

At the time, I thought it was a money issue and they were just irresponsible spenders because they were wasting their money on pricey beer in bars while I was drinking bargain beer back in the room. I'd spend eight dollars for a case of America's Best and get shit-faced. They'd spend four times as much in a bar and barely catch a buzz — and the next day they didn't have any beer money for the rest of the week. I thought I was just better with finances. I couldn't think of any other reason they'd stay sober all week.

ONE FRIDAY EVENING IN 1987, four of us were in my dorm room trying to shotgun a case of cheap beer in thirty minutes. To shotgun a beer, you use a key to punch a hole near the bottom of the can, then put your mouth over the hole while pulling the tab to open the top. If you do it right, the beer drains straight down your throat in about three seconds. If you do it wrong, you're an idiot and it takes about ten seconds. Since the only point of the game is to get drunk, it's impossible to lose.

Before we could finish, my father called and ruined the game. My father never called. But now he wanted to have our first-ever serious conversation where I wasn't in trouble. As soon as I heard his voice, I realized something was wrong and I cleared the room. I thought he was getting ready to tell me he had cancer and I froze in fear.

"Your mother knows I'm talking to you," he said. "I need to get out from underneath this thing so I'm going away for a while but I'll be back and everything's going to be fine."

I didn't know what to say because I had no idea what in the hell he was talking about. I just continued to listen, hoping he'd say something to give me a clue about what he was trying to tell me.

"It's not the end of the world," he said. "I just need to get this monkey off my back."

What monkey? I thought he was drunk. I knew I was.

By then, one of my friends had tiptoed back into the room to make sure everything was okay. While looking at my friend, I said to my father, "So you're going to go get a monkey off your back"?

My friend gave a confused look. He didn't know what it meant either. Then my father said something about "booze and pills."

I talked to my mom right after that. "What pills?" I asked her.

In addition to being an alcoholic, my dad was addicted to a narcotic painkiller, which he was prescribing to himself. When I was younger, I used to crawl under the hanging suit coats in my father's closet looking for loose change. The plush carpet was always littered with pink pills. Turns out, they were Darvon, a popular narcotic among addicts with an impressive street value. If I had known that at the time, I would have swallowed a few to see how it felt. God only knows what would have happened after that.

When I went home a few weeks later, my mom was alone in our gigantic house and my dad was at a treatment hospital in New Canaan, Connecticut. The next time I saw my father, he was a Bible-thumping Alcoholics Anonymous groupie with an earring and a tiny braided ponytail fashioned from the one strand of hair left on the back of his head.

Never, I told myself.

But one night, he asked me to go to an AA meeting with him. The only reason I went was because my mother told me to. "Just go," she said. "You need to see what he's doing. Do it for me."

We went to a seven pm meeting in the basement of a church on Highland Avenue in Rochester.

As I followed my father and his ponytail down the steps into a meeting room, a bunch of mostly young people cheerfully welcomed him with "Hi John" and "Hey Doc." A girl in her twenties who looked like a deadhead rushed up and gave my dad a hug. "Yay, Doc is here," she said.

I was speechless. *My dad hugs people now? And excuse it, but what's up with Doc?* My dad hated that name. "Call me an asshole if you want," he once told my girlfriend, "but stop calling me 'Doc.' That's what my Medicaid patients call me and I hate it."

I thought it was odd that he didn't forbid his new Manson family of alcoholics from using the word. I couldn't wait to hear what my brother Greg had to say about all of this.

A few days later, me and my friend Brian Sweeny were in the kitchen of my parent's house. We were heading out to Preps, a bar in downtown Rochester where we always ordered pitchers of beer four at a time. My brother, Mark Glickman, Jeff Vigneri and Rich Tassone were waiting for us in the driveway. My father came in and said he wanted to have a word with me so Brian went outside.

My dad said, "You know, drinking is a choice, but it's not your choice if it affects my sobriety."

I was stunned. My father and I didn't have conversations like this.

"I'm no different from him," I said, while pointing to Brian on the other side of the glass door. By the time my father looked, Brian, who heard what I said, was nowhere in sight. "I'm just one of five guys going out for a few beers," I said. "What about [my brother] Greg?"

"You're not like them," he said.

It's amazing how often my dad left me at a loss for words. This wasn't just some off-the-cuff remark; it was an announcement. I didn't know what to think about it then, and thirty years later, I still don't know what I think about it. I've contemplated it drunk and I've contemplated it sober. I didn't know what to think about it either way.

For all I know, his alcoholic father dropped the same line on him. It didn't influence my behavior in or out of the house, but it was kind of a big deal. It was his way of saying: "I see you've caught the bug, but I'm just getting over the same thing and I don't want to re-catch the family strain, so stay the hell away from me." Fair enough.

I didn't go home for a long time after that, mostly because I didn't want another sermon on drinking from my father and his ponytail. And I sure as hell didn't want the scrutiny of my mom, a former Emergency Room nurse and a professional in the alcoholism and chemical dependency field. She could smell alcohol on my breath before I even got home.

Our house had two staircases. When I came home late at night, no matter how quiet I was, I'd hear my mom walking down the front staircase. Then she'd walk toward me slowly looking directly into my eyes without saying a word. It was ten times scarier than being interrogated by a cop. A lot of times, as soon as I heard her going down the front staircase, I'd run up the back staircase and disappear into one of the many unused rooms. Other times, she'd wait for me in the kitchen like a triage nurse.

But I was good — evilly good — at reassuring her. I told her what she wanted to believe about my behavior, just enough to give her peace of mind until the next time I came home drunk.

On one of those nights, I promised I'd go with her and my father to talk to someone about my drinking. That someone was a guy named Bob. He was the Director of the Chemical Dependency unit of a major hospital, a position my mother assumed a few years later. He was also a recovering alcoholic and my father's AA sponsor.

The four of us met in Bob's office. Since I was there against my will, I wanted them to know I was going to be stubborn and uncooperative. All three of them were experts in this area.

My mom was a nurse and a chemical dependency professional. My dad was a medical doctor with a ponytail. And Bob was an addiction specialist. I knew why I was there and I knew that it would look bad if I was defensive. But I was ready to deflect any insinuation that I had a drinking problem.

At first, that's what I did. When they asked me why I was drinking every day, I said it only seemed that way because they only saw me when I was home on break from college. When they said I was at risk of being an alcoholic because my father and grandfather were alcoholics, I said I had nothing in common with either of them. When they said I was in denial, I said, "No I'm not."

After twenty minutes, Bob was exasperated. At one point, he looked at my mother and clenched both of his fists in front of him and said, "Uggg! It makes you just want to shake him and say, 'Listen to me!'"

"It's no big deal; I'm just drinking with my friends," I said.

I could tell they weren't going to let me go home until they made at least some progress with me, however little. Towards the end, they would have been satisfied with anything. I agreed to drink less, read some pamphlets and think about everything we had talked about.

In other words, they accomplished nothing because I wasn't going to do any of that. I wanted to get out of there so badly I would have agreed to anything — unless they asked me not to drink that night.

Chapter Two

Life with Eric and Andy… and Father Jim

I DROVE BACK TO SPRINGFIELD THE NEXT DAY. It was my senior year and I was living off-campus with Eric Jackson, an obnoxious, cocky womanizer who was my closest friend, enabler and accomplice throughout college.

We formed an instant friendship during the first week of our freshman year in Gulick Hall at Springfield College. The first time I saw him, he was running through the female floors of our coed dorm wearing nothing but a dark blue ski mask. The first time he saw me, I was javelin-tossing fluorescent light tubes out of a second-story dorm window.

Yet somehow, it still managed to go downhill from there. For four years, we played off one another to break the barriers of bad taste and rotten behavior, from robbing churches and dropping acid to drinking urine and working as male strippers.

At the beginning of our senior year, we left the dorms and moved into a house owned by Andy, a burly, middle-aged, former Navy SEAL and Vietnam veteran who had graduated from The Citadel where he played football. He was a Springfield firefighter and a lacrosse referee — a loud and imposing man's man, complete with a big, bushy Mike Ditka mustache.

That was the public Andy. The private Andy was what the gay community might call a "flam boy" — a big, middle-aged, effeminate gay man who liked to roleplay as the naughty sissy, running around the house on his tiptoes, giggling and trying to spank our asses with a kitchen spatula.

In 1988, that was the kind of thing people still kept in the closet. But when Andy wasn't screwing around, he was the adult presence and role model Eric and I needed in our life. We always respected him and we grew to love him.

The sissy play was irritating if you weren't in the mood to run away from a groping, three-hundred-pound horn-dog with an egg turner, but he'd snap out of it in an instant when we asked him to. He called it his "naughty mode" and ninety percent of the time it was funny.

The other ten percent usually included "Father Jim," a creepy friend of Andy's who was a Catholic priest and the chaplain for the Massachusetts State Police.

Father Jim used to come to the house late at night for one of Andy's specialized, therapeutic massages. Andy had this special massage tool. It was a softball-sized motor that strapped to the back of his hand to create a vibrating sensation in his fingers.

I let him do it to me once, briefly, on my back — only because he promised not to snap into sissy mode in the middle of it. He contained himself for about nine seconds. I said, "Wow, that feels cool."

He said, "Roll over, sweetie, and I'll make it twice as cool." And he sat there laughing his ass off as I rolled off the bed and ran for my life.

Father Jim came to the house when his bad back was acting up. Eric and I weren't stupid, but we played stupid anyway because we just didn't care. Eric didn't care because he lived in the basement. I didn't care because, by the time Father Jim got there at night, I was too drunk to care.

Occasionally, Father Jim would swing by in his Cossack and collar, which added a whole new element of awkward to the situation. Still, Eric and I respected Andy enough to not bust his balls about it — even though he was a relentless ballbuster.

Father Jim came by one afternoon while I was winding down from a morning of classes with a twelve-pack of Miller Lite and Knots Landing. He walked into the living room in his full priest attire and he stared at the twelve-pack long enough to make his disapproval obvious. "Andy just ran to the store," I said. "He'll be back in a minute."

"Yes, I saw him going down the road," he said, as he sat down in the chair across from me.

After a minute of small talk, he said, "You know, Andy came to me for a word of advice and it concerned you. He expressed some concern about your drinking."

"I'm in college," I said. "Everyone drinks."

"I'm not an expert on that issue and I don't judge," he said. "You can come to me and I will steer you in the right direction. Are you Catholic?"

"Okay, thanks," I said. "I don't know if I'm Catholic. I'm Presbyterian or Protestant… whichever one is the P in WASP."

"There's a surprise," he said, extra snottily.

About eight hours later, Father Jim came back. It was about eleven o'clock at night on a Friday night, he wasn't wearing his priest clothes and he was visibly drunk.

"Hello, Father," I said. "Andy's in his room and I was just heading downstairs to see Eric." He didn't say anything.

When I went downstairs, Eric was poking the seeds out of a pile of pot.

"Father Jim is upstairs," I said. "Can I hang out down here?"

"Yeah, I'm heading out with Kristen soon," he said. "Wanna get high?"

"I'm already drunk," I said. "Pot will put me in a coma, so yes, I want to get high."

We shot-gunned a few beers for effect, then took way too many deep bong hits. "I think we smoked too much," he said. "Now I don't feel like going out."

He told me to hang out and finish the pile. "Smoke a little more, then go upstairs," he said. "Make sure you do the Sign of the Cross before you drop to your knees."

As soon as he left, the combination of pot and alcohol hit me like a train and I was seeing everything in triplicate. I passed out right there on the couch in the basement.

I'm not sure what woke me up. It could have been Father Jim's hand fumbling with my zipper or maybe it was his mouth on my ear. When I realized what was happening, I body-rolled right off the couch and across the floor, a move I'd learned while getting massages from Andy. Father Jim didn't say a word. He just sat on the edge of the couch with a blank stare on his face.

"You were sleepwalking," I told him. "I'll get Andy to help you back upstairs."

And that was the end of it. Andy said Father Jim drank too much and didn't know what he was doing. I'm sure Andy knew why Father Jim went downstairs but I didn't burden him with the details. I just said he was trying to get in the wrong bed.

I didn't need to make a big deal about it. I didn't need to kick Father Jim's ass to prove I wasn't' gay. I didn't need counseling. I didn't need to rebel against organized religion. I didn't need to barge into one of his services and call him a fraud in front of his flock. He got drunk and made a mistake, a defense I'd be using for the rest of my life.

Besides, to me, getting groped by a drunk priest was a story I could tell repeatedly, and it would never get old. I never did that, though — not because it haunted me, but because it got replaced by other stories that were just as funny but more believable.

That same year, Eric talked me into going to the Magic Lantern one night to apply for jobs as bar-backs. It was a giant strip club on the outskirts of Springfield, and Eric had heard they needed bar-backs.

On the night we went, it was "Jack and Jill Night" which meant there would be male dancers with a female audience on one side, and vice versa. One of the professional male dancers canceled at the last moment, which just happened to be the same moment Eric and I strutted in there looking for jobs.

We were standing in the kitchen when the owner, Tony, caught a glimpse of us as he breezed through the kitchen. "I'll be right with you guys," he said.

Almost simultaneously, we looked at each other and said, "Danny DeVito." That's exactly who Tony looked and sounded like. Then we heard him squealing something about the "goddamn ice machine."

Right then and there, Tony had given Eric and I the gift of a lifetime: the sheer joy of mimicking his bitchy, 1930's gangster dialect. When he came back to the kitchen, Tony was suspiciously happy to see us.

"I'll hire you guys to stock the bar and work in the kitchen," he said. "But I have an idea for tonight. Can you guys dance? I'll pay each of you sixty bucks."

Two hours later, Eric and I were dressed like gay prostitutes, and instead of "John and Eric," we were "Butch Cassidy and the California Kid." We agreed — Eric agreed for both of us — to split the absent dancer's half-hour set and go on stage for fifteen minutes apiece. "We'll call it the 'audition set' for the 'All-College Male Revue.'"

We had a couple of hours to pick out outfits from a big box of stuff that other male strippers had left behind over the years. Tony told the bartender to give us whatever we wanted, but added, "Just don't let them get drunk." If he didn't want us to get drunk, he shouldn't have given us a dressing room in the basement where they kept all the liquor.

Dancing naked in front of drunk women was nothing new for Eric. He worked the stage like a pro, made a lot of money in tips, and miraculously kept his G-string on the entire time. He was surprisingly smooth, even classy.

I wasn't so smooth. First of all, I couldn't dance so I needed to find a different way to entertain seventy-five women for the duration of four songs. The DJ told me to keep most of my clothes on until the fourth and final song. But when I came out to ZZ Top's "LaGrange," I got caught up in the moment and took everything off in the first thirty seconds.

For the next three songs, I stayed off the stage, opting instead to work the floor doing lap and table dances for wildly-intoxicated women while stealing their drinks. The only people not cringing were the ones who were too drunk to care, and even they were cringing.

Eric said it looked like I was committing a battery of domestic violence offenses out there. Tony banned me from the stage forever. "You're like a goddamn gorilla," he said. "You're going to get this place shut down."

"I did fine," I told him. "They gave me $21 in tips."

"They gave you money because they were afraid of you," he said. "They were paying you to go away."

Tony liked me, though, and he gave me regular hours as a bar-back, bouncer, and eventually, manager.

After graduation, my girlfriend was doing a summer internship in Florida so I decided to keep working at the Magic Lantern until she was done. I moved into the house Tony owned next door to the dance club with three of the dancers.

One Saturday night, five bouncers were trying to remove a guy who was picking fights and groping the dancers. At the door, he called one of the bouncers a "juiced-up half-breed," and I coldcocked him. He pressed charges and the police gave me a court appearance ticket for Monday.

I locked up the Magic Lantern that night and went next door, then came back two hours later for more beer. The back door was unlocked and when I walked in the big main room, I saw light coming from under the door of the back dressing room. I couldn't hear anything going on inside so I opened the door and turned on the lights.

Tony, a family man, was laying on his back naked as the bottom end of a sixty-nine with one of the male dancers. At first, neither one of them reacted to me at all. After a few seconds, Tony pulled the penis out of his mouth and calmly said, "Close the door, John."

That's when I suspected that the rumors about Tony being gay might be true.

I didn't stick around for an explanation. As soon as I was sober enough to drive the next morning, I packed my stuff and hightailed it back to Rochester. Awkward as it was, I wasn't running away from Tony, although I knew I'd never be able to talk to him again without seeing his hand on that penis, as he casually pulled it out of his mouth to have a word with me.

Mostly, I was running away from a court appearance that I knew wasn't going to go well for me.

As soon as I got back, I called Dennis, the foreman of a lawn crew I used to work on during my summers home from college, before everyone got uptight with political correctness.

"Cracker John!" he said.

"Uncle Tom!" I replied.

"Oh good, we're still friends," he said. He spared me the trouble of having to ask. "Come help us out," he said. "We need a white boy so we can get into nice places for lunch."

I went back to work with them the next day. It was the same group of guys I worked with before. After a week, they accused me of going off to college and coming back full of shit.

In previous summers, they laughed at my stories, but they weren't buying any of the material I brought back from Springfield. They began making jokes about "A priest, a landlord and a strip club owner" walking into a bar. And of course, they wondered why all the stories I took the time to fabricate had gay underpinnings.

The following summer, my girlfriend and I got married in her hometown, Norwich, Connecticut, then bought a house in Rochester. In the months leading up to the wedding, I tried to scale back my drinking in an honest effort to be more responsible.

I didn't drink at all for about two months. But the night before the wedding, my groomsmen — led by Eric Jackson — took me on a surprise trip to the Magic Lantern. It was late and they were just closing for the night, but Tony, who was coming to the wedding the next day, happily opened the cooler doors and let us have free reign of the front bar. I tried to drink moderately, but by the time we left, I had drunk about fifteen beers, not to mention four kamikazes.

I was hungover for the wedding and it didn't take my groomsmen long to convince me that the best cure for the hangover was to keep drinking, which is what I did at the reception and what I continued to do when I got back to Rochester.

I didn't feel like I needed to drink every day, but I did it anyway. I needed something to look forward to at the end of the day, and drinking always put me in the perfect mood. But I only got drunk on the weekends… and sometimes Thursdays and Sundays.

I was trying to figure out how to turn my English degree from Springfield College into a career. I didn't know what I wanted to do, but my mother was throwing out ten ideas a day so finally I took one of her suggestions: Substitute teaching.

That landed me in the small town of Elba, New York, just east of Buffalo, which prides itself as the "Potato Capital of the World," even though it's not. I was a permanent substitute teacher, and the head varsity wrestling coach. I loved the coaching part, but as a permanent sub, I was nothing more than a spitball target at the front of the classroom.

After a few months, the principal asked me if I was interested in getting out of the classroom for three months to teach a seventh and eighth grade girl's gym class.

"These are wonderful girls," he said. "They need someone like you; you're a coach and they'll respect you."

No. They were evil and what they really needed was jail time, lots of it. Thirteen-year-old girls are calculating, manipulative and heartless and they will ruin your world just for a laugh.

I was in the gymnasium office one day after class when one of the girls ran out of the locker-room screaming for help.

"Mr Wolfe, you need to do something," she said. "Katie slammed her head on the floor and she's bleeding all over the place!" Other girls were also screaming for me from inside the locker room.

"Make sure everyone's dressed!" I yelled before running in.

Once I was in the locker room, they formed a big circle around me and started screaming "Rape!" and "Mr Wolfe's a pervert!"

That was in 1989. If it had been 2016, I'd either be going viral on YouTube or anal in Sing Sing.

BACK THEN I WAS DRIVING A PONTIAC FIERO, which was a practical joke General Motors played on American car owners in the mid-80s. It was designed to look like a sports car, but it was made of plastic and it had a weed-eater-sized engine that fit in the trunk. The car itself was only about the size of a prize pig, but not as fast. On snow, the thing handled like a drunk wildebeest on skates.

Every night during the winter of 1989, that's what I was — a drunk wildebeest, careening here and there along a desolate county road that runs through the farmlands between Buffalo and Rochester. When the winds began whipping over the pastures, the white-outs weren't just blinding… They could make a Fiero change lanes against its will.

The first time it happened, I bounced between the guardrails on either side of the road like a pinball in a series of collisions that would have totaled a real car. But the only damage to my Fiero was a big crack. When my friend Mike West saw it the next day, he said the damage was probably covered under warranty. "I'll bet Toys 'R' Us will give you a new one," he said.

A week later, I treated my wrestlers to a night of bowling in Batavia. While they drank pitchers of soda, I drank pitchers of beer — three of them. On the way home, me and my Fiero slid off the road and landed on its side. Fortunately, the guy who came by and helped me shove it back onto the road wasn't a cop.

But it was enough to make me rethink my commuting policy. So instead of driving home after a day of substitute teaching and coaching, I'd stop in Batavia to decompress at a corner bar.

I tried to limit myself to five pints of beer before making the one-hour drive home. But there were times when I just couldn't stop. Each beer gave me more and more of a calming effect that felt helpful, healthy and necessary to me. Cutting myself off suddenly from that unwinding process felt like an unnatural shock to my system and my state of mind. After a while, I stopped trying.

At the end of the day, I just made the decision. Either I was going home or I was spending the night in Batavia. I found myself incapable of doing anything "moderate" so I took the option of "stopping at the bar" out of the equation. I knew I couldn't go there and limit myself to two, three or even five. I also couldn't afford to drink in a bar and stay in a hotel every night.

So, most nights, I picked up beer at a convenience store near the school and raced home to drink it. Sometimes I'd drink along the way, but there is literally no place to hide empties in a Fiero. They don't fit under the seat or in the console and there's no back seat — and cramming them in the glove compartment with the registration and proof of insurance didn't strike me as a brilliant idea.

About once a week, when I was especially tense, I'd end wrestling practice a little early and drive straight to the bar. I'd put off worrying about the expense of it all after I was too drunk to care.

We ended the year with a record of 7–8, a dramatic improvement from the 0–15 record they had the year before I got there. But ever since I'd stepped into a classroom of screaming kids, my eyes were wide open for something better-suited for my temperament.

I started searching for a new job the day after a kid called me an "old dork." I was never going to be a teacher, at least not a good one, unless they made it okay to hit the bad kids, which was bound to happen eventually, whether they made it okay or not.

I got a message one day from the American Resume Service, which I'd used a year earlier to "lay out" my resume. It seemed the resume they produced for me somehow migrated to the resumes they were collecting for a job opening they had in Rochester for a resume writer.

They asked me to bring in writing samples and a copy of the resume their company designed. I got the job, which entailed sitting in a one-person field office with a waiting room, and setting up appointments with people who needed resumes.

They'd come in and tell me their life story, then I'd write and design their resume on a nice Macintosh Computer (something most people still didn't own in 1990).

I thought I was doing a good job until a regional manager from American Resume Service called and said someone would be coming by my office to check in with me. A woman who looked and talked like the "Ice Princess" Lilith on *Cheers* showed up and said, "Thank you for helping out. We don't need you any longer."

I didn't know what to say so I said something stupid. "Do you want to see the resumes I've been writing?"

"No, we're all set here," she said. "Thank you."

"But wait, I've been sending copies of all the resumes I've been writing to the main office along with the checks people have been giving me," I said.

"Listen," she said. "I'm just here to keep the office open until they get someone to replace you. You're sending them resumes and that's fine, but you're only charging people thirty and forty dollars for a resume. Those checks should be four times that."

"I'm just sending you the checks they give me," I said. "Most of these people are out of work and can't afford more than that. They see the ads that say our resumes cost ten dollars and when I ask for more, they get mad and say it's false advertising."

"Our ads say, 'from ten dollars up,'" she snapped. "That means the price starts at ten dollars, which would get them nothing more than a piece of paper with their name and address typed on it."

"But who would want that?" I asked.

"Apparently, you will, so gather your things please."

I put all my stuff in a briefcase Andy had given me as a going-away present, said goodbye and started to leave.

"You forgot your name thingy," she said, pointing to the nameplate on the desk Andy had given me with the briefcase. She snickered a little as I grabbed it and left.

It was my first experience in the working world and as I walked down the hall of the office building I felt like an idiot. I was just about to open my car door when I turned around and marched back to the office.

I thought for a second, which probably wasn't long enough, then knocked on the office door.

"I'm on the phone," she barked as she opened the door. "What do you need?"

"You have no personality and you're an asshole," I said.

She just stood there and looked at me like I was boring her, like she'd heard it a thousand times.

Writing resumes isn't really writing; it's just stacking sentences. But after my brief experience in the little resume office, I knew I needed to get experience however and wherever I could so I'd have something to put on my resume and eventually build a portfolio.

Proofreading isn't really writing either, but I did it for six months to land a job as an advertising copywriter with a Young and Rubicam subsidiary.

For more than a year, I thought I had found my calling. Two things changed my mind. One, I got laid off (that was the main thing). And two, there was too much interaction with people who were chic and cool and trendy.

Instead of saying "yes," they'd say, "Yahtzee." Instead of saying, "that's great," they'd say, "that's gangbusters." One time I tried to fit in by saying "shazzam" instead of "yes" but it just wasn't in my heart.

I worked as a freelance copywriter for about a year. My first major project was rewriting the Baseball Hall of Fame's 1991 gift catalog. The Hall of Fame shipped all of it — every piece of merchandise in the catalog — to my townhouse in boxes that were stacked to the ceiling of my living room.

The next day, with a box cutter in one hand and a beer in the other, I opened the boxes and wrote a little paragraph about every item they sent me, from baseball bats to nostalgic uniforms.

To keep the project interesting, I put a little spin on the process. I would chug one beer for every product description I wrote, but if the description was more than fifty words, I would chug two beers, which was why the Hall of Fame's catalog was a lot wordier in 1991 than it was in 1990.

The featured item that year was an exquisite $2,000 solid silver baseball atop a mahogany base. They only cast fifty of them and I had the one with "2" engraved on the bottom. I wrote two hundred and fifty-two words for that, which meant that I got to chug six beers. I had just run out of beer when my friend Boz showed up with a case of Molson.

Boz drank like I did. In fact, Boz did a lot of things like I did. It was his idea to use the Baseball Hall of Fame's $2,000 Sterling Silver baseball to play bocce in the front yard. I tried to stop him.

"Are you fucking nuts? That thing is hand-engraved, minted silver," I said. "There's only fifty of them in the world."

"Come on, let's play," he said while rolling it across the grass. "They wouldn't have sent it to you if they didn't want you to use it."

Boz always had a way of explaining things to me in a way that made sense.

Chapter Three

A Work in Progression

AN IDEA CAME TO ME one night while I was guzzling beer and typing a letter to an advertising agency that was infuriating me by ignoring my phone calls and resume. It began as a fantasy revenge plan but the more I drank, the smarter the idea seemed. By the end of the night, I was a drunk genius.

The next day, I bought some supplies and a case of Miller Lite. I made three billboard signs — three feet wide and five feet long — out of extra-thick white foam core.

Using spray paint and black marker, I turned the first one into a giant prototype of my resume. The second one was just a giant headline that read, "Got Your Attention?" The last one was my phone number. Each number was about two-feet high. Under that was a headline that read, "Call me or else I'll come back tomorrow."

Late at night, I went to Rumrill-Hoyt (a large ad agency in Rochester) with the signs, a ladder and lots of heavy-duty duct tape. I plastered them straight across the front of the building, right on the giant windows of the three offices belonging to the people who were ignoring me.

The next morning, I sat in the parking lot across the street and watched people showing up to work. Several cars paused on the street and stared at the back of my signs, wondering why there were three giant white rectangles on their building.

Unfortunately, there was no way for me to witness their reactions when they walked into their offices. I could just imagine them yelling to each other:

"What does yours say?"

"Mine has his resume," says the first.

"Mine is asking if we're paying attention," says the second.

"Mine has his phone number," says the third. "And the asshole says he's coming back tomorrow."

Through a friend of a friend, I heard that the folks at Rumrill-Hoyt were talking about me that day... but not in a good way. For starters, the maintenance guys had an impossible time getting the signs off the windows. And the people in their offices, the ones I'd targeted, bitched and complained all day about the clean-up workers hanging outside of their windows.

The bigger problem for me and my fledgling reputation was that I'd apparently left a few cans of beer on the window ledges — which had the agency snobs ridiculing me as a disgruntled drunk.

The Rochester Democrat and Chronicle — which had a soft spot for social degenerates like disgruntled drunks — wrote about my exploits in an editorial about the 1990 recession. The editorial caught the attention of the owners of Rochester Business Profiles, a medium-circulation monthly magazine in Monroe County.

After a few conversations, they made me their new editor. Right off the bat, I phased out the magazine's prevaricating puff pieces about local business leaders and replaced them with commentary-laced articles on current events. Right after I was hired, I was joined by Nadine, a young art director who was just as eager to irk local officials and mock political correctness as I was.

She was a reliable drinking buddy. Whenever we were working late, I'd buy a twelve-pack of Miller Lite, which I easily drank by myself, and a six-pack of Zima, which we "shared." The legal limit for drinking and driving was still .10 and the laws weren't nearly as severe as they are today, so we didn't think twice about driving home afterward.

I only got pulled over once back then, and it was for a tail light. The officer asked me if I'd been drinking. "Yeah," I said, "but it only was four or five and it wasn't even beer... it was just Zima."

"Okay then," he said. "But you need to get that light fixed."

If I had given the same answer ten years later, I would have been arrested. It wasn't a very bright answer back then either, especially since Zima had more alcohol than beer.

After about five issues, the magazine's distribution went up dramatically. Not surprisingly, we began getting a lot of angry letters to the editor, including Congresswoman Louise Slaughter's five-page rant over an editorial in which I accused her of billing taxpayers for her manicures.

The magazine's owners loved the attention, but they were concerned about pissing off the advertisers. After the Rochester City School District hinted at a lawsuit over an article I wrote about their spending abuses, the magazine's owners got nervous and changed the name of the magazine to *The Rochesterian*.

GIVEN MY GENERAL DISTASTE for government and politics, I was surprised to get a phone call, a meeting request, and ultimately, a political appointment, from Monroe County Executive Robert L. King.

He offered me a large salary and a host of other benefits that a responsible young man with a pregnant wife should have. I didn't want to do it, and I told them that.

My wife and my mother thought I was being selfish and tried to guilt me into taking the position.

I stood my ground and told them: "I'm not giving up my free reign of unencumbered speech; I'm not surrendering my First Amendment rights to the regulations of the State; I'm not falling on a government sword just for more money and a pension."

I am not taking this job. Period. And the subject never came up again.

Sigh.

My new office was in the historic County Office Building right on Main Street; I had comprehensive dental; and my parking was validated monthly. The set hours and paid holidays were a godsend, and I was generally pleased with the college savings plan.

Up until then, I was a heavy daily drinker but the compulsion hadn't yet trickled into the work day. I drank at *The Rochesterian*, but only after five o'clock. That was my rule, a rule that lasted about three weeks into my new position, when King became the first boss to catch me drinking on the job.

We were at a fundraiser with New York City Mayor Rudy Giuliani at the Hyatt Regency Hotel in Rochester. It was seven o'clock in the evening and I wanted to drink... not a drink, to drink. I'd never had a drink in my life.

I said I was going to the bathroom. Instead, I snuck into an adjoining room where there was an open bar for the cocktail reception. I ordered three different brands of beer so it didn't look like they were all for me, which they were.

I brought them to the men's room, and while I was pretending to comb my hair while guzzling beer, King walked in and said, "Thirsty?"

I just laughed, as if he said something ridiculous.

I drove us to the event in his official County car. As we were leaving, he said, "I'll drive." That was the closest he came to mentioning it.

About a year into my job with King, a little-known state legislator named George Pataki shocked the political class with an upset victory over Mario Cuomo in the 1994 race for governor of New York State.

Pataki, a long-time friend and close colleague of King, took a vacation to celebrate his victory. He brought King with him, and at some point during the geek-getaway, the subject of speechwriters came up. Pataki said they were talking to a former speechwriter for George H.W. Bush, but they hadn't made a final decision.

Despite what King must have suspected about my drinking problem, he recommended me for the position. At first, Pataki wasn't blown away by my one year of speechwriting experience, but he threw my name in the hat as a favor to King.

Vying for the job as Pataki's speechwriter took nine months. Throughout the process, I was writing speeches for the interim County Executive — Jack Doyle, a highly-educated, street-smart Irishman who loved an old-school political brawl. Doyle, a former State Supreme Court Judge, took an instant liking to my irreverence, blunt talk and ruffled appearance.

Each time they summoned me to Albany for another interview, I had to ask Doyle for a day off and spend seven hours in the car. They kept asking me to write mock speeches, which were supposed to be spec samples of my writing.

One day, I read a line from one of my "mock speeches" in an article about a speech the Governor delivered to the "Association for A Better New York." I was flattered until I realized I should be pissed off.

And I was starting to have mixed feelings. During the day, when I was sober, all I could think about was being the speechwriter for the Governor of New York.

At night, after a few hours of drinking, I wanted to withdraw my name from the process and tell them to fuck themselves. One night, after several hours of intense drinking, that's what I did.

As a general rule, I never fully discounted feelings I had or decisions I made while drinking. I assumed that if I felt strongly about something when I was drunk, I probably felt just as strongly about it when I was sober. In fact, part of me believed that my drunk feelings were more honest and accurate.

But as the days went on, I began to question myself. I wasn't proud of my "safe" decision. I was a lot prouder of the guy who was studying his ass off for a job he didn't have yet — the guy who was confident enough to bet on his own abilities.

In this case, I wasn't proud of my decision, drunk or sober — so it was unanimous. I called the Governor's Office and told them I made a mistake. They called back the following day, and suddenly I was looking for an apartment in Albany.

Chapter Four

A Change of Venue

I LIVED ALONE on the second floor of a house on Whitehall Road in Albany during my first year in the Governor's Office and drove back and forth to Rochester on the weekends. My apartment was basically the second floor of Archie Bunker's house — same exterior, same interior, same street. That was' where the similarities ended.

My landlord was an academic, left-leaning forty-six-year-old widow who would literally set aside time to talk my ear off.

I didn't have a refrigerator upstairs, so I had to keep all my beer in her kitchen, which was in plain sight of the couch where she spent every minute of her life.

Every time I came downstairs for more beer, she'd torture me with the same questions.

"Ya thirsty?" she'd ask.

"Just trying to wind down," I'd say.

"This is the seventh beer for you already," she'd say.

I'd never respond to that, so she would invariably fill the silence with another story about her dead husband.

It was February, which gave me an easy solution to the problem. Every day I'd load as much beer as I could fit into a large garbage bag and hang them out of my upstairs window.

One night, I left five or six beers hanging there overnight and they froze and broke through the bag. From my bed, the frozen cans hitting the roof right outside my landlord's bedroom window sounded like bodies being dropped from a plane. God only knows how it sounded from hers.

I spent virtually all my time at work, even though they didn't trust me to write a speech at first.

For the first few weeks, I was crammed into the Governor's small Press Office writing op-ed pieces for newspapers and quotes for press releases. I felt like an intern, but I expected there would be some sort of probationary period where I would have to prove I could script the governor the way he wanted.

After a few months, I began writing full-blown speeches. The first one was a relatively easy address to the Business Council that played very well with the audience.

Paradoxically, my first speech to get widespread attention and praise was the result of a disaster. I wrote it quickly and nervously following the tragedy of TWA flight 800, which exploded mysteriously off the coast of Long Island in 1996. It was, and still is, the worst airline disaster in U.S. history.

The next day, family members of the victims rushed to East Moriches, New York, looking for information and answers. That's where the bodies of the victims were being taken so they could be identified and prepared for transport.

The Governor addressed the family members the following day with a speech that was carried live by FOX and CNN. The Governor was obviously too busy to discuss what he wanted to say, so he reviewed the speech once, then read it exactly the way I wrote it.

The next day, the words that I struggled for hours to write were printed in every major newspaper across the country from the *LA Times* to the *New York Times*. *The Daily News* ran one of the quotes as a front-page headline.

It was a horrible time to prove myself, but helping people in their darkest hour was the Governor's greatest strength and giving him the words to do it quickly became mine. That's when I wrote with relative ease — and I say "relative" because, many times, I wrote with tears in my eyes. Making sense of human suffering was almost a natural response for me. It came intuitively and without palliating, pomp or pretense.

Shortly thereafter, I was given my own office, a substantial raise and the title "Chief Speechwriter." It was clear that I had proven myself and that I wouldn't be leaving the Governor's Office anytime soon.

The speech warranted a sequel of sorts which I wrote in 1997 on the one-year anniversary of the disaster. That speech, which I titled "A

Mother's Love," was delivered on the beaches of the Long Island Sound where the victims were taken from the water. The Governor included the speech, almost in its entirety, in the final chapter of his autobiography.

Chapter Five

Working the Capitol Steps

THE GOVERNOR'S OFFICE occupies most of the second floor in the state capitol building in Albany. My office was one of the few on the Governor's Floor without a front office and a secretary. I liked it because I didn't have to say hi to everyone in the morning, no one was tracking my movements, and no one was counting the beers coming through the door.

It was a single office right off the main floor, big enough for everything I needed: A full-size couch for overnights, a matching lounge chair and coffee table (all circa my date of birth). And about fifteen feet in front of my desk, I had the biggest television money could buy in 1977.

One colleague used to call my office "The Paragraph Factory." As the years went on, everyone just called it what it was: a man cave. Of course, I arranged for a refrigerator — not one of those square little things that college kids have in their dorm rooms. No, I finagled a full-sized, phlegm-green, stand-up refrigerator.

If the State Capitol was a prison — which is where a lot of state legislators wind up — I was friends with that guy who could get you anything. People visiting for the first time all said the same thing: "How and where and why did you get that big-ass refrigerator?"

IF YOU'RE A VISITOR, getting into the Capitol Building sucks because you have to jump a hundred hurdles. If you work there, it sucks even more because you have to jump a hundred hurdles — every day.

They were always rotating the State Troopers and Corrections Officers working security and the metal detectors, so in the outer areas of the building you never really got to know the officers enough to just walk by. Oftentimes that meant having to hold a thirty-pack with one hand while showing my ID with the other.

I parked in an underground lot cordoned off for legislative leaders and a few members of the Governor's staff. And from there I walked through a tunnel up through the main concourse of the Empire State Plaza, then up the escalator and through the Main Lobby of the State Capitol Building and to the base of the monstrous "Million-Dollar Staircase."

They call it that because a million years ago, that's how much it cost to build. Something like that.

This was the only beautiful leg of my daily pilgrimage to work. It's four massive staircases that wrap around each other. Each is made of carved stone winding up five floors around a hollow pedestal… like four snakes crawling up an elephant's leg. It's vexingly confusing the first fifty or so times, especially if you hate certain things in the morning, like people.

I learned everything I need to know about the Million-Dollar Staircase while shoving my way through the countless tours flowing through the Capitol every day. Each tour consisted of forty or fifty kids with ear splitting voices echoing off the marble floors into the stone walls straight into my office, in one ear of my hangover right through the other.

Over five hundred stonecutters worked on this project and it took them fourteen years to complete. And they carved faces into the stairway walls. Some were famous Americans like Washington and Lincoln and Grant and Susan B. Anthony. Others were friends and family members of the sculptors.

The giant staircase was lit with a tennis court-sized skylight, but during World War II, state officials were afraid of giving away their position to Japanese bomber pilots so they painted the skylight black. Today, if Japanese pilots got lost on their way to bomb Albany, a lot of people would point them in the right direction.

The Million-Dollar Staircase, with all its intricate carvings and majesty, will always hold a special place in my heart because, through the years, I have paused to die on it a million times.

Almost every day, I was having trouble walking from my car to my office without experiencing these strange attacks.

Everything would be normal, then I'd have a sudden thought — an evil, horrific one, although I could never remember exactly what it was

— that caused an abrupt change in my attitude and everything around me. It would come out of nowhere, like a bolt of lightning shooting down to my head, spiking my mood.

The thought always came and went in a split second, but it left me light-headed and panicky. My heart would race and my forehead beaded up with sweat.

It always felt like I was having a heart attack and I would have to convince myself every step of the way that it was just a panic attack because that's what the doctors told me it was. But I know now that it was neither. I was in withdrawal from alcohol. And on most days, I was somewhere on the Million-Dollar Staircase when it struck.

One morning, I hadn't even gotten to the staircase when I became so disoriented that I was using the wall like a handrail. I was heading to the staircase when a trooper friend came by and said, "What the hell is going on? Your face is white. What happened?"

I could never talk when this happened. Sometimes it felt like I was dying and my mouth was paralyzed. My trooper friend called another trooper and the next thing you know, we were on our way to the emergency room.

After I saw the triage nurse there, I convinced the trooper to go back to the Capitol. I said whatever I had to say to get him to leave. When he did, I took the hospital band off my wrist and headed straight to the sports bar across the street from the hospital.

There was nothing in the Emergency Room that would cure my condition faster than alcohol (well, there was but they weren't going to give it to me). I began to feel better after the first beer so I continued to drink for several more hours.

They call that "self-medicating." I called it survival. In addition to keeping my heart beating properly, I drank for my mental health. These weren't just excuses. In my mind, both reasons were legitimate.

A MONTH AFTER THE TWA Flight 800 disaster, the Governor summoned me to San Diego for the 1996 Republican convention. He had just been asked to deliver the nominating speech for the Vice-Presidential nominee, Jack Kemp.

I caught the first flight out of Albany and made it all the way to the

Hotel del Coronado in San Diego without a drink, despite my best efforts to get alcohol every step of the way. As soon as I got there, the Governor began reviewing a draft of the speech I wrote on the plane.

Our work area was a room next to the Governor's suite. There was a kitchen and bar area that opened to a large sitting room where he was going through the speech with a pen.

I positioned myself at the bar counter, right over a hospitality fridge that I assumed was filled with beer. Every time he leaned over to write all over my speech, I crouched down and guzzled a beer.

The troopers standing near the door were trying to keep a straight face as they watched me stand up and talk to the Governor, then kneel down to pound a beer, over and over again until the speech was done.

By the time the editing session was over, there were nine empty Molson bottles lined up on the floor of the kitchen area. As we were leaving, the Governor saw the line of green bottles and said, "What happened there?"

After traveling four-thousand miles to write the Governor's nomination speech, I didn't even stick around to watch him deliver it. I'd gone to the San Diego Convention Center earlier in the day to watch the techs load the speech into the Teleprompter.

The Governor and I stood on the stage for about fifteen minutes waiting for former Vice President Dan Quayle to finish rehearsing his speech.

After we rehearsed ours, I made a couple changes on the Teleprompter and headed for the Mexican border with three State Police investigators and one of the Governor's spokesmen. We made it from the Convention center to Tijuana in less than an hour.

Crossing the border would have landed all five of us into varying depths of deep shit. The investigators would have gotten the worst of it.

We started on the main strip where every Corona or Dos Equis came with a complimentary shot of tequila. As the evening wore on, we wandered further and further off the beaten path, going from bar to bar down narrow streets with no street lights without paying attention to our surroundings.

By eleven o'clock that night — which is when we were supposed to be at the San Diego airport in time for my flight — we were in some scuzzy neighborhood bar spilling drinks all over each other. When someone shouted out the time, we all yelled "Shit!" and ran, then collided in the doorway while trying to run through it five at a time.

Before we even got to Tijuana, we agreed to keep a low profile, but now we were taking up the entire street as we ran back to the main strip in a loud, drunken formation that was about as subtle as five gorillas walking through an airport. Make that five gorillas walking through an airport holding open containers of alcohol.

We were about a hundred yards from the checkpoint at the border when five or six Tijuana cops on bikes began circling us. They wanted to arrest us for — get this — violating Tijuana's open container law. Meanwhile, there were a couple of twelve-year-old hookers smoking a joint on the corner.

They wanted money. When the investigators identified themselves as New York State Police investigators, even more Tijuana cops showed up and they began talking amongst themselves. The most senior investigator with us was handling the negotiation process and that's the last thing I remember before waking up to an airline stewardess nudging my shoulder in Albany.

Chapter Six

A Crisis of the Heart

IF YOU'RE THE CHIEF SPEECHWRITER for a Governor — and that's not a big club — there's nothing more draining and unrewarding than writing the bureaucratic, politically laced, annual nightmare known as the State-of-the-State address at the beginning of the year, which is unmercifully followed two weeks later by an Annual Budget Address.

For me, it entailed a month of walking back and forth from my office to the Governor's with the twenty-page draft of the speech in my hand — a draft riddled with his thoughts and ideas scrawled on both sides of either page in illegible patches of verbal guesswork.

In the beginning, the dysfunctional process irritated me so much I literally drank until I forgot how much I wanted to quit. I'd stay buzzed just long enough to write for another hour. Then I'd get pissed off and drink some more.

Problem was, once I started drinking, I couldn't stop — at least, not for very long. After a while, if I couldn't duck back into my office to keep enough alcohol in my system, the cravings would turn into withdrawal symptoms, like sweating and heart palpitations, that were too severe to hide. The first time it happened, I was writing the 1997 State-of-the-State address.

It took me by surprise. I thought I was having a heart attack. I walked up the Million-Dollar staircase to the nurse's office on the legislative floor. She took my vital signs and called another nurse and they put me on oxygen and called an ambulance. For some reason, they sent a fire truck instead, and four firefighters carried me out of the State Capitol on a stretcher.

This was the first of countless trips to the emergency room. And the drill was always the same. They would monitor my vital signs and hook me up to an EKG then let me go after a few hours. Before I left, they always made an appointment for me to see a cardiologist. They detected some irregularities with my heartbeat but they were never able to make an informed diagnosis because I always lied about my drinking.

I lied to the cardiologist too, without technically lying. I twisted my symptoms, steering his examination away from anything alcohol-related and towards something cardiovascular.

When he asked me if I smoked, which I didn't, I didn't just say "no," I said, "Oh, God no!" — giving him the impression that I would never do anything so unhealthy, like smoking... or drinking too much.

In this case, the cardiologist sent me home with the prefect prop to divert people's attention away from my drinking — a conspicuous Holter monitor strapped around my waist and attached to my chest to record the rhythm of my heart. I was sure my drinking was causing my heart palpitations. But I also knew that, if alcohol was causing a serious heart problem, the Holter monitor would reveal it.

The cardiologist said I had an "ectopic heartbeat." I researched it when I got home and discovered it doesn't really mean anything. It's just a small change in an otherwise normal heartbeat. People get them all the time for a variety of reasons. I was getting it from alcohol withdrawal, but per my research, it wasn't going to kill me.

I had an official diagnosis from the Chief Cardiologist at St. Peter's Hospital in Albany, and I made sure everyone knew about it so I could excuse myself in any situation to drink it away. That's how I explained away my relentless bouts with severe alcohol withdrawal.

For the time being, I had resolved my withdrawal issue. I didn't see the addition of a giant beer fridge to my office as a sign that my drinking was getting worse.

I saw it as me rising to a new challenge. To me, the problem was that I was having "faux heart attacks" throughout the day that were distracting me and threatening the quality of my writing. The attacks happened when I was craving alcohol and couldn't get it — so as far as I was concerned, not having alcohol was the problem.

My dad once told me about a guy who was in the hospital in serious condition due to his alcoholism —yet he still thought he could make drinking work in his life.

The guy ended up on a feeding tube, so he paid someone to pour vodka into it. I guarantee he was proud of himself for coming up with the idea. And I was proud of myself for finagling a refrigerator from the basement of the State Capitol into my second-floor office.

Drunk or not, I was writing a lot. The Governor insisted that I write things that he wanted a certain way, including portions of his book. And I was rewarded for it.

When I joined the Executive Chamber in 1995, my salary was $48,000 per year. Four years later, with no change in job title or responsibilities, my salary was $134,000. They knew how hard it would be to find another person who could absorb mountains of information on any subject at any time and turn it into a speech or an op-ed an hour later.

I had faults, a number of them, depending on who you asked, but writer's block wasn't one of them.

I had a state car, too — a black Crown Victoria with a police placard and dark-tinted windows — but that was sort of a double-edged sword. Most cops didn't pull it over because it was clearly an official car — identical to the cars that state police investigators drove. And since the windows were so darkly tinted, no one could see what was going on inside of the car, like me opening a beer.

But sometimes, the car's official, cop-like appearance drew the attention of people who were always on the lookout for a scandal.

Mounted inside the trunk, it had two big red warning lights and they'd flash and flicker like police lights every time I loaded beer in the back. Occasionally, I'd catch a condemnatory stare.

One time, a guy walked up behind me and wrote down my plate number. I yelled over to him, "You know where to stick that pen, right?"

They gave me the car because I was spending two or three days a week in Manhattan. The car, my room and the office were all within a block-and-a-half of each other — East 39th and East 41st Streets — and I kept all three fully stocked with beer.

On the streets of Manhattan, the black Crown Vic looked right at home. Whenever I was in New York City, it took the place of the refrigerator back in Albany.

It was usually parked less than one hundred yards away, on East 41st Street or Third Avenue, and the trunk was always loaded with beer. The backseat was large enough to spread out with a notepad and electronic devices.

And it was equipped with a second phone so I could sit back there and drink, work and take phone calls five feet away from people walking by on the sidewalk, and — thanks to the tinted windows — no one had a clue.

It seems silly that a refrigerator and an official car with tinted windows would play such a significant role in my daily life, but having those two things at my disposal allowed me to drink whenever, wherever.

THE REASON I WAS SPENDING so much time in NYC in 1998 had to do with the Governor's political ambitions. At that point, Pataki was the twice-elected Governor of, arguably, the most important state in America.

Once a week, the Governor would meet behind closed doors with his chief pollster and three or four senior members of his administration to make political decisions about what the Governor should be doing and saying. I was included in those meetings, primarily because whatever was decided upon had to be articulated and I was the articulator. Around that time, the Governor decided to form an exploratory committee for a possible Presidential run.

The plan was to announce a series of high-profile speeches that the Governor would deliver over the course of a few months. To prepare for the speeches, the Governor would meet with some heavy hitters to pick their brains on certain subjects. I would play the third wheel at these meetings.

Basically, I was there to bring up certain subjects and incorporate some of the answers into speeches. We scheduled meetings with former Secretary of State Henry Kissinger, former UN ambassador Jeanne Kirkpatrick, author and former Reagan speechwriter Peggy Noonan, and a leading economist named Stephen Moore.

We met first with Noonan and during that meeting she agreed to actually write the first draft of the speech, then pitch it over to me for revisions. It was the Governor's idea. In fact, he asked her to do it while looking at me to see if I was offended.

My mind was going in the opposite direction. I was more than happy to work with Peggy Noonan, especially because she was taking a giant headache out of my inbox.

After the meeting, one of our drivers was getting ready to take her home and she suggested I come along for the ride. It was rush hour in Manhattan, which meant I was going to have plenty of time to pick Noonan's brain while we sat in traffic on 5th Avenue.

She authored Reagan's *Challenger* Disaster Speech, which is and will always be among the great speeches in history... but I never got the chance to talk to her about her Reagan days.

Did I think about plopping a thirty-pack between us in the backseat? I thought about it... I really did. Then, I decided it would be more gentlemanly to guzzle four tallboys in the black Crown Vic before we left.

I could tell she was either bothered or puzzled by something. I had a feeling it was the presence of the Governor's pollster — Arthur J. Finkelstein — in a meeting about speeches. It was either that or the beer on my breath.

It was the former. She was put off by Finkelstein's posturing and pontificating, which was obviously intended to impress her. It didn't.

Once we were in the car, she cut right to the chase.

In a soft and almost sympathetic tone, she asked, "How do you write speeches like that?"

"Well, you know how it is with pollsters," I said.

"No," she said, "I don't know how it is. Ronald Reagan knew that [most Americans] didn't agree with his position on abortion, but when his advisors would show him those numbers, he didn't care. He'd say that he believed abortion was taking a human life. He stood by his principles, and even the people who disagreed with him respected his convictions."

"It's gotten better," I said, trying to be tactful and loyal.

"It used to be worse?" she asked. "The political guru in a corduroy suit thing isn't working for your boss. It's so clichéd and 1970s. Reagan would have laughed that guy out of his office."

As we sat in traffic, I began to get uncomfortable, but it had nothing to do with what she was saying... all of which was true. Then I just left. I told Noonan it was an honor to meet her but I was getting called back to the office, then got out of the car and walked to the nearest bar.

I ordered two pints of beer, slugged them down, then ordered another round and wondered, *Why in the hell did I do that?*

A couple weeks later, we were scheduled to meet with Henry Kissinger and Jeanne Kirkpatrick. To prepare for the meetings, the Governor and I would meet about a week beforehand and go over a list of issues the Governor would bring up at lunch. Then I would go back to my office, turn the list into an outline and print it out.

The Governor — much to his credit and insight — sent the first outline back to me with "TERRORISM" scribbled in big letters across the top. He even circled it a hundred times. It's an issue that wasn't on many people's radar screen in 1998. I included terrorism on the list of issues to raise at the lunches, but both Kissinger and Kirkpatrick disregarded the topic as inconsequential.

On the way to the Kissinger lunch, the Governor saw me loading batteries into a small tape recorder.

"What are you doing with that?" he asked.

"Kissinger's got a tough accent. "I'll keep this in my briefcase and take notes later."

"You're going to secretly record Henry Kissinger?"

"No," I eventually said, once I remembered how tape recorders destroyed Kissinger's boss, President Nixon, during the Watergate Scandal.

The Kissinger meeting was at Club 101 on Park Avenue in Manhattan. I went separately from the Governor so I could walk there and stop for a drink along the way if I had to. I put some beer in my briefcase and began walking.

Everyone hated my briefcase. They were always telling me to leave it at the office or in the vehicle. In the 90s, briefcases weren't cool or chic or hip. The premise was that if you had to carry information into a meeting, you weren't confident enough to rely solely on the information in your head — a premise that didn't bother me since my briefcase was loaded with booze, not information.

I had planned on having a few drinks in the restroom once I got in the restaurant, but one of the Federal Marshals was standing ten feet away in the lobby. The echoing sound of me cracking open a beer in a men's room might freak him out. I decided it was worth the risk.

I sat in a stall, and used one hand to crack open a beer while simultaneously coughing loudly and flushing the toilet. I drank a couple more beers, flattened the cans, wrapped all the evidence in paper towels and threw it away.

I walked out of the restroom coughing, just to keep that part of the ruse going. The restaurant manager and the Marshal were standing right there, as if they were waiting for me to come out.

"You're John Wolfe?" the Marshal asked.

"Yes," I said. "I'm a few minutes early and the Governor is about ten minutes behind schedule, which is pretty good for him."

"Everything okay in there?" he asked.

"Yeah, now it is… that time of year," I said.

"So, it's just you and the Governor along with Secretary Kissinger," he said, while looking down at a little notebook. "That's what we have."

"Yes," I said.

"Okay," he said, while eyeballing my briefcase. "Secretary Kissinger will be here in a few minutes and I'll direct him to that room. That's where you'll be meeting," he said, pointing to a corner room with glass walls.

The entire table was glass, end to end, with no tablecloth. So much for discreetly taking notes under the table.

I had a comfortable buzz going when Kissinger walked in, looked me up and down in sort of a grandfatherly way and said, "Hi, I'm Henry Kissinger."

Prior to the meeting, I promised myself that I would get through the entire meeting without saying anything stupid — a promise I broke the second I opened my mouth. "This is an honor, Dr Kissinger," I said. "I grew up with you and Nixon."

After that, I didn't have to worry about saying the wrong thing any more because he talked the entire time. It wasn't what I expected. I was afraid that being alone in a room with Kissinger with nothing to say would be painfully awkward. I assumed his demeanor would be arrogant and his conversations would be more like lectures. It was the opposite. He didn't talk about himself once.

The first thing he asked me was, "Where did you go to college?"

The alcohol in my system was telling me to say, "Dartmouth."

For some reason, I thought he'd take me less seriously if I told him I went to Springfield College, but I told him anyway and he acted impressed — at least I assumed he was acting.

"Oh, Springfield College in Massachusetts," he said. "One of the best schools in America for sports medicine. Good for you."

He was right; it was a great school for sports medicine, which is why I was an English major... me and some other guy.

The meeting lasted about an hour and a half, and I was feeling good about the experience, but I was also on the verge of losing my alcohol buzz, which was typically when I crashed and burned.

I figured I could take care of that problem on the way back to the office. One of my favorite bars was four blocks away on Lexington Avenue and I was headed in that direction until one of the troopers waved me down.

"The Governor wants you in there with him," he said, pointing to the black Suburban.

"Oh, I can't. I've got to..." and that was when I remembered the Governor can veto whatever excuse I was getting ready to fabricate.

So I got in the back of the Suburban and when the Governor got off the phone, he said, "I thought that went really well. Was it helpful?" That was all he wanted to say.

By then, it seemed like all of the alcohol had left my body. My heart was beating out of my chest and I could feel the sweat on my forehead.

"Yeah, it was great," I said. "I just need to get to a computer while it's fresh in my mind. I've got like twenty themes in my head." I needed to get to a bodega or a bar — fast.

FOR THE FIRST TIME, I was worried about my drinking. I wasn't worried about what it was doing to my health or my reputation or my family. I had accepted the fact that I needed beer close by always.

I had accepted the fact that I probably wouldn't be able to write a speech if I had to do it sober. I had even accepted the fact that I was an alcoholic. I wasn't worried about any of that; I was worried about the logistics of keeping alcohol within reach 24/7. That's all I mean when I say I was worried about my drinking. But I was determined to figure it out... the logistical problem, that is.

I had to. There were times when I'd get a sudden feeling of impending doom. My heart would start racing — it would skip and stutter, then race again. I could feel sweat beading up on my forehead like condensation on a cold glass of water. The top of my head would tingle and go numb. I'd have to remind myself to breathe, and if I missed a breath, it felt like I was going to die.

After a while, in my own mind, I just thought of it as the "feeling." When the feeling struck, I would do anything to take it away. If it meant doing something drastic and reckless, like sneaking alcohol right under somebody's nose, I did it, and I didn't think twice about it because I was desperate and felt like I was dying and going crazy at the same time.

Once the feeling struck, and once I set my sights on the solution, there was no turning back. I was going to drink. It didn't matter where I was or what I was doing or who was standing next to me.

I would excuse myself if I had to. I would run into a bathroom. I would rush out to my car. I would walk out of meetings. I would crawl under anything or anywhere to get the alcohol in my system. The chaos in my chest felt like an alarm going off in my heart. My whole body went into full panic mode.

The only thing I knew would take this feeling away was beer, lots of it... one to start, then two, then six, and then I couldn't stop. It felt like if I drank enough, I could eradicate the problem forever.

I could actually feel the alcohol going down my throat and into my chest and drenching my heart like medicine. I would pour beer into my mouth like I was putting out a fire in my chest. And I could feel my chest responding right away to the ameliorating effect of the alcohol and I could feel my heart calming down and relaxing and beating normally. It was the most relieving sensation I've ever felt... like I was saving my own life with alcohol.

My worst fear was being stranded somewhere without it or being cut off from it, which is exactly how I felt when the trooper called me back to the Suburban after the Kissinger meeting. I had been fighting the feeling for over an hour, and when the meeting was over, I was two blocks away and closing in on the sanctuary of a bar when the trooper stopped me dead in my tracks. I came very close to ignoring him and figuring out an excuse once I was feeling better in the bar.

I started to see alcohol as my heart medication. I was convinced that this awful feeling would never go away on its own. I couldn't ignore it. I had to chase it away. I had to bombard it with alcohol.

I knew deep down that this wasn't the way it was supposed to be. I knew that there had to be a better way to stop the feeling. I promised to figure it out as soon as I felt better, but I only felt better after several drinks, then I was in no condition to figure out anything.

I promised myself I would find the correct way at some later date. But the next time the feeling struck, the last thing on my mind was developing a sensible, long-term solution. I drank the feeling away, over and over again without ever making any real effort to solve the problem permanently.

Sometimes, when the feeling struck suddenly, it lulled me into a state of dumb, stunned silence. If someone was there, I would just stare at them without being able to say a word.

They would say, "Hey, what's wrong... your face is white!" I wouldn't be able to answer because I was too scared to move a muscle. That's when whoever was there would call an ambulance. I can't remember how many times this happened. It was a lot. If I left in an ambulance, it meant the feeling struck me so hard I couldn't get to a drink. And that's all it meant.

A few weeks later, we had our lunch meeting with Jeanne Kirkpatrick. I had been with the Governor the entire morning, but I hadn't planned on speaking much at the meeting so I didn't feel like I needed a drink to make me happy, outgoing and interested.

Of course, as soon as I saw the opportunity to drink, I seized it without thinking twice. The opportunity was when Kirkpatrick ordered a mixed drink. So, when the waitress took my order, I pointed to the fancy beer menu and said, "Then you know what? How's the Olde English High Gravity?"

Of course, I knew exactly how it was; it was fourteen percent alcohol by volume, nearly four times the alcohol content of Budweiser. I remember thinking, *This is a major faux pas, but he knows how I am and she's too old to care.*

Fifteen minutes later, the Governor left the table to take a call, which was the opportunity I had been impatiently waiting for. I motioned the waitress for another high-test beer as I polished off the one in front of me. She was back in less than a minute, before the Governor returned to the table. I liked her. .

Kirkpatrick didn't notice, and the Governor didn't return to the table until after the waitress delivered the new beer and took away the one I'd inhaled at the last second.

For me, that was a victory, but instead of sitting back and savoring it, my instinct was always to go for more. I pounded the new beer, which wasn't easy because of the alcohol content, then ordered a third. To the Governor, it looked like I'd only had two beers when, in reality, I'd had the equivalent of thirteen Coors Lights.

THERE WAS A DYSFUNCTIONAL dynamic at the Capitol — hundreds of them actually — and I took full advantage of it. The Governor's Executive Services, or Governor's Detail, provided security for the Governor and the State Capitol. About half of the detail was comprised of uniformed Troopers and the rest are plainclothes State Police investigators who protect the Governor.

Although he went on to become a major, at the time, Charles was a sergeant on the Governor's Detail. His commanding officer, the Colonel, oversaw the entire detail. Hands down, the Colonel was the most complicated person I've ever met, a walking enigma.

He either liked you or he hated you. There was no middle ground. If he hated you, he'd just ignore you, even if you were bleeding to death on the steps of the Capitol. If he liked you, he'd break a million rules to help you.

Hence, the enigma: He hated alcohol, but he loved me. He hated drunk drivers, but he gave me a full-blown unmarked State Police car to use for months at a time.

When my wife was pregnant with my son, Jackson, I jokingly told him I was concerned about getting her to the hospital quick enough. I said he should loan me something with lights and sirens. The next day, Charles called and told me to pick it up.

But this thing looked too much like a cop car, so when the big day came, I drove the family car. I knew I'd be going out for beer, and I was worried about the optics of loading alcohol into a police car. I was less worried about the optics of smuggling beer into the delivery room where Jackson was born.

The Colonel routinely held court with key members of the governor's senior staff and top campaign donors. He knew when sensitive discussions were taking place and where big decisions were being made — and he planted himself right in the middle of it. No one ever questioned his presence because they assumed the Governor wanted him there. Besides, he had a gun.

I wasn't even good at pretending to like that crowd, probably because I never practiced. They were power-hungry, superficial, arrogant, rich and full of shit. Besides, they didn't drink like me, and I wasn't willing to drink socially just to be with them.

I would rather guzzle beer from a paper bag with a hobo in an alley than sip pomegranate martinis at Elaine's with the Governor's millionaire buddies.

Even though I didn't like those people, in the Colonel's mind, I was one of them. He saw me in meetings with them; he saw my name on the schedule with them; and he saw me walking with them into very private meetings with the Governor.

Since I was always on the verge of some kind of trouble, the Colonel saw me as an opportunity to make himself look like a savior by keeping me out of the newspaper and out of jail.

I was the only high-value member of the Governor's staff who was constantly going to need the kind of rescuing that only the Colonel could provide. I had friends who were investigators under the Colonel's command. They said the Colonel frequently mentioned "keeping Wolfe out of trouble because the Governor needs him."

The entire dysfunctional dynamic worked perfectly in my favor. Did I take advantage of it? Of course, but not for malicious purposes or financial gain; I was just keeping myself entertained and out of jail.

Even though I was already assigned a state car for personal use — a black Crown Vic with a police package — during certain times of the year I would swap it for a "slightly different" model.

The one I always asked the Colonel for was "X88." It looked exactly like mine — a black Crown Vic with blacked-out windows and a big black antenna in the back. The difference is it had a police radio with "no hit" license plates. It also had lights and sirens, which I never used except to scare my kids in the driveway. But the radio and plates made it next to impossible to get pulled over on the thru-way.

Before I even met the Colonel, I saw him featured on an episode of *America's Most Wanted* where he was credited with helping then-prosecutor Eliot Spitzer bring down the Gambino crime family.

His critics say he used his alliances from that experience to get himself promoted from Sergeant to Colonel in warp speed. But the guy was always in my corner.

It may seem odd that, as the Governor's Chief Speechwriter, I needed the State Police to have my back. As a group, speechwriters aren't an especially unruly lot. But someone thought I needed the Colonel's protection, and I did... repeatedly.

It was important for me to remember that the Colonel was my best friend's boss, and although Charles moved up the ranks the old-fashioned way, the Colonel supported his rise.

Charles appreciated the support. He just didn't like his style and he hated reporting to him. Despite the Colonel's perceived power, Charles knew enough to keep him at arm's length. Charles was smart about it. He made his hierarchical relationship with the Colonel strictly military, like an infantry officer reporting to a bird Colonel. There wasn't a lot of small talk. Charles would sooner change his name to Vanilla Ice than be known as one of the Colonel's cronies.

I thought the Colonel was an idiot for giving me a police car. But I never drove it drunk or did anything else that was overtly obnoxious or improper that would make him regret giving it to me... well, until I began writing about it.

But here's the thing: If there had been someone else in the Colonel's position — and I didn't realize this until there was — a lot of things about my time in the Governor's Office might have turned out much differently, and not in a good way.

Right around 9/11, the Colonel disappeared from the Governor's power circle the way top people who run into trouble always disappear: quietly, with a raise, into state agency land.

With everything else that was disappearing around that time, like the

World Trade Center, I didn't appreciate the importance of my affiliation with the Colonel until years later, when I actually needed him and he was no longer there.

Chapter Seven

Life in the War Room

ONE MORNING IN MY OFFICE at the Governor's Office, a guy from the Division of Budget was in my office fact-checking some numbers for me. When I grabbed a beer from the fridge and opened it, he said, "You're drinking beer in the morning?"

"Well, yeah," I said. "I don't want liquor on my breath this early."

"You do it right out in the open?" he asked.

"Of course," I said. "Only alcoholics try to hide their drinking. It's no big deal. I've got this thing where I start shaking and sweating. Drinking a few beers is the only thing that makes it go away."

No one ever said, "Maybe all the drinking is what's causing you to feel that way in the first place."

Deep down, I must have known that.

By the dawn of the second millennium, I no longer felt the need to hide my drinking from anybody. By then I had transformed my corner of the State Capitol into a virtual corridor of unacceptable behavior.

On most days, the smell of alcohol, candles and the general scent of immorality permeated my office, then wafted out of the door and infiltrated all that is sacred, from one hallowed hall to the other, from the historic War Room to the blessed Flag Room, and straight up the Million-Dollar Staircase.

People who regularly passed through that part of the Executive Chamber were no longer shocked by anything. Every type of outrageous behavior had already been reported to the State Police or some other authority and either ignored or swept under the rug.

Every so often, usually for an hour or two on Friday afternoons, SUNY or the State Legislature or some lobbying group would get permission to use our War Room, a forty-foot-high domed rotunda with historic hand-painted ceiling murals. The War Room is an open area, surrounded by the four main hallways of the Governor's floor, so I'd walk past or through it ten times a day.

Whenever I saw them setting up for one of these gatherings, I'd get excited for the fancy beer I knew I'd be stealing from them later. Fancy to me was Molson or Guinness because I was so accustomed to drinking Coors Light for speed and effect. A lot of times, I was drinking with one hand while opening the next beer with the other. I never slowed down long enough to taste anything.

When one of these cocktail receptions pitched their beer and wine tent on my doorstep — the War Room was forty feet from my office — I would throw on a sport coat I kept on my office floor for various occasions, slide into the reception and head straight to the provisional bar. I'd pretend to be the guy they sent to get drinks for the group.

While ordering, I'd look up in the air like I was trying to recall what everyone wanted, and I would order four different brands of beer, then say, "I'll send one of the ladies back to get the wine." With four bottles of beer in my hand, I'd walk away from the bar looking wide-eyed and excited at some imaginary thing a hundred feet away as if I had just caught sight of all my friends. I'd keep walking to that make-believe place until I got to the real place, which was my office.

Usually I would just put the beer in the fridge and hit up the reception again before they left or until I cleaned them out, whichever came first.

The person tending bar always knew what I was doing. One time, I was walking by as they were cleaning up, and the bartender said, "I've got two left."

"Oh," I said, as I pretended to be indecisive about it.

"Your office is right around the corner, isn't it?" he asked.

"There's like ten of us in there," I said, "and they always make me get the drinks."

He laughed and said, "Next time, I'll give you and the guys everything that's left over. It's better than lugging it all back."

"Anything I... uh, *we*, can do to help," I said.

I did have friends in the office, but they were all troopers I gave keys to so they could hang out there during their overnight shifts. It was a perfect break room, complete with a couch, TV and a fridge for their food.

I ran into a problem with that arrangement, a problem that's far more amusing now than when it was happening. Every so often, I'd leave a speech open and on the screen so people in the New York City office could access it remotely and print it out. It was a "read only" file so the only place anyone could make changes to the speech was from my office, which a couple of the troopers thought would be funny.

It was funny the first few times. The problem is that they kept doing it, and at least twice, I didn't catch the prank soon enough.

In a commencement address to Albany Law School grads, they changed a sentence to read, "When confronted with cynicism [about the law profession], remind the cynic that it was a vagina named Hillary who ended slavery." By the time I changed it back to "Lawyer named Lincoln," there was already a draft sitting on the Governor's desk.

The other one was written into a final draft that was already formatted for the teleprompter. I'm not sure how a bunch of conservative economists at the Detroit Economic Club would have reacted if the Governor said, "When I took office, we had a regulation in New York that mandated the precise length and width of penises that daycare centers had to keep on the premises."

The prompter operator called me from Detroit a couple hours before the speech and said, "I don't usually question the content of a speech unless it looks like a formatting error, but can I ask a question?"

"Of course," I said, "What's up?"

"In New York, do they really measure penises at daycare centers?" he asked.

He read me the sentence. "Okay," I said. "Let's go ahead and change 'penises' to 'Band-Aids.'"

"Whoa," he said. "Your C drive did that?"

I wanted to say, "No, the State Police did," but I was too busy scanning the speech for more surprises.

DURING CERTAIN TIMES OF THE YEAR — usually in December or January — it was customary for me to spend one, two, even three nights in a row sleeping in my office. One night, as I was preparing a budget address, I passed out on my office couch next to a table covered with empty beer cans.

Loud knocking on my door woke me up the next morning. I opened the door without getting my bearings first, and I was standing in the doorway wearing nothing but underwear and socks, squinting my eyes to see who was standing in right front of me. There were four number-crunchers from the Division of Budget, including the deputy budget director and the Governor's budget spokesman.

"What's up?" I said.

Joe, the unflappable and meticulous Budget spokesman, didn't miss a beat. "You want us to come back?" he asked. It took me four years to realize they never did.

When things like this happened, no one in the Governor's Office was ever shocked. The Deputy Budget Director apparently complained to a Governor's aide that she tried to fact-check the Governor's speech only to find his "Chief Speechwriter in his underwear, hungover and surrounded by booze in the State Capitol."

"You should have called first," the aide said.

My reputation in and around the Capitol as a lush, a partier or a full-blown alcoholic didn't bother me. I assumed my sense of humor, healthy appearance and writing ability canceled out the one unsavory thing.

On paper — if you subtract the drinking — I was the poster child of good health. I went to the gym every morning, religiously. I ate five fruits and vegetables every day (I did it just like I drank — all at once and for effect, not taste) and I took a milk thistle supplement to promote healthy liver function.

I crammed all this healthy shit down my throat because I thought it would counteract the harmful effects of drinking too much. Obviously, I didn't tell anyone that; I said it was part of my routine.

During one of her visits, my mother saw the bottle of milk thistle and asked, "Why do you have this?"

Like a fool, I said, "To repair my liver."

THE TROOPERS AND CLEANING PEOPLE who worked overnights at the Capitol wouldn't have batted an eye at the sight of me wandering around the Capitol in boxers.

There was a God-fearing, elderly black woman named Marilee who cleaned the Executive Chamber offices and liked to lecture me about the condition of my office and torture me with grandmotherly advice on a range of social issues. The first time she saw me walking down the hall in my underwear with a beer in my hand, she stopped what she was doing and just shook her head.

"What?" I said.

"White people get away with everything," said Marilee.

"Oh God, here we go," I said.

"Don't use His name in vain," she said. "Tell me, what would happen if these troopers saw a black man walking around the Capitol like that?"

"I give up," I said. "What?"

"They'd shoot his black ass. That's what," she said.

"No, there's too much ricochet in here; they'd tase him," I said.

Marilee had a clear plastic bag hanging from her cleaning cart where she kept empties. Every Friday, she'd bring them back for the deposit and every Monday, she told me how much she got for them.

One night she poked her head into my office and said, "I put black garbage bags in your closet. Put all of your empties in those bags from now on."

"Okay," I said. "Why, so people can't see the beer cans?"

"So I can't see them," she said. "I made forty dollars off you last month, but I feel guilty profiting off your sinning. You drink too much and if this job is doing it to you, you should quit before people start talking."

People were already talking. At the State Capitol, where defamation of character is a required skill, there were two things I couldn't control: my drinking and what people said.

Most people knew I drank a lot. Others knew my drinking was problematic, particularly the administration officials and State Troopers at the Capitol who fielded the complaints about my behavior. And some of them, including the Governor, thought I drank too much. But I only discussed the issue in a serious way with a few people.

One of them was Boz. Through most of the early '90s, Boz and I drank ourselves to oblivion every single time we got together. On weekends, Boz drank as much as I did, but he could stop for a few days in the middle of the week.

One night, while we were sitting bare naked in my rec room shot-gunning beers and listening to old records, we made a pact. We promised to say something if we ever thought the other's drinking was becoming an issue — as if shot-gunning beers naked wasn't all the proof we needed.

One day as I was in the process of relocating beer from the War Room to my office, I got a message marked "urgent" to call Mike West, my longtime friend from Rochester. He didn't waste any time getting to the point. After a night of drinking, Boz had driven his car into a cement wall on a Rochester expressway and he was dead.

Years ago, everyone said that Boz and I were awful for each other, that we were codependent alcoholics. It was hard to dispute that back then, and it was even harder to dispute now that he'd been killed in a drunk driving accident and I was in my office getting drunk in the middle of the work day. But at the time, we just weren't ready to grow up and act our age, so for four years, we put our maturity on hold, did the next wrong thing, and laughed at everything that crossed our paths without stopping long enough to care how it looked to everyone else. And we were lucky because most people will never know the freedom and the joy of acting like a six-year-old while enjoying all the legal, civil and God-given rights of a twenty-five-year-old.

ONE SATURDAY, I WAS at the Capitol finishing up a speech about the "Y2K" scare, which we were hyping relentlessly to win over the doomsday set. I thought I was the only one on the second floor that day until there was a knock on my door. It was Bill, a veteran uniformed trooper at the Capitol.

"Hey John, are you leaving soon?" he asked.

"In about an hour, why?" I asked.

"An hour is good. There was an accident right by your Crown Vic and they're cleaning it up," he said.

It wasn't really an accident. Some guy drove from Massachusetts to the State Capitol Building and jumped head first out of a fourth story window and landed near my car.

"It's not a pretty sight," Bill said, "And I knew you were here so…"

"Did you think it was me?" I asked.

"No... but I'm glad you answered the door," he said.

"Thanks," I said. "If I have to write the words 'new millennium' one more time, you may see me going upstairs too."

IT WAS NO SECRET that I was tired of writing speeches. So, when Zenia Mucha, the Governor's Director of Communications and most trusted advisor, asked me if I was willing to move to Burbank, California, to work for Disney, I said yes without hesitation.

Zenia was the much-revered and feared Chief Spokesperson for the Governor — so infamous for her toughness that George W. Bush once joked that his first choice for a Vice President was New York's most powerful Republican... but "Zenia Mucha didn't want it." The joke (kind of) was that Zenia wielded more power than the Governor.

In 2000, Zenia announced that she was leaving the Governor's Office to become an Executive Vice President with Disney CEO Michael Eisner. Later that same day, she asked me to read Eisner's book, *Work in Progress*, and tell her what I thought.

When that time came, I asked her, "Did you want to know what I thought of the book, or what I think of him after reading the book?"

"Both," she said.

I hated the book but I knew where the whole thing was going so I tried to say something nice. "Well, there's a lot of stuff in there I didn't know," I said. "He's a driven guy, really motivated. He's got a healthy ego."

"Would you have a problem writing for that ego?" she asked.

"No," I said. "Look at the one I'm writing for now."

"That's what I need at Disney, the same thing," she said. "You'd be writing for him but doing stuff for me too... just like here."

The next day, I realized she had already told the Governor. I was reading a speech under a portrait of FDR in the "Hallway of Governors" when I was approached by Brad Race, the Governor's now-deceased Chief of Staff, which was rare.

Our relationship was cordial, but never especially warm. Zenia once told me that he resented having to sign off on all my raises, especially the one that put my salary in his ballpark.

"I guess congratulations are in order," he said.

I didn't bite.

"What do you mean?" I asked.

"I was just in there," he said, motioning towards the Governor's office, "and the Governor pointed at Zenia and said, 'She's stealing Wolfe.'"

"Oh, that," I said.

"Don't worry about it. Take it as a compliment," he said. "You have a rare talent and he thinks the world of you. It's just… this is more change than he wanted right now,"

Two days later, Zenia called me into her office and said Eisner wouldn't sign off on my hiring. He said he needed to be a hundred percent comfortable with his writer and he wanted a Hollywood insider, not a political one. Fortunately, I'm neither.

Zenia felt bad, partly for me and partly because Eisner overruled her on one of her first decisions. She tried to soften the blow by telling me that Bob Iger, the President of Disney who succeeded Eisner as CEO in 2005, supported my hiring, but Eisner overruled him too. She said I could still have a job at Disney but only Eisner could sign off on the package deal we had been discussing.

Truth is, I wasn't a hundred percent comfortable with Eisner either. His own book portrayed him as power-hungry and arrogant, or he liked to portray that image. Either way, he was right: I wasn't his guy. And of course, there was no way my drinking would be tolerated at Disney.

Still, my ego was wounded. My friends, my family and the people I worked with believed I was an alcoholic. I had a vulgar mouth, I dressed like shit and I got into trouble. The only unassailable thing about me was my talent as a writer. But Eisner never got that far with me.

When I pressed Zenia for more information, she told me that Eisner said, "I'm not sure why; I just don't like the guy." I'd never even met the douchebag.

A lot of people, including the Governor, had already heard that I was going to Disney with Zenia. I wasn't about to admit that I got shot down by their top mouse.

Almost immediately, I tried to save face by resuscitating an invitation by Dell to discuss an executive-level position at their headquarters in Austin, Texas. Around the same time, the Governor signed off on an $18,000 per year raise for me, which I didn't even ask for.

But I had already accepted the invitation to go to Austin. I wasn't a tech guy. I couldn't even connect a Dell computer to a printer. Until I joined the Governor's Office, I had the kind of cell phone that came with a shoulder strap.

Without putting any thought into the absurdity of me working for a computer company, I went flailing to Austin like a drunk boxer who gets knocked out and starts fighting again before regaining his faculties. (The boxer in my analogy was drunk and that's how I was when I got to Austin.)

When I stepped off the plane in Austin, a Dell limo was waiting for me in front of the airport. But it was already late in the afternoon so we just drove past Dell's headquarters in Round Rock then to the hotel. The bartender in the hotel bar was having trouble keeping pace with me, so after two or three pints of Rolling Rock, I told him to bring a kamikaze with each subsequent beer.

I wasn't used to that kind of drinking, and in about two hours, I was plastered. I fell asleep in my suit and tie, which saved time in the morning because I was still sleeping when the limo came back to get me for a nine am interview at Dell. I never bothered to look in a mirror but I knew I wasn't a pretty sight.

I had time to walk off the Kamikaze aftermath as they were showing me around the place. I don't even remember who I was with because, right off the bat, I hated the place.

"Where are the walls?" I asked.

"Dell is an open-office company," she said. Then she explained why but I had already stopped listening. I needed walls.

For whatever reason, Dell felt walls created a hierarchical animosity that was bad for morale, so everyone — from high-level executives to office assistants — worked under one giant ceiling, separated only by cubicle partitions. As soon as I saw that, I knew I had no future with Dell, not because I didn't like people — I just didn't like people watching me drink beer at lunchtime, a perk I wasn't willing or able to give up.

My next meeting was at two that afternoon so I said I needed to go back to the hotel. On the way there, I made the limo guy stop at a convenience store so I could get a case of Miller Lite. I wanted to crack one open in the limo so I said something loud to the driver as I pulled the tab. "So," I said loudly. "Someone at your company said there were five lakes around here. Are we near one?"

"Well, they're called lakes, or reservoirs, but each one is just a sectioned-off piece of the Colorado River," he said.

"Oh, that's interesting," I lied, as I inhaled my first beer of the day.

Back at the hotel, I only had two hours to prepare for my next interview. I went to the hotel bar and drank, but I didn't want to go back to Dell smelling like beer so I chased three beers with two lemony Kamikazes.

Since I had already decided I could never work for Dell, I'm not sure why I even went back. It wasn't even an interview; it was four Dell executives bragging about their company to a half-drunk speechwriter who couldn't give a shit.

One of them seemed to like me about as much as Michael Eisner did. She was disparaging about New York, condescending towards Republicans (knowing I worked for one), and paradoxically, jingoistic about the overwhelmingly Republican State of Texas.

At one point, in front of two other Dell executives, she said, "I'm trying to keep an open mind about you even though I assume you're a Republican since you report to one."

"What do you mean?" I asked.

"Exploitation doesn't make you guilty by association," she said.

I will die not knowing what in the hell that means, or caring. The senseless syntax makes the thought guilty by association.

A few days after I got back to Albany, one of the Dell executives who was in that meeting sent me an email asking me about my impressions of Dell. I replied saying, among other things, that I was "trying to keep an open mind about Dell even though it was headquartered in the backward state of Texas."

After a week of silence, I got an email that said everyone at Dell was "surprised and taken aback by [my] snot-o-gram."

I'd never heard that term before… snot-o-gram. In my email back to them, I wrote, "I'd like to use that if you haven't trademarked it already. I get snot-o-grams all the time from condescending Democrats, usually in the form of a letter, but sometimes in a job interview."

Before sending it, I remembered the advice of Abraham Lincoln. He said that, before sending out hot and angry letters, you should set it aside and get a good night's sleep. Then, according to Abe, you should re-read it in the morning, just to be sure it still makes sense to send it.

I didn't do any of that. I just fired it off... and that was the end of my relationship with Dell.

At the time, the luster of working for the Governor was starting to dull, and my days in the Capitol were becoming increasingly unrewarding and tedious and long — and the longer the days got, the earlier I started drinking to get through them.

With nothing else going on — compounded by my fear that I had cursed myself by staying in the Governor's Office too long — my conflicts with Dell and Disney were disproportionately discouraging.

It didn't help that, right around this time, someone in the Executive Chamber sent out a directive saying the Governor wanted a briefing for everything on his schedule.

One day, a new person in the Scheduling Office walked into my office and said, "I just got this today so I brought it right down to you."

It was — I'm not making this up — a request to provide the Governor with written remarks for a big event that was being held to celebrate his wife's fiftieth birthday party.

"Wait, don't leave yet," I told her. I've got those remarks right here.

I wrote "Happy Birthday" on a post-it note, stuck it to the paperwork and said, "It's ready for the teleprompter."

OUT OF FRUSTRATION AND BOREDOM, I found myself drinking at work before noon. At first, it was just while I was in Manhattan where I didn't have to drive, but once I developed the pattern there, it was hard to stop when I got back to Albany.

The IT guys in the Executive Chamber knew I drank at work because they were routinely in my office and I didn't feel compelled to hide it from them. I was especially close to Kevin.

About twice a week, he and I would meet for a few beers after work at a place called Mahar's — a beer connoisseur's paradise. Mahar's imported beer from every corner of the globe, and they used a computer to keep track of how many different beers you drank. When you reached one hundred and twenty-five beers, you were given a personalized beer stein, which they kept on a shelf behind the bar.

The goal was drinking five hundred different beers. The few people who managed to hit that number were memorialized with a little gold plaque mounted somewhere in the woodwork of the bar.

I was about to hit the two-thousand mark when, as I was talking to Kevin at Mahar's one night, I realized two things: One, I really didn't need to advertise my drinking any more than I already had; two, if I ever got pulled over while leaving Mahar's, the police would be able to go back and see how many beers I drank, along with the alcohol content of what I was drinking.

In the same conversation, I confided in Kevin… At least, I thought I was confiding in him.

"I'm having a little trouble at work," I told him. "It's getting hard to get these speeches done unless I'm drinking… and by drinking, I mean drinking a lot."

He was unfazed. "You write the Governor's speeches when you're drunk… I knew that," he said.

"Right, they're better that way and I can do it quicker," I said. "But I can't do it at the Capitol. I need access to the Executive Chamber server from my house."

"We'd have to put a state computer at your house," he said. "If someone asks the Governor about this, will he be cool with it?" he asked.

"Oh, hell yeah," I said.

A few days later he came into my office with a yellow box. "When can I come over to your house and hook up the computer? It's ready," he said.

He installed a program called "Reach Out" on my computer. The advent of the cell phone made it obsolete a few years later, but at the time it was cutting edge. It allowed me to bypass the Executive Chamber's firewall and access its server from home. That meant I could write speeches from home and anyone with credentials, like the Governor, could literally see the speech as I was writing it.

Simply put, it allowed me to work at home — which is to say, I still went to the State Capitol every day, but I wrote all the speeches at home.

Drunk.

"I feel like I'm enabling you," Kevin said, "but it's better than the alternative."

"Don't feel that way," I told him. "It's not like I was going to stop drinking if you couldn't do it."

The refrigerator I finagled into my office years earlier allowed me to drink at work, but because I still had to drive home, I wasn't getting bombed at the office. Now that my home and office were linked, that barrier was gone.

It's not that I was a better writer when I was drunk; I was just a more patient writer when I was drunk. I've always had a low threshold for boredom, and most of what I was writing was, for me, boring to the point of being intolerable. Drinking made writing less boring, so I put more effort into it, which made it better.

Commencement addresses were a different story. I assumed the graduates would be drunk when they listened to the speech, so I thought it was appropriate for me to be twice as drunk when I wrote it.

Drinking was working for me, and it appeared to be working for the Governor. Invariably, the drunker I was when I wrote something, the more he liked it.

The Governor especially liked what he called "soaring rhetoric" in certain parts of the speech. The rhetoric he loved most was the rhetoric I wrote when I was too drunk to spell rhetoric. After a night like that, I'd wake up in the morning, correct all the spelling errors, and send it along.

The day the Reach Out software was installed was the last day I wrote anything while I could still walk a straight line. Writing at home removed the last of the limits I had imposed on myself.

During the day, I'd meet with the Governor or whoever else could give me the information I needed for a speech. Most of the time, I didn't need to talk to anybody except the people in the Scheduling Office who had details about the event.

For most of the day, I'd stay in my office and assemble hard copies of everything I'd need later and make sure everything in the computer was saved in the proper place to access it from home. I wouldn't write per se, but if a speech required a lot of research, I'd do it sober in my office because my drunken research inspired bad habits, like making shit up.

I'd drink five beers in my office (never more than five but never fewer) then drive home and log right back into the Executive Chamber server from there.

So, if someone were standing in my office while I was working from home, they could see me moving the cursor with the mouse and everything else I was doing. I didn't even have to format the speech in large type and bring it directly to the Governor any more.

With Reach Out, I could enlarge the type and print it out right onto his secretary's lap. Short of pelting an intern with spitballs, there was nothing I could do at the Capitol that I couldn't do at home in a fraction of the time.

So, for the most part, I stopped writing at work. I spent my time there acting as my own secretary, marking speech dates on the calendar, returning emails and stuffing file folders with back-up materials that I would need later, when I was too drunk to read a calendar but perfectly fine to write a speech.

Other than that, I was just drinking and killing time, time that I should have been using to advance my career and get out of the Governor's Office. After I finished writing my first State-of-the-State address in 1997, the Governor raised my hand in victory for the cameras. As he was doing it, I was thinking that I needed to find another job before it was time to write the next one.

By the summer of 2001, I realized I wasn't going anywhere soon, so I purchased a lake house in the Adirondacks. The euphoria of fulfilling that dream lasted less than a month.

Chapter Eight

A World of Grey

THE BLACK CROWN VICTORIA didn't get pulled over very often so I was surprised to see police lights in my rear-view mirror one morning while I was driving to New York City. I was less than fifty miles from Manhattan, going about seventy-five mph, which usually wasn't fast enough to attract the attention of a State Trooper on the Thruway.

The trooper walked to the front of the car and took a quick look at the "Police Vehicle" parking placard on the dashboard, as if he expected to see it there. He didn't ask for a license or anything. He just said, "Hey, you're with…?"

"The Governor's Office," I said.

"Okay. You know there's something going on down there, right?" he asked.

"No, I was listening to Led Zeppelin. What's going on?" I asked.

"I don't know, something about a small plane hitting one of the Twin Towers so Lower Manhattan is probably jammed," he said.

"Holy shit… okay, I'm only going to East 39th," I said.

I was on the New Jersey Parkway heading for Harlem River Drive. I was almost to the George Washington Bridge when I had to slam on my brakes for fifteen or twenty guys with shotguns. They were lined up across the road, stopping cars from getting any closer to the bridge into the city. Some were cops in uniform, or partly in uniform; others were just heavily-armed guys who looked like they could have been mowing their lawn fifteen minutes earlier.

Parked all over the median was a scattered variety of New Jersey and New York State Police cars and a lot of pickup trucks with gun racks. I drove straight towards the bridge and they saw the "Police Vehicle" placard on my dashboard. I showed them my Executive Chamber ID and they waved me through.

I was the only vehicle on the entire George Washington Bridge until I got close to the end of it. That's when a firetruck on the wrong side of the bridge headed straight towards me. There wasn't enough time or room to weave and bob. Thank God we both picked a side and stayed there. It was headed away from Manhattan. To this day, I have no idea where it was going.

I could almost hear the door to Manhattan slamming shut behind me like a jail gate as I drove off the bridge onto Harlem River Drive. When I got on the FDR, I began looking for ways to get off because I could see dump trucks and construction vehicles blocking the access to about half the streets along 1st and 2nd Avenues.

As I got closer, I realized that the ones that weren't blocked had Humvees and National Guardsmen with M-16s. As soon as they let me in, I abandoned the Crown Vic on East 39th and started walking to the office.

Along the way, I looked in the open doorways of the bars. The first tower had just collapsed and every bar was packed with a cross-section of people who would normally be walking by and a few who looked like they were jogging by when they sought cover. I ducked into one of them, promising myself I'd leave in fifteen minutes.

Like a lot of the people in the bar, I was wearing a suit and tie. So, I simply acted like everyone else who was only drinking to cope with the circumstances or calm their nerves.

I already knew the key details of the attacks, but to fit in, I felt I should stare at the TV screens and act shocked and aghast with every bit of breaking news about what I already knew.

It was only noon and everyone was drinking... one of those rare times when I had a little company in my world. It reminded me of those occasional Saturdays in college when everyone would wake up, brush their teeth, and resume drinking from the night before.

For the first time in years, I felt normal. And for the first time in a long time, I didn't have to take any steps to conceal my drinking. Is this what it took, I wondered, to feel less shame, less alone and less of an outcast... a terror attack?

Part of me wanted to stay there forever and savor the feeling of being normal. I had the rest of my life to worry about what was happening on

TV, a couple miles down the road.

The other part of me was being paged by the Governor's Office. Before I could return the page, my phone rang. It was one of the troopers on the Governor's detail wanting to know exactly where I was standing on Third Avenue. I ran out to the sidewalk and yelled, "About fifty feet from East Thirty-ninth!"

"Okay, now I see you," he said. "Did you have one for me?"

"I had one for everyone," I said.

"Get ready to walk right into the middle lane of Third Avenue and jump in the second car, the Suburban," he said. "We're not even pulling over."

Not only did they not pull over, they barely slowed down. I dove head-first into the backseat a little too hard and collided with the Governor. From the backseat, someone yelled, "Dumb fuck!"

It was the only other Governor's aide from Albany who was in Manhattan when the towers fell. As I spun around to get in his face, a trooper yelled and said, "Wolfe, don't!" The Governor, who was sitting right next to me, said nothing.

The motorcade's lights and sirens blared as we headed to what was left of the World Trade Center. I wasn't even paying attention to where we were as we passed through one roadblock after the other. Suddenly, everything turned light grey, then grey, then dark grey. There wasn't a color in sight... just different shades of grey.

When we got out of the Suburban, the air was gritty. It had an aftertaste... like drywall dust. I couldn't shake a recurring thought that made it hard to breathe. The dust in the air and the grit in my teeth was an amalgamation of everything that was obliterated when the towers fell — the buildings and the planes, but also the people in them. The stuff was everywhere — in the air, in mounds and drifts on the ground, and in our mouths and lungs. I didn't know what was more sacrilegious — spitting it out or letting it drip down my throat. I did both.

Ground Zero (the fourteen-acre area around the collapsed towers) was like the inside of an urn, except for the occasional item left intact, like leather shoes. They were scattered on the ground, just sitting in piles of dust and debris.

It wasn't a good time to contemplate things like how they got separated from the person wearing them, but it was hard to block those thoughts. My policy was to look away from the shoes; I wasn't prepared to see what might be inside them.

Every so often, someone would tell me to wipe my face. Alcohol was dripping from my head in the form of sweat, mixing with the dust and leaving grey lines on the side of my face. It was like cement dust, and the next day we were chipping it off our shoes.

It had been at least an hour since my last drink, which was normally when my heart would start racing and I would feel like I'd have a heart attack unless I got another drink. I kept thinking about how pathetic it would be if that actually happened and I had to co-op the services of emergency personnel at Ground Zero.

I was supposed to stay close to the Governor and the troopers, but every time I got more than twenty feet behind them, they'd disappear into the gray clouds of dust.

The whole time, I had no idea where I was, except when I could see the mangled remains of the Twin Towers, which I avoided looking at. I heard people say it didn't seem real and after a while they started calling it "The Pile." To me, it looked so real that I could barely distinguish the pile of debris from a pile of bodies.

We stayed at Ground Zero for a few hours before heading to a series of emergency meetings and briefings led by Mayor Giuliani and Governor Pataki. Along the way, we stopped at Bellevue Hospital and the now-closed Cabrini Medical Center.

The hallways of Cabrini were lined with paramedics and nurses and doctors. Officials there told our advance guys that the victims of the attacks were either "walking around wounded or dead because they're not here." They weren't at Bellevue Hospital either, at least not many of them.

The sad reality is that the clear majority of people who came in contact with the crashes or the collapses were killed immediately, as were almost all the firefighters who ran up the staircases. Even in the lower floors and the lobby, where emergency command centers were set up, there weren't many safe places to be when the first tower collapsed. You were either obliterated or you weren't.

At Bellevue, we were in a recovery room where there were four guys with serious injuries. Two of them were unconscious and the other two were awake but in a lot of pain.

The governor leaned over the bedrail of one of the patients, stared silently into the man's eyes and said, "You're a hero and the nation thanks you. We will get through this."

The man struggled to push words out of his mouth. I was resting my notepad on the Governor's back, waiting to write down exactly what the man was getting ready to say.

Finally, in a hoarse voice, he said, "I fell off some scaffolding in Midtown two days ago."

There was some faint laughter from the three other patients in the room — all NYFD firefighters who suffered serious injuries when the first tower collapsed. They were in rough shape. One of them told the Governor, "We'll get through this because we are New Yorkers."

It was a line the Governor wanted me to use in speeches whenever possible, and I did for several months until it grew corny and old and crossing it out became a guilty necessity.

As soon as we got back to the Third Avenue office that evening, I walked from the Governor's Suburban to a corner bodega and grabbed as many sixteen-ounce Miller Lites as I could carry to the register. I liked sixteen-ouncers because it took me five gulps to finish one instead of just three.

As always, the bodega guy handed me one beer with a separate brown bag because he knew I was going to open it while I was still in the store. Opening the can inside the store didn't make it any more legal; I just did it that way because, if I ever got caught, it seemed more plausible that I would think it was more legal. But it was September eleventh. Except for terrorism, everything was legal.

I still had a full thirty-pack of warm beer in the trunk of the black Crown Vic but I assumed both the car and the beer were in an impound lot or a landfill by now. It didn't matter; cold beer was always better — not necessary, just better. And nothing is colder than a bodega beer. Don't ask me why.

I went back to the bodega two more times that night before passing out in my room at the Eastgate Hotel.

We weren't texting in 2001. We had grey government flip phones with little screens that showed numbers and nothing else.

We also had to carry special pagers that were the equivalent of third-party texting. To send someone a message, you had to call a number and tell an operator what you wanted to say, then she would text the message to the other person's pager… but they had to be in the same secure government network. It made no sense, so naturally we did it that way.

That's what I woke up to the next morning. Coming from one side of the room was the unrelenting government chirping of the pager; from under a pile of clothes on the other side of the room was the ringing of the flip phone. When they went off simultaneously like that, it evoked a rote, psychological response from me that would have made Pavlov's dog run in front of a bus.

In my case, it meant one of two things. Either the Governor needed something, or someone else needed something and they thought that saying it was "for the Governor" would compel me to do it faster. We worked in the Governor's Office; everything we did was for the Governor.

Whenever I woke up still drunk — and that morning I did — I was in the habit of counting the things I needed before running out the door. It was always six things: Keys, pager, phone, wallet, briefcase and booze. The booze usually went in the briefcase, but on this morning, I anticipated a serious logistical problem.

I probably could have found a way to sneak drinks at Ground Zero, but even I had boundaries. Besides, every law enforcement agency in America was down there. It wasn't a good place to look sneaky.

The day after the attacks, the dust was still in the air at Ground Zero. Everything was encased in thick, almost uniform, layers of dust that was like a mixture of grey flour and papier-mâché.

I'd seen this stuff once before. It had been at a summer camp in the Adirondacks in 1980.

In May of that year, Mount St. Helens erupted and a kid from Washington State showed up to camp with a coffee can filled with ash from the fallout. It looked and felt almost identical to the stuff we were walking over now. Three inches of the stuff blanketed everything within three blocks of Ground Zero. It was static and found its way into tiny, bad areas.

In the shower that night, I kept wondering, *How did this shit get all the way up there?*

Towards the end of the first day, I was standing next to a group of firefighters. One of them was talking about climbing up the stairs and seeing a man's body falling past the stairway window. He said, "I tried to imagine what the guy was thinking... if he still had hope that there was a net on the ground."

They probably didn't have the luxury of giving it much thought. Most likely, the intense heat forced them to the window, then out. Maybe the slim chance of a net was their last thought before jumping, but the heat made the decision for them. These people had just gotten to work. One minute they were stirring their coffee and logging into their computer and the next minute they were hanging out of the window knowing they had ten seconds to live. I thought about that longer than I needed to.

AS WE WERE LEAVING Ground Zero that day, there were hundreds of people gathered outside of the restricted zone — somewhere along Canal Street — and a few of them were holding signs that said, "Ground Hero" — a sentiment aimed primarily at the dust-covered cops and firefighters involved in the recovery effort.

That's when I realized that, for every hero at Ground Zero, there were at least five idiots on Canal Street, which was as close as the public could get to the World Trade Center.

There were barricades and police tape and cops and dogs and Guardsmen with M-16s stationed there to separate the onlookers from the restricted zone. People were lined up all along the police tape, peering around barricades and vehicles or whatever else was in their way to get a better view of... whatever.

As dumb as they seemed to be, they must have realized you couldn't see the World Trade Center any more. They were just trying to witness... something. In the process, they were getting in the way.

Maybe it was because I was craving alcohol, but these people annoyed the shit out of me, especially the ones aiming their cameras to the point in the sky where the Twin Towers used to be.

They were taking pictures of the empty space in the skyline. They weren't volunteers or people looking to donate blood. They were morbid curiosity-seekers trying to see what everyone on the other side of the tape would spend years trying to forget.

Other people were swarming around the destroyed emergency vehicles being towed away from the site. They were grabbing clumps of dust and soot to keep as souvenirs or keepsakes or proof that they were there.

I had already contemplated the soot caked on the sides of my shoes and everywhere. There were people in that dust, and I spent the night of September 11 plucking gravel-sized deposits of it from my nose. I would have gladly offered up my grey boogers to the souvenir seekers.

I never drank at Ground Zero. In fact, I never thought of sneaking alcohol down there or even felt the compulsion to drink once I was there. Looking back on it now, that's amazing to me because, by 2001, I always made sure alcohol was an option. I always kept a sufficient quantity of it close by and easily accessible because I wanted — I needed — the security of knowing that I could drink myself through any situation... any way, anytime and anywhere.

I'd like to think that, on that day, my sense of decency was stronger than my compulsion to drink. The truth is, for the first time in my life, I was too shocked to even think about drinking. That's how bad it was.

IN THE HOURS after the attacks, I braced myself for news about friends who had been killed. The last thing I expected to hear about was a friend from Rochester.

Brian Sweeny — who was there when my father confronted me about my drinking — was a tough, strong-minded Irishman from the Boston area. We worked together on a lawn crew during college breaks.

His ex-fiancée was a violinist with the Rochester Symphony Orchestra, and he was in Rochester trying — desperately — to get her back. He didn't know anyone in Rochester so I introduced him to my brother and the guys we hung out with.

Everyone liked Brian instantly. It was hard not to. He wasn't afraid to do any of the stupid things we did daily. He liked to drink and he was funny as hell — especially when he did his "Rat" voice. Rat was a hooligan Brian knew from a rough Irish neighborhood in South Boston who'd provoke people he didn't like with, "Fahk yah muthah!" Brian's imitation of it, in his thick Irish accent, left me doubled up and spitting beer every time.

Brian was also a babe magnet — tall, tough and tailor-made for the cover of *Men's Health Magazine*. For all those reasons, especially the last one, Brian was quickly indoctrinated into the group, even though he stopped being a babe magnet as soon as he opened his mouth.

Gorgeous girls used to come up and hit on him and he'd ask their advice on how to get his girlfriend back. They always pretended to be sympathetic at first, but as soon as he paused to take a sip of beer, they seized the opportunity to run like hell, taking their hot friends with them.

She's all he talked about — everything they did together, how they were going to get married and how miserable he was without her. To his credit, as devastated as he was, he never uttered a negative word about her.

After a year of trying to win her back, Brian surrendered to reality. He had done all he could do, and now he had to go back to Massachusetts and get his life back in order. I drove him from Rochester to his parent's house in Spencer, Massachusetts.

I had been talking Brian off a ledge for so long, I didn't know what to say to him any more, especially because I was always saying she'd take him back. I never actually believed that; I was just trying to cheer him up so he'd be more fun to drink with.

Now, it was definitely over, and we had five hours in my Cutlass Supreme to talk about it. But for the first time ever, Brian never mentioned her name. He just sat and stared out the window in a defeated trance. I put "Chicago's Greatest Hits" in the tape player to keep the mood light.

The song "Make Me Smile" came on and Brian began mumbling his own monotone version of it with zero enthusiasm. I looked at him at a key point in the song as he wearily moaned the words, "I'm so happy... that you love me."

I didn't say anything the first time. Then he did it again, but this time he sang it slower than Chicago was singing it, so his words dragged glaringly into the silent parts to get my attention.

"Oh my God!" I yelled. "Are you shitting me?"

We got to Spencer and hung out for a little while before I headed back to Rochester. I talked to him over the next few years but as we both moved around and advanced in our careers, we talked mostly through a mutual friend.

On September twelfth, while I was at Ground Zero, our mutual friend called the Governor's Office and left a numbing message. Brian Sweeny was on Flight 175 from Boston to Los Angeles, the plane that crashed into the South Tower. With everything else that happened that day, it was hard to get any more shocked than I already was. I decided to process the whole thing later.

As soon as we got back to the offices on Third Avenue, I ran to the black Crown Vic parked on East 39th Street. I drank as fast as I could for about twenty minutes, hoping to get nice and drunk before my pager went off again.

I tried to imagine what Brian was thinking about on that plane. I couldn't help thinking about the car ride back to Massachusetts. Years after that ride, Brian met his true soulmate, a woman who deserved his unconditional loyalty.

A few weeks after the attacks, CNN aired the message Brian left on the answering machine for his wife.

From the plane, he said: "Jules, this is Brian. Listen, I'm on an airplane that's been hijacked. If things don't go well, and it's not looking good, I just want you to know I absolutely love you. I want you to feel good, go have some good times. Same to my parents and everybody. And I just totally love you and I'll see you when you get here. Bye, Babe. Hope I call you."

AROUND THE TIME OF THE ATTACKS, the Colonel left as head of the Executive Service Detail to become, of all things, an Inspector General for a state agency. He was replaced by an asshole named Major Brock, who hated the Colonel so much that his hatred extended to everyone the Colonel liked. So, Brock hated me more than anyone. He didn't like Charles, either.

Brock was a clone of that infamous prick on *Law and Order SVU*, the Internal Affairs guy, who was always trying to destroy the careers of other cops. He presented himself as morally superior to the around him and I often wondered if he thought he was genetically superior to Charles.

When the Colonel was still in charge, we were civil to one another. When the Colonel was in transition, we didn't like each other. After the Colonel left, we hated each other. By 2004, I don't know what he thought, but I wanted to beat him to death with my bare hands.

Immediately after the attacks, the Governor called for an emergency session of the State Legislature in Albany. On September 14, he and I flew back to Albany so he could address the legislature with a twenty-minute speech that I was only halfway through writing by the time we got to the helipad. I wrote the other half with the governor in the chopper, which was hard because he didn't feel like talking.

For about fifteen minutes, he stared down at my shitty handwriting, occasionally making changes in his shittier handwriting. The speech was in rough shape and the Governor was deep in thought. I didn't know what to do.

He knew so many people that died that day, including his close friend, Neil Levin. Now he had the weight of the world on his shoulders. He had to set aside his own emotions and govern his state though its darkest day.

I sat next to him with a partially written speech as he stared quietly out of the window with his chin on his hand. The last thing I wanted to do was bother him about the speech but I had no choice.

"I have those last two pages for you," I said.

He looked down at the paper for about thirty seconds and said, "Looks good; we're done."

I knew what that meant.

I ditched the pen. For the rest of the flight back to Albany, I dictated what I knew the Governor wanted to say to the Teleprompter guys in Albany.

After another hour of extreme chaos in the Assembly Chambers, I reviewed the speech on the teleprompter and the Governor delivered it. Amazingly, the haphazardly written speech was published in two books.

I went straight from the Assembly Chambers to my office and began the process of inhaling every ounce of alcohol in the refrigerator. People kept knocking on the door and the phone wouldn't stop ringing.

A trooper stuck his head in the door and said, "The helicopter is leaving in forty-five minutes. You're driving to the helipad with the Governor, right?"

Since I planned on drinking on the way to the helipad, I said, "No, I'll get to the helipad on my own but I'll be there."

Forty-five minutes later, I was still drinking in my office when Charles called from the Command Center.

"They had to leave without you," he said. "Everything okay?"

"Yeah, well... you know," I said.

"Oh, okay," he said.

"I've got to get you on another chopper," he said. "You ready?"

"Yeah," I said, "but..."

"Oh... got ya," he said. "I'll be there in fifteen minutes."

It's Charles's fault we talked to each other that way. Unless we were talking cell-to-cell, it's conceivable that someone on his end or mine could listen in on our calls. At least, that's what he said.

So Charles limited the number of nouns and verbs I could use to one per conversation. He said he was being "private." I called it paranoid. Over time, though, we had created a language of our own that relied more on tone and inflection than words.

On the way to the helipad, Charles said, "Brock is gonna be on this chopper."

"Good thing I'm drunk," I said.

"Don't throw him out, okay?" Charles said.

When we got to the helipad, the chopper was ready to go. It was one of those small bubble helicopters, and I was crammed in there with an asshole who had a gun. Maybe it was God's way of punishing me for getting drunk. More likely, it was the Governor's way of punishing me for missing the first helicopter.

It would take about an hour to get to the East 34th Street Helipad in Manhattan so I thought I should start it out on a civil note.

As I climbed into the chopper, I looked at Brock and said, "Hi Major."

He leaned forward and made an audible sniffing sound and said, "The Colonel's gone, you know."

"So what?" I asked.

He was insinuating that my drunken behavior was no longer appropriate, as if there was a time when it was.

After about a minute of awkward silence, I turned to the camera guy who was traveling with us and did my best impression of the Major: "Uh, uh, uh... The Colonel's gone, you know."

Brock just glared away, plotting.

He would eventually get the last laugh, but for now I was content leaving things just the way they were. It didn't matter whether I was nice to this guy or not. We already hated each other and he was never going to have my back.

THREE WEEKS AFTER THE 9/11 ATTACKS, my wife brought Mallory and Jackson down to New York City so I could take them to the Bronx Zoo for a few hours. After that, we drove to Times Square.

It was my first day off since the attacks and I couldn't relax. I was edgy and irritable and sweaty and craving alcohol — basically the same way I'd been for the past three weeks.

Jackson had been in FAO Schwarz for about a half hour entertaining himself with his signature pastime, which was lining up random things on the ground in a formation that made sense only to him. At the lake, he'd do the same thing with rocks in the sand for hours at a time. (I wondered at first but he's fine now.)

My cravings and irritability were exacerbated by the frustration of not being able to get a three-year-old out of FAO Schwarz... at least not without making a scene.

Nothing I said could convince him to leave the store. I told him that the ice cream guy outside had a surprise for him; he didn't care. I offered to buy him everything he was playing with; he didn't care. I told him there was another wave of terror attacks and this one was heading for FAO Schwarz; he didn't give a crap. He wanted to stay right where he was.

Finally, I led him out by the arm, and he was going berserk every horrific step of the way. I did what most parents do: I waited until I was outside to deal with it. That's when I lost my head and started carrying on like I just "cheeked" my meds and ran away from Bellevue... but going outside to have a meltdown doesn't get you much privacy when you're at Times Square.

It was one of my worst moments ever.

In retrospect, maybe it wasn't as bad as I've made it out to be in my mind over the years. It's actually the kind of thing that happens at Walmart ten times a day. But for me it was uncharacteristic and shameful. I got down on my knees and grabbed his little arms and yelled at him to stop whining.

When I came to my senses and looked up, everyone within a hundred feet was staring at me… almost out of pity. This city had just been attacked by terrorists, and everyone was in the feel-good spirit of unity, strength and love. And now they were looking at me like I was helping the terrorists win.

That's when the doorman from FAO Schwarz, who was dressed up like a big toy soldier, came over, pointed to an ice cream wagon, and cheerfully said, "It's okay, daddy. It's nothing a little ice cream can't solve, right little guy?" Jackson immediately stopped crying, and the big toy soldier said, "See, Dad?" and happily marched away.

And there I was, still on my knees, praying for an aneurism to take me right then and there.

As it turned out, the toy soldier was right. Ice cream made my obsessive-compulsive little boy forget about the perfectly straight line of cars he had to leave behind at FAO Schwartz. And it was enough to make everyone else forget about my ugly episode. But for some reason, I've never been able to smooth it over with myself.

After it happened, like manna from heaven, I saw a beautiful neon sign, the kind that spelled out the word "Corona."

"Are you guys as hungry as I am?" I asked.

As soon as we were seated, I went into the usual routine. I said I had to go to the bathroom, then headed for the bar.

About a week later, I started to push for permission to leave Manhattan and go back to Albany. By then, most of the 9/11 funerals had been held. The ones that hadn't were on hold until search crews gave family members something to bury. For some families, that could mean never.

I wanted to leave New York City so much, I blew off the opportunity to meet The Who, my favorite band. They were going to be at the Concert for New York City at Madison Square Garden on October twentieth. The Governor was speaking there, which meant I could have gone with him and stayed backstage impersonating someone who was working.

The Governor was giving the only kind of speech a politician should deliver at an event like that: a speech barely long enough to form a complete sentence.

By my own rules, I should have gone to the event, not to meet The Who, but to ensure there were no glitches when the speech was loaded onto the teleprompter. I always insisted on doing that myself.

In this case, the teleprompter wasn't a pair of glass plates; the words were projected onto a giant screen facing the main stage. It's not just a matter of proofreading. It's a matter of spacing and formatting and breaking up the text at certain spots based on the speaker's pace and cadence.

The speechwriter is really the only one who can do this, but in this case, despite The Who, the speechwriter wanted to go home and drink away the past month.

I arranged for the Governor's advance guy to act as sort of a remote set of eyes for me. A couple hours before the start of the show, he stood on the stage and read the speech to me from the giant screen. I made some changes while laying on a couch with a case of beer in the Adirondacks.

Before I hung up, the advance guy said, "I almost forgot. He's speaking in between acts. They wanted to know if we had a preference about where he should be in the lineup."

"Just make sure he speaks after someone like James Taylor or Elton John," I said. "Don't put him after The Who."

Once all that was taken care of, I hung up the phone, grabbed another beer and watched as The Who riled up the crowd with a hard-hitting rendition of "Won't Get Fooled Again." The crowd was still going crazy as George Elmer Pataki walked out to the stage to deliver my short little speech, and that's when I turned off the TV. I was done obsessing over 9/11... at least I thought I was.

Chapter Nine

The Long Mourning After

WHEN I LEFT MANHATTAN, I drove straight to the place that made me feel the way John Denver must have felt when he wrote "Rocky Mountain High."

The Adirondack Mountain region of New York is the exact opposite of New York City, and my wife and I had bought a vacation house there two years before the 9/11 attacks — a two-and-a-half story lake house, about sixty yards from a private beach and dock on Loon Lake.

The lake house was in Chestertown, home to Loon Lake, the 1964 White House Christmas tree, the grave of William Butler Yeats' father and that's it. The house was my heaven... saturated with the smell of mossy rocks, evergreen needles and knotty pine, a smell that brought me back to my summers climbing the Adirondack Mountains as a kid.

I was about ten beers into a thirty-pack — which, for me, was an appetizer — when my pager went off. I had to go back to New York City. After a couple days there, I dragged myself kicking and screaming up the Million-Dollar Staircase. It was my first day back to work in the Albany office since the attacks.

Along the way, I wondered if someone got into my office and took the beer I'd heisted from the SUNY reception the month before. Surprisingly, it was all there, and even though it was only ten o'clock in the morning, I decided to drink one, which meant I decided to drink them all.

After drinking slowly but steadily in my office for about an hour, I turned on the computer, knowing my email inbox was going to be filled with eulogy requests. I dreaded these, not because each one required hours of research and writing, but because each one required me to dive straight into people's deepest despair. Sometimes I felt like an intruder. Always I felt helpless.

Writing eulogies came easy to me, yet when I spoke to family members on the phone, I constantly found myself at a loss for words.

At times, while talking to the loved ones of victims, certain details would connect with images I saw at Ground Zero.

To write the eulogy properly, I had to imagine I was the person on the other end of the phone — people who had suffered a sudden and immeasurable loss. To relate to that person with a speech, first you have to feel what that person is feeling. You have to imagine you suffered the same loss as them. In the weeks and months after 9/11, I did that too many times.

To put it in perspective, on September eleventh, I wrote the Governor's first official statement about the attacks and saved the document under the filename "WTC-1." A year later, I wrote the Governor's remarks for the one-year memorial service at Ground Zero. I saved that document as "WTC-163." About half of those 163 speeches were eulogies.

That's a lot of consoling words being written by a guy who was drinking himself to bed every night even before 9/11.

Once I began writing a eulogy, I didn't stop until I was done because it usually took a while to get in the proper frame of mind for that kind of a speech. A little drinking helped a lot; a lot of drinking helped more. I did the latter.

A week earlier, when I had still been in Manhattan, the Governor's Scheduling Office sent me a list of 9/11 funerals, with asterisks next to the ones where he was speaking. I pulled it out of a giant envelope filled with all the other things I was in denial about. There were a lot of asterisks. The first day back was going to be a long one.

Before doing anything, I needed to secure a ride home because I planned on being several times over the legal limit when it was time to drive home. This was one of the few areas of my drinking where I exercised at least some degree of responsibility.

I'd like to think that a smart problem drinker, as a general practice, would take pains to protect their drinking by not driving drunk. Being put in a jail cell is a serious drinker's second-worst nightmare. Being put on probation is the first, because if you get five years of probation, that's how long it's going to be till your next drink.

My closest friends at the time were my greatest enablers; they really couldn't be one if they weren't the other. That's why most of my friends were State Troopers. And maybe "enabler" projects the wrong connotation.

It's fairer to say that my trooper friends were very good at managing my behavior. As self-destructive as the behavior was at times, they kept it legal and non-lethal. They rarely preached. When they did, I simply asked, "Am I free to go now or am I under arrest?"

AFTER A MONTH AT GROUND ZERO, it was hard to focus on things like charter schools and tax cuts while I was still writing 9/11 eulogies. A lot of families were waiting for some sort of remains — or even a piece of jewelry — to bury before making funeral arrangements for their loved ones. I was in the process of preparing for the 2002 State-of-the-State Address when I stopped to write the last 9/11 eulogy. That was in the middle of November.

The very next day, it was time to start writing the dreaded State-of-the-State Address. It was always an inverted challenge for me, as a writer, to use as many words as possible to say absolutely nothing while living up to the expectations of everyone by keeping it intensely boring. But I got very good at it, which made me worry about my future, both as a writer and as a person. It was great for my future as an alcoholic.

One day, the Governor was reviewing a draft of the speech in his office. Whenever we got to this part of the process, he'd sit at this desk with a pen in his hand and start reading. I'd sit on the other side of the desk with nothing to do except study his facial expressions and pray for his writing hand to stay still.

One time, without even changing the expression on his face, he crossed out three full pages from the middle of a thirteen-page speech. When he handed the speech back to me, he said, "We need to do something different in the middle."

This time, the Governor said he didn't want any distractions until we finalized what he called a "problematic section of the speech" that didn't seem to flow with the rest of the speech.

"Stop changing the shit before and after that section," I always wanted to tell him, "and it'll flow." Instead, I'd just say something like,

"Okay, I'll just change it back to the way I had it three drafts ago."

We had already been in there for over an hour. My forehead was beading up with sweat. My heart was pounding and I was getting irritable and restless and desperate for a drink.

We were on the verge of wrapping things up when the Governor's secretary asked if we had a few minutes to say a quick hi to someone. I thought I was going to explode.

As I stormed toward the door leading out of the Governor's Office into the reception area, I bitched out loud, "We're never gonna get this fucking speech done."

I accidentally said it right into the face of the guy walking in. It was LL Cool J.

"Oh, you guys got work to do," he said. "I was just saying hi. I didn't mean to…"

Then the Governor walks up and says, "LL, what's up? You know John, right?"

I was thinking, *No, he doesn't, John. How the hell would he?* But out loud I said, "Holy shit, it's LL Cool J."

I was quick to seize the opportunity.

"Governor," I said, "This is actually a good chance for me to run down to my office and make some of these changes and then I'll run right back."

"Yeah, yeah, good idea," he said.

I ran to my office and I still had the speech in my hand when I inhaled two beers. I sat down and made a few changes while I drank several more, and stuffed another one in an interagency envelope so I could digest the others while I walked back to the Governor's office then drink one more in the little bathroom right outside the Governor's office.

Along the way, I kept telling myself, *This speech is going to suck. Then again, it's a State-of-the-State address; all it can do is suck.*

Interagency envelopes, or "pouches," were the heavy, tan-colored 11" x 17" envelopes used by state mail rooms. They weren't meant for carrying cans of beer, but I never used them for anything else.

For my purposes, they were far from ideal. Some of the envelopes had marble-sized holes punched through both sides so the mail room workers could tell just by looking at them if there was anything inside.

I didn't realize it for a long time, but one of my State Trooper buddies told me that my silver Coors Lite cans shone right through the holes. That problem was easily fixed with a piece of paper, but it was just another thing to remember for a routine that was becoming increasingly high maintenance.

I was still wiping beer dew from my chin when I walked back into the Governor's office. The Governor and LL Cool J were standing just inside the door, like they were saying goodbye. I walked in all bubbly, with a fresh glow, and said, "Hey, can we get a picture with the three of us?" People have looked at that photo and said, "Why are you sweating?"

THE PROCESS OF WRITING the State-of-the-State address is excruciatingly tedious. It's like shoveling snow off the field at the Super Bowl. You're the center of attention, and technically, you're in charge because the game can't go on until you're done, but no one with a brain would trade places with you. And by 2001, I had already been through the process five times.

After the first one back in 1996, I promised myself I'd change bedpans at a nursing home before writing another one. Sometimes, I thought the end product at a nursing home would be better.

Every year, no matter how hard I fought to keep it out, the speech would get weighed down with programmatic nonsense, government jargon and the unavoidable, squishy pandering to women, Hispanics and "enviros."

Sometimes I couldn't hide my irritation, especially after a long night of revising revisions, editing edits or moving paragraphs back to where they were before they got moved everywhere else.

Writing "final draft" on the Governor's copy of the speech meant nothing. The Governor was surrounded by bean counters who'd whisper in his ear in between drafts.

I'd walk into the Governor's Office and he'd say: "What about women? What do we have in there for women?"

And I'd say something snippy like, "I think women are getting the tax cuts in the speech."

And if the whispering bean counter was still in the office, they'd look aghast, as if I'd just urinated on a picture of Susan B. Anthony.

Or he'd say, "We only have three things in here for Hispanics."

And I'd say, "Which is three things more than we have for Asians."

Comments like that elicited a cold, short look from the Governor. Usually, he would pause for a second, then go right back to doing whatever he was doing. That was especially annoying because it was like he was saying, "Yes, I heard what you just said, and it warrants nothing in return."

Everyone knew I hated the politics of pandering, and I did. But it wasn't a matter of principle. I had abandoned those when I accepted this job. I hated pandering because it was impossible to write a speech that spoke individually to every group of New Yorkers... one group at a time. So maybe it was a matter of principle.

Every step along the way, I argued that the speech was getting too long and way too boring. I could barely stay awake when we rehearsed it the first time, much less the third. I wasn't the only one. Midway through the first State-of-the-State address I wrote, one of the State Troopers standing at attention beside the lectern collapsed at the Governor's feet. That was encouraging.

Over the next few years, I refined the process a little, which, I confess, entailed a fair amount of deceit and manipulation. State-of-the-State time was a time to boast about the Governor's past accomplishments and push his agenda items for the coming year. So it was a time where all the governor's top people tried to assert themselves and not only be part of the process, but to some extent, control the process.

One of the Governor's most trusted advisors, who was also his close friend, was constantly trying to get his pet projects mentioned in the State-of-the-State address.

Obviously, I was the gatekeeper of what got in and what didn't get in. The only way something got in was if the Governor specifically told me to put it in or if I got paper with his writing on it telling me to put it in.

This one advisor would actually come down to my office with a paragraph or two he wrote and say: "I talked to the Governor about this proposal. He said we should put it in the speech but the language isn't very strong so you'll probably want to rewrite it."

Oh yeah, I'd rewrite it. I'd intentionally make it worse. I'd rearrange the concept of the thing to make it sound awkward and ridiculous. Then I'd spring it on the Governor when no one else was around to defend it and he'd say, "What the fuck is this?"

I'd say, "Yeah, I didn't like that either; Mike said you wanted it in."

"Get rid of it," he'd say, then Mike would get yelled at later, but by then I had already deleted the shitty text so he didn't know why.

Another thing I did to control the process was kind of funny. Every year, I made a big deal about how many words were in the speech. Throughout the entire process, I'd loudly announce the word count at key times.

Whenever we went through a round of changes and I brought the revised speech back to the Governor, I'd write the word count on the front with a short comment like, "perfect" or "a little long."

No one, especially the Governor, wanted the speech to last more than an hour. Over time, the Governor and everyone else believed I could actually calculate the time — right down to the minute — by cross-calculating the word count, the number of applause lines and the Governor's cadence.

To really sell the concept, I'd secretly tell key people how many words were in the speech as if it were some sort of nuclear code. Sometimes I'd even write it on a tiny piece of paper and slip it to them.

Even the Governor fell for it. He was constantly saying, "Wolfe-let…. What's the word count now?"

I'd throw out a big number and a little hint.

"It's almost seven thousand words. As long as we don't add anything more, I think we're okay," I'd say.

It doesn't matter, of course; I just told everyone it mattered. Here's how it worked.

During the final week of the process, the Governor would bring his top ten or so advisors into the Red Room and rehearse the speech. It was basically a gathering of over-inflated egos that always turned into a dick-measuring contest with everyone trying to show the other who had more influence with the Governor.

Halfway through the rehearsal, an advisor might interrupt and say, "Governor, at this point in the speech you should talk about what we did in Newburgh with the Brownfields program."

And the Governor, who always had a hard time saying "no" to certain advisors, would say, "Wolfe-let, did you hear that?"

And if I hated the idea, I'd say, "Yeah, I guess we could shoehorn that in there. It would need a transition but we're at about seven-thousand-four-hundred words so I'd have to take out the two paragraphs on the Adirondack Land Purchase." I made up the word count and the false choice about the Adirondack Land Purchase, but it would kill the Brownfield idea right then and there.

The Governor would say, "Oh, hmmm... well, Wolfe-let will look at it and we'll see if it works," which was another way of saying, "Fuck you and your stupid idea."

Obviously, the word count of a speech does determine how long it takes to deliver it. But during rehearsal, the cadence is different and there's no applause. That's why I used a stopwatch to determine exactly how long it took him to deliver one-hundred words. I timed him at about eight minutes. I (generously) estimated an additional two minutes for applause. That makes the math very easy. Six thousand words equals one hour; I did whatever I had to do to limit the speech to that number. When I shouted out the word count during rehearsal or revisions, I was just making up numbers to keep stupid ideas from the peanut gallery out of the speech. If the speech was still too long after the final revisions, I could surgically remove five-hundred words without anyone noticing.

This process was a large part of my life and my drinking for nearly a decade.

We rehearsed in the majestic assembly chambers, usually for two nights in a row prior to the day of the speech. On average, there'd be about twenty of us in there: me and the Governor and three people who needed to be there, and fifteen staffers who didn't mind staying up till three am just to get a little ass-kissing time with the Governor.

Every run-through of the speech took at least an hour, and it got more boring each time we did it. I would hang out near the Teleprompter with a hard copy of the speech in my hand.

The Governor stood ten feet away at the lectern. And right behind me there was a control room where they operated the audio and lights. That was where I kept my beer. I could stand in the doorway of the control room and everyone could see the one half of my body holding the speech but not the other half holding the beer. Every few minutes, the Governor would pause and ask me a question.

"Wolfe-let, do we need these last four words?" he'd ask. From inside the control room, I'd pull the beer away from my mouth and yell back, "No, Governor. I'm crossing it off now."

None of this even raised an eyebrow from the tech guys working back there. They saw me do it every year. And when they came to my office for the file transfers, they'd walk straight to the fridge and grab a beer.

Half the time, I doubt they even wanted one, but I'd insist on it because it would look bad if the Governor walked in and I was the only one drinking... not that it would look better if we were all drinking. When it was time for them to leave, I'd finish their beers for them. When they looked at me sideways, I'd say, "I don't have a sink in here."

My office was like Tijuana. As soon as people set foot in it, they felt like they were in a place where rules no longer mattered. "What happens in Wolfe's office stays in Wolfe's office," they used to say.

One time in the middle of a Tuesday, I was drinking while working on an education speech with one of my assistants. The Governor's education advisor — a brainy workaholic square — walked in to see if we had any questions. As soon as he walked in, I said, "Want a beer?"

"Oh sure," he said, and he actually finished it. After he left, my assistant said, "Everyone who walks in here is instantly corrupted."

When we were done rehearsing for the night, the governor would say, "I guess it's time for everyone to go home and go to sleep while Wolfe goes back to his office and works for another two hours." It was his way of feigning slight guilt in a light-hearted way. The reality is that they were going back to the mansion to drink wine and I was going back to my office to drink beer.

Besides, usually when I had to go back to the office and work on the speech, a handful of other people had to go back to their offices to dig up information for me. At three or four in the morning, they'd pop their heads into my office to see if I needed anything before they went home.

One by one, they'd come to the door and I'd look up from the couch wearing boxers and a T-shirt and say, "No, I'm all set. It's a one-man job from here." As soon as I was sure everyone except the troopers were off the floor, I'd drink until I passed out on the couch.

As they walked to their cars, they must have been wondering how the speech would get done with me laying on the couch, drinking and watching TV. That's how I got mentally prepared for the challenge, and I never missed a deadline.

On the day of the speech, I always sat in the Assembly Chambers right next to the Teleprompter operator while the Governor did his thing. At that point, my job was done, but I always kept a paper copy of the speech in my hand in case of an emergency.

One year, Assembly Speaker Sheldon Silver had the Assembly chambers renovated and re-carpeted for the sole sake of wasting other people's money. In the middle of one of our rehearsals, I walked up to the Teleprompter operator and touched his metal chair. The static shock from the carpet traveled from my finger, through the chair and into the computer and blacked out the entire system.

When I explained to the Governor why he was staring at two blank glass plates, he said, "Okay, Wolfe-let. You're in charge of figuring out what we do if that happens tomorrow."

I roped off the teleprompter guy, then sat next to him during the speech with a can of static guard. Every few minutes during the hour-long speech, I sprayed the operator, his chair, the floor and the feet of anybody who got within three feet of the monitor.

Anywhere from two days to two weeks after the annual State-of-the-State address, the Governor is required to submit a budget to the legislature and deliver a Budget Address. It doesn't take nearly as long to write as the first speech because it's shorter and has a lot of numbers in it, which allowed me to pack it with twice the tedium in half the time.

IT WAS GETTING HARDER to delay the first drink of the day because it was getting increasingly hard to find friends to help me kill the time.

By 2002, most of my closest friends in the Governor's Office had jumped ship. Back then we called it "four and out," meaning you put in your four years with the Governor to get the experience on your resume, then used it to "cash in" with a top post in one of the agencies or in the private sector. That's what seventy-five percent of my original colleagues had already done.

Now, after seven years with the Governor, I was the seventh-highest paid member of the Governor's staff. I started in 1995 with a salary of $48,000 and now I was making $135,000. That's an unprecedented salary jump for someone whose job title only went from "Speechwriter" to "Chief Speechwriter." *The New York Times* thought it was unusually high too, so they published it, highlighting my name, title and salary in a glaring graphic that ran with a story on state spending.

Many of the people working in the offices around mine were interns when I first started. The people they interned for were the same people I used to work and drink with. Prior to 9/11, I had squandered the opportunity to move onward and upward into the private sector. Now, given the way I was drinking, it was hard to imagine making that transition.

I tried looking at the bright side. I was making great money doing a job that was easiest to do when I was drunk. Who else was going to not only tolerate that, but accommodate and reward me for it? It was hard to ignore the fact that, as my drinking increased, so did my salary. In fact, it nearly tripled… and they threw in a very fast Crown Victoria. Why would I leave?

Someday, I convinced myself, I'd stop drinking so much and shoot for a job as speechwriter in the White House. After a few years doing that, I would move into the private sector. That was always my end goal. For now, I'd stay right where I was until I could figure out what to do about my drinking.

Chapter Ten

The Difference a Day Makes

I DON'T REMEMBER what prompted the occasion, but on the Labor Day after 9/11, my ex-wife's family reserved a row of rooms at one of the nicer chain hotels on the Lake George strip. It sticks out in my mind because, for me, it was the perfect weekend. And it was the last time I can remember when drinking was fun. I could drink as early and as much as I wanted — while being around other people — without having to sneak around.

Thanks to my ex-father-in-law, a wonderful man who drank the way I did, there was an endless supply of beer at the hotel. And thanks to the proximity of the hotel, there was an endless line of bars within walking distance. For me, having a room on the Lake George strip was pure heaven. Bars everywhere, lots of lights and lots of happy people and a big comfortable bed to pass out on so I could sleep it off and start all over again.

The best thing about Lake George in the summer was that I could drink at any hour of the day and it was okay because someone else was doing the same thing. It was like 9/11 without all the dust and horror.

For me, the amount of fun you can have on the Lake George boardwalk is limited only by your imagination.

One night, I was leaning against a post on the boardwalk with a pint of Guinness in one hand and a Bud Light in the other. I was positioned in front of a gangway leading to a giant pontoon boat and it must have looked like I owned the boat.

A group of about fifteen Chinese tourists came by and the comedian in the group walked right up to me — his face got way too close to mine — and said, "We like your boat and now we take the ride?" The rest of the group laughed longer than they should have for a joke that wasn't funny. Then I realized they were laughing at me. I guess they thought my dumbfounded non-reaction was funny.

"Ha, ha, ha," I said. "No, I can't let you take the boat. I use it for tours."

"You are the boat man?" he said, "Then we get on the boat now.... Ha, ha, ha"

And the whole group laughed again, which made me feel less guilty about what I was about to do to them.

"Yep," I said. "We start here and then we go down the east shore to the Narrows and then we circle around the islands and come right back to this dock. It takes about an hour."

Now the group he was closing in around me, listening intently. Suddenly, the source of their amusement was offering them something of interest. And when the comedian relayed what I said to the rest of the group, they all nodded to each other with excitement.

"When do we go?" the comedian asked in a sort of a demanding tone.

"The next ride is at nine o'clock," I said. "So I'm going to go get my assistant and you may want to go grab some snacks for the ride and then we'll meet right here in twenty minutes."

A few of them whipped out their cameras (of course) and aimed them at me as I walked down the gangway and stepped into the boat and pretended to be checking the navigation lights.

"Yep, we're good to go," I said as I stepped off the boat. "I'll see you at nine o'clock."

While they scurried off to get their snacks, I went back to the upper deck of the bar, which was overlooking the pontoon boat. I had been hanging out there earlier with a rowdy group of people and they were still there.

I asked them, "How much will you guys give me if I can do a dance and make a group of Chinese people materialize right there?" as I pointed down to the boardwalk.

They laughed and said things like "shut up" and "you're drunk" then laughed some more.

At about 8:50, I started doing my dance, very slow and subtle at first. I was discreetly looking down the boardwalk waiting for my Chinese tourists. When they finally appeared about one-hundred feet away, I picked up the pace of the dance and timed my crescendo perfectly for when they arrived at the boat.

Having won the bet that really wasn't a bet because I didn't win anything, I went down to the boat and greeted my Chinese guests.

I opened the gate to the boat. "Come on in," I said. "Make yourself comfortable. There's plenty of room for all of you."

They laughed at absolutely nothing as they boarded the boat with cameras and food. I was pleased that they still thought I was their lackey clown. Now, I could write this whole thing off as revenge, instead of mean-spirited.

I told the group to look up to the deck where my drunk friends were still watching. I pointed out one guy, a big Irish wiseass named Mike who had been busting my balls earlier in the night.

"See that man there?" I said, pointing to Mike. "That's Mike. He's got your tickets and he'll be driving the boat. I'll go tell him you're ready." And they stood there smiling up at Mike.

I went up the stairs to the deck and told Mike, "Dude, they love you. They want to meet you."

Then I just left out the side door and walked a half-mile down the street to Duffy's, my favorite bar in Lake George.

THE NEXT DAY WAS THE last full day of Labor Day weekend. As soon as I woke up, I went for a forty-five-minute run. It was sunny, hot, maybe eighty degrees, and there was hardly a cloud in the sky.

As I ran through the village heading north to Diamond Point, people with their sunglasses and coffee were just emerging from their condos and hotel rooms and checking out the perfect day. The strip was slowly coming back to life. The souvenir shops, arcades and even the bars were gearing up for one of the busiest days of the season.

Once I got through the strip, I ran north towards Diamond Point. When my watch hit twenty-two minutes, I turned around and ran back to the village.

The sidewalks were crowded now as people went in and out of the arcades and souvenir shops carrying beach bags, pushing strollers and walking dogs.

After a shower and a few beers back at the room, a bunch of us headed to the Million-Dollar Beach on the south end of Lake George. I dumped the remains of a thirty-pack of beer into a large plastic bag I stole from the maid's cart, added a bucket of ice, grabbed a towel and started walking with the group.

It was a rare opportunity to drink out in the open, right on the street. I guess "opportunity" is the wrong word since it was illegal. But everyone in my group was from Connecticut. I wanted them (me) to have fun so I told them that New York had abolished open container laws.

The beach was almost full. We set up right next to a lifeguard station with three large blankets, a few chairs and a big umbrella in the middle. I sat, very happily, in a beach chair right next to my plastic bag of beer, loving life outside of the shadows.

The Million-Dollar Beach (there were a lot of million-dollar things in my life) was hopping. Every inch of sand was alive with summer. A group of about ten teenagers were playing a variation of volleyball that allowed throwing sand in the face of the person trying to hit the ball.

There were a few Frisbees sailing around and there was the requisite pair of awkward-looking twenty-year-olds playing hacky sack for some reason. Kids were running in and out of the water and a few boys were ambushing their sunbathing parents with Super Soakers.

There was the occasional lifeguard whistle followed by the pimply warning, "No throwing sand please," and that was followed by another warning from the guilty child's mother, "Do it one more time, Kyle, and you're coming in!" There were people wearing bathing suits and eating hot dogs who shouldn't be wearing bathing suits and eating hot dogs.

When there was no more beer, a few of us made our way to the nearest bar, then to the arcade because studies have shown there's nothing more fun than playing air hockey when you're drunk.

It was almost five o'clock and I could feel the end of summer closing in on me. I was still in the arcade watching a kid running from game to game with a big casino cup of quarters in one hand and a string of game tickets from the other, flowing behind him like a long red dragon tail.

Back at the hotel, we sat outside getting drunk and listening to the belly flops and cannon balls coming from the pool. It was nice to drink like a normal person for a change — well, like a normal person who's an alcoholic — without having to sneak around slugging down beers behind closed blinds and parked cars. It was nice to be just another guy walking around with a beer instead of having to duck below the dashboard to steal a swig. It was nice to have the rest of the world join me for a drink in the middle of the day, especially because I knew I'd be drinking alone tomorrow.

I've never understood how other people could just stop drinking after the weekend. And they didn't just stop; they'd make cute little jokes about it. They'd say Mondays are like men because they come too fast.

For me, it was no joking matter. For me, Sunday afternoons were like that last hospital visit you make to a loved one… and you know the next time you see them they'll be in a casket and everyone will be lying about how good they look.

I referred to the day after Labor Day as "Suicide Tuesday" because "Terrible Tuesday" didn't sound bad enough. Labor Day is summer's death. The day after Labor Day is the wretched burial. And the entire month of October is the mourning period. For me, it was a harsh reminder that I had to keep drinking when everybody else went back to coffee.

On that Suicide Tuesday, I woke up in a fog. As expected, everything seemed grey and dismal, and just to dampen my spirits further, it was cold and drizzly. On the dreadful, sober drive to work, a stupid thought popped into my head as I was trying to lighten my mood: "I was going from the Million-Dollar Beach to the Million-Dollar Staircase."

I felt like I should pull over and punish myself just for having the thought.

When the car phone in Crown Vic rang, I took a deep breath before looking down to see who it was. It was the Governor's Office.

"Hey John, it's Mary, how was your weekend?" the phone said.

"Oh, it was… good," I said. "Hey, let me call you right back, okay?"

"Oh, okay, we'll be here," she said.

Mary was one of the secretaries in the Governor's Office and I liked her too much to subject her to my miserable mood.

On the way up the Million-Dollar Staircase, I paused every few steps to check my pulse. I could feel my heart pounding against the inside of my jacket like someone was punching me in the chest. Halfway up the first set of steps, I began to worry about passing out and crashing down the rock staircase. I crouched down and took deep breaths so my heart would stop racing.

Sweat was rolling down my forehead and into my eyes. I just wanted to get to my office and I was praying no one would see me before I got there.

Fortunately, this section of the staircase was rarely used because the entire Second Floor was the Governor's Office, which the *New York Post* called "Fort Pataki." It was sealed off in a way that made using the Million-Dollar Staircase inconvenient.

The legislators who worked on the third and fourth floors would never deign to walk up that many stairs, no matter how historic and majestic they were.

I loved the Million-Dollar Staircase, despite the abysmal condition I was always in while climbing it. I was sure I'd get my last rites there.

I stayed crouched down for several minutes staring up to the top stair. After a minute, I stood up slowly and moved cautiously onward, using the same, carefully-planned motion to lift each foot up to the next step.

When I got to the top, I wiped my forehead and took another series of deep breaths, unlocked my office and collapsed on the couch without turning on the lights.

There were only two beers in the refrigerator. After drinking both as fast as I could, I felt a little better, a little more relaxed and a little less worried.

I walked the perimeter of the Governor's Floor, which is four hallways that form a square around the War Room, then went back to my office and printed out the Governor's Schedule. There were a few speeches coming up… nothing I couldn't write from home tonight.

Then I had the kind of thought that becomes a promise the second you have it. It was the thought that, no matter how grey life gets, happy people are drinking and having fun just down the road. I jumped into the black Crown Vic and drove right back to Lake George.

IT TOOK AN HOUR to get to the Lake George strip and along the way the temperature dropped from fifty-two degrees to forty. I drove straight to the Million-Dollar Beach and sat in the parking lot sipping beer and staring at the wet sand where people had been playing and having fun just two days earlier.

I sat there taking measured gulps of beer and trying to imagine the kids throwing sand and the lifeguards with their whistles. I could see a thousand yards in every direction but there wasn't a single person in sight. It didn't look like the same place. It didn't even look like a place where anyone could ever be happy.

The strip itself was just as desolate. There was only one car parked on the street and it looked like the rest of Lake George: abandoned. The streets that, the day before, had been lined with people and scooters parked cars and motorcycles were bare now. It was a ghost town, minus the whistling wind, boarded windows and tumbleweed.

I sat in my car for a while and stared at the strip of the unlit neon signs, dark arcades and gated storefronts. A cop went by. I knew he'd see the black Crown Vic and wonder what was going on. It wouldn't be the first time a cop mistook it for an investigator's car and came up to shoot the breeze. I tried to think about what I'd say if his curiosity got the best of him.

It didn't happen; he kept driving. But I'm not sure what I would have said if he pulled up and asked, "Everything okay?"

In a troubling sort of way, it's a good question.

There were a million people here two days ago. Why was I the only one here today… doing this? Why didn't I see other people standing by themselves contemplating the contrast between festive and gloomy? What was wrong with me?

I turned around and drove slowly back to the southern end of the strip. All along, I had been keeping my eyes open for a neon beer sign that was lit. I didn't just want a draft beer; I wanted to find a place where other people were drinking exactly the way they were drinking two days ago.

Duffy's didn't just look closed; it looked like it was in foreclosure. The upper deck was enclosed in plywood. All the other bars on the boardwalk that I had gone to over the weekend were cold, dark and deserted. There wasn't a soul in sight… just a handful of ducks who were too depressed to quack.

Finally, about a half mile past the strip, I saw a sign in a window that looked like it had electricity running through it. It was either a bar or a restaurant or a hotel or all three. I'd seen the place before but for some reason I'd never been in it. The name of the joint, "The Lemon Peel," didn't provide much of a clue about what was inside.

I went in, of course, and was relieved to see a nice long bar with a bartender and two working TVs. At the far end of the bar, there were several older guys who looked so much alike it was as if someone had copy-and-pasted the same old man on four different barstools.

They stared at me hard for five seconds, then never looked at me again. It was like they downloaded every ounce of information they needed about me in one long stare, then deemed me unnecessary and deleted me.

The bartender was more cordial, although his greeting was unusual.

"So... what's the big story over here?" he asked.

"I'll have the usual," I said, trying to be funny. He just looked at me with no expression.

"Okay, then," I said. "I'll have two Coors Lights."

He laid out two napkins, while looking out the front window to see who the second beer was for.

I tried to drink the first one slowly but it was gone by the time the bartender got to the register. And by the time he came back with my change I was almost done with the other one. He just looked at me with a cocked head, as if to say, "Do you wanna talk about it?"

"Oh, yeah, I'll have a couple more," I said.

I knew I'd have to leave after the next two. It was obvious I was my own designated driver and I didn't want to test my luck with this bartender. I tried to nurse the next two.

I didn't feel like making eye contact with anyone so I just read the *AP* news alerts on my digital pager. And after that, I re-read old messages and checked the weather a few times until I was out of beer and whatever optimism drove me here.

This wasn't what I'd had in mind. I didn't know what I thought would be happening there. I guess I was hoping everyone was still drinking and in a good mood. I hoped the kids were still playing, and the dogs were still running loose, and the parents were still drinking and laughing.

Sometimes I think that's what I was always hoping for when I drank alone.

The contrast between what I was hoping for and what I found wasn't surprising but somehow it was still disappointing, like scratching off a lottery ticket and being disappointed when you lose. I guess I knew there'd be no crowds of happy people drinking and having fun in Lake George that day, but for some reason I had to make sure.

Apparently, the party was over. Unless there were hundreds of drunk and happy people hiding behind the cold, dark buildings, no one extended Labor Day weekend without telling me.

As I walked back to the black Crown Vic, I wondered why I was stupid enough to park an official state car so close to a bar. I don't know why I suddenly cared about appearances. The day before, I was using the same car for tailgate parties.

I stood on the sidewalk for a few minutes, pretending to stretch and yawn, while looking around to make sure no one was watching me, then ducked into the car and headed back to my office and my refrigerator.

Chapter Eleven

A Time for Choosing

AT FIRST, I THOUGHT I was imagining it, but in the year since I returned to Albany following the 9/11 attacks, it seemed like it was harder to get drunk. I say "harder" because it wasn't simply a matter of drinking more; I had to drink more and faster.

Kevin, the IT guy in the Governor's Office, saw me shot-gunning beer one Saturday as I was writing a commencement speech for Siena College.

"So you have to be drunk to write a speech now?" he asked.

"That's old news," I laughed.

There was a time when I *didn't* have to, but there was also a time when I believed in the programs and policies I was writing about. But after a few years in Albany, I had been in enough back rooms to realize that even well-intentioned politicians like George Pataki are powerless to make government any better or the political ruling class any less corrupt.

I was surrounded by people who took this stuff seriously. They talked about legislation and legislators and polls and primary races and power brokers with an inexplicable reverence and awe. I never understood it. To me, they were just a cartel of propaganda pushers with a dumbed-down, dog whistle message that's aimed, not at real people, but at masses of people.

They're trying to appeal to one giant idiot with a generic, clichéd set of statements and ideas whose phoniness is, to me, glaring. And I should know; I was writing it.

But after 9/11, I didn't want to write it any more. Now, no amount of alcohol could make anything I was writing seem important or worth putting effort into. I tried to drink myself towards a purpose and it just didn't work. All it did was make my sober moments less frequent and harder to endure.

At some point of every day — usually in the afternoon but sometimes earlier — I'd get a tense racing sensation that would start in my chest and radiate to the tips of my fingers and my head as a tingling sensation. I'd start shaking, sweating and craving alcohol. Sometimes I'd even forget to breathe and get short of breath. It was like my episodes on the Million-Dollar Staircase, just a lot more intense and debilitating.

The whole thing came on suddenly, like a heart attack. The fact that I had survived these episodes in the past gave me no comfort. Each one felt worse than the one before, and I detected little nuances that, in my mind, made them different and unrelated.

Sometimes it would stun me so much I couldn't even speak. When it first started happening, I would run to alcohol out of fear. I thought that a few beers or more would ease my mind. But it worked better than that. One or two beers made the entire episode disappear in two minutes. My heart stopped racing, the feeling of doom went away, and I stopped shaking. Alcohol was an instant cure.

These episodes scared me — a lot. But after they went away, I made no effort to prevent it from happening again. I didn't Google it. I didn't talk to anyone about it. Instead, knowing that alcohol made them go away, I looked for more efficient ways to get alcohol in my bloodstream when they struck — which was important because they never struck in a convenient place... like a bar.

It always happened someplace where drinking a beer was either risky or impossible. It was almost as if my body revolted if I got too far from alcohol, like when I was stuck in stop-and-go traffic on the FDR trying to leave Manhattan. One time, it scared me so much that I put the car in park while on the FDR, got out in plain view of dozens of other drivers, and grabbed a thirty-pack from the trunk.

I wished there was a mini beer that would fit in my pocket, something that would go down just as easily warm as it did cold. I don't know why it took me so long to realize there is such a beer. It's called vodka.

My past experience with liquor had been short-lived. I'd stopped drinking it the day after I started.

I was fifteen and me and a friend walked to his house after school and began experimenting from his mother's liquor cabinet. I don't remember what the exact tally was, but I lowered his mom's bottle of Old Grandad by several inches.

The full effect of all that alcohol didn't really hit me until I staggered home and tried crawling inconspicuously past my parents and brother who were eating dinner in the kitchen.

Three months later, my friend's mother killed herself right where we had been drinking. That scared me — a lot — because the exact same thing happened a year earlier. That time, me and a different friend got into trouble with his mother at his house for starting a fire.

A week later, his mother committed suicide by dousing herself with gasoline and lighting herself on fire in the middle of a suburban street. It was a tragic coincidence but I didn't know that at the time.

I never touched Old Grandad again. Thirty years later, the smell of it still brought me to a bad place. In fact, there have been times when I've been desperate enough for alcohol to drink mouthwash or even rubbing alcohol, but not Old Grandad.

I'd always preferred the rapid, mass consumption of beer. The "liquor is quicker" concept isn't true for those of us who can drink a beer as fast as someone else can do a shot.

I didn't want to get in the habit of drinking liquor. I just wanted to have it close by to stop these sporadic attacks from crippling me throughout the day. It was for peace of mind.

Goldschlager was great for drinkability, breath and alcohol content, but harder to hide than most other liquor bottles. It was shaped like a big hand bell and wouldn't fit in my briefcase or under my car seat, so I poured it into Evian water battles. The only problem with that was the little gold flakes floating around. It made a water bottle look like a Trump Tower snow globe.

I started hating Goldschlager the first time I spilled it. It's like minty Gorilla Glue. And once you spill a little of it on the outside of the water bottle, the secret is over. Everyone knows it's not water because, not only can they smell it a block away, they can see it coagulating on the outside of the bottle like sap on a Maple tree.

I switched to flavored vodka because it went down easily and it was clear so I could put it in any clear container and pass it off as water. I vowed, however, that I wouldn't drink it like water... except in times of great distress. It didn't take long.

In the past, whenever someone had questioned my drinking, my defense had always been, "I don't drink liquor or do drugs." It was a weak defense to begin with and now it wasn't even true.

RASPBERRY-FLAVORED SMIRNOFF VODKA worked well for me. It was seventy-proof and came in a long thin bottle that fit right under the car seat. I could gulp the stuff like beer for a quick high and it left my breath smelling more like Skittles than booze.

I left work early one afternoon to meet John and Eric, two uniformed State Troopers on the Capitol detail whose shift ended at three o'clock in the afternoon. We agreed to meet at my house between four and five o'clock.

On the way home, I bought a fifth of vodka, which I had to keep hidden because my wife was already complaining that my drinking was getting out of control.

I knew she was counting how many beers I drank at night but I didn't make it easy. For starters, she didn't know I was drinking at work so she couldn't count those. She was only counting the number of empties I left on the counter above a mini-fridge I used in the basement. But since I knew she was counting them, I'd leave three or four empties there and put the rest in a garbage bag in the garage, then restock the fridge with beer from the trunk of the car.

By the end of the night, she'd say, "You're drinking a whole twelve-pack every day."

I pretended to be shocked. I knew how many empties I left for her to see on the counter and sometimes I'd point to the counter, accuse her of exaggerating and say, "Look, it's only eight," even though I knew it was closer to thirty.

If she knew I had introduced vodka into the mix, it would be impossible to defend myself because she knew I hated liquor.

When I pulled up to the driveway that day, Jackson came running up to the car so I hid the vodka under the seat. He went off to play with his friends and I went inside and began drinking while waiting for John and Eric. Ten minutes later, beer in hand, I walked back out to the driveway to get the vodka out of the car.

Jackson was playing with a few neighborhood kids in the street in front of the house, which was common on our street because our street had a cul-de-sac. Just as I was opening the car door, I heard the neighborhood nuisance coming down the street on his Harley-Davidson, which was modified to be ten times louder than a normal Harley.

He had a reputation for hating the neighborhood kids and every day he did his part to bolster it.

He was speeding, as usual, so I made sure he could see me standing in the driveway watching him as he passed by.

As he approached the kids, he revved the engine, apparently to scare them, then sped up and actually aimed right toward them, forcing Jackson and another boy to jump out of his way.

Without thinking to drop my beer, I jumped into the Crown Vic and flew after him, hoping to get a hand on him before he could pull into the garage and shut the door behind him, like he normally did.

From inside his garage, he saw me coming and ran straight towards the car as I pulled into the driveway. He threw his whole body against the car door to prevent me from getting out, while yelling, "Get the fuck off my property."

Once I pushed his fat ass off the door, he high-tailed it back to the garage while throwing blind punches behind his back and yelling, "You and your fucking kids!" All I could think about was how close he came to plowing over Jackson and the other boy. When he got to the garage, I pushed him to the wall but he kept swearing and swinging like a lunatic. His wife poked her head out of a door and he yelled to her, "Go get my gun and call the police!"

I wanted to punch him in the trachea and just walk away and let someone else figure out how he got that way. His wife ruined that plan, which was a good thing since I was only a few hundred yards from home, my state car was in the driveway and a dozen people saw me chasing him down the street. The police probably would have pieced it all together.

He put the fear of God into Jackson; I wasn't leaving without doing the same thing to him.

I was already in a little trouble for having him jacked up in his own garage, so I didn't think I'd make it any worse with a few words. His wife was standing in the doorway leading from the garage to the house talking to the police on the phone and I knew it was time to leave.

I loosened my grip and calmly and quietly said, "Your neighbors hired me to kill you, and I could do it right now but instead I'm going to pick you off the next time you're riding down the street like an asshole."

I walked back down the driveway to the car... calmly at first, until I remembered there was an open beer and a bottle of vodka in my state car which was parked in the driveway of a man I'd just threatened to kill. I raced like hell to get the car back to my own driveway. I knew I could avoid a DWI, on top of whatever else I had coming, if I could get into the house before the cops got there. I just barely made it.

Neighbors were yelling "thank you" as I ran into the house, which made me feel guilty for not finishing the job. I was only in the house for a minute when my two trooper friends showed up. I had about thirty seconds to tell them what happened when five Guilderland Police got there.

As the Guilderland cops filed out of their cars to investigate, John and Eric identified themselves as State Troopers. A couple of the Guilderland cops went down to the end of the street to talk to the lunatic and his wife. A couple more were talking to the neighbors in the street and the rest hung out and talked to John and Eric.

The cops knew Cahill was a bully and a reprobate, and the neighbors they talked to were all on my side. On top of that, my two trooper friends were doing whatever they could to smooth things over without stepping on toes. But I knew I'd broken a bunch of laws and there was probably no way to make this thing just go away.

For a while, the cops just hung out and waited, presumably for the Guilderland Police captain who showed up with a State Police sergeant right behind him. Now there were six or seven police cars there. All of them, including John and Eric, gathered together for a few minutes and listened to the captain and the sergeant. Then, all at once, they just got in their cars and left.

I looked at my wife and said, "What in the hell just happened?"

When the police cars were all gone, John said to me and Eric, "You guys ready? First two rounds are on Wolfe."

I had dodged a bullet, a big one. My wife wasn't impressed.

EVERY NIGHT WAS THE SAME drill. I'd get home from work and hang out with Mallory and Jackson in the downstairs rec room, which was equipped with all the comforts of a corner bar: twelve arcade games, two juke boxes, more than twenty neon signs, two TVs and a beer fridge.

When they went to bed, I stayed downstairs until I passed out. Increasingly, I found that I couldn't drink beer fast enough to be as drunk as I wanted — needed — to be. That's when I reached for the vodka, which I kept locked up in the coin compartment of a Space Invaders game.

On most nights, I made it upstairs and passed out on the couch. Once in a while, I'd pass out somewhere along the way and my wife would eventually wake me up so I could stagger to bed.

A few times, she used a camcorder to record me walking from the couch to the stairs, then played it for me the next day. Her intentions were good. She wanted me to see what I was doing to myself. Admittedly, I was shocked by what I saw on the recordings. It wasn't funny drunk; it was pathetic drunk and I didn't like it.

But I still wasn't surrendering to the growing pressure from family and friends to do something, because I knew that "doing something" meant going to a rehab.

It's not that I didn't need help; I just didn't want it.

I wasn't afraid of dying young from drinking too much. I was afraid of growing old while living a long and uneventful life. I was afraid of being bored and predictable. I was afraid of living without being able to adjust my mood with alcohol.

When I was a kid, I always asked my mom what kind of a mood my dad was in before I got anywhere near him. I wasn't afraid of getting beaten; I was afraid of his bad moods. They were toxic, and worse, infectious.

He could depress an entire room full of happy people with his caustic moods without saying a word. The only thing that cured his dreadful moods was an hour or two with a book and six or seven beers. After that, he wanted to read my English essays and talk about Jethro Tull and wrestling. I loved what alcohol did to my father.

And I loved what it did for me, especially when I was scratching and clawing my way up the Million-Dollar Staircase. It was an instant cure. Why in the hell would I want to quit drinking?

My typical argument back then was that I wasn't harming anyone. Then I would throw out facts and figures in a slurred justification defense that went something like this: "I've never gotten a DWI and I make a lot of money and I go to the gym religiously and I don't hit my wife and I spend a lot of time with my kids and they love me."

The people in my life who weren't afraid to debate me on the subject pointed out that I couldn't go a day without drinking. Friends at work, including State Troopers, were quietly saying things to my wife.

My mother, an alcohol and chemical dependency professional, was pressing me to get help but I was good at changing the subject.

But my wife... my wife had those damn recordings, which made it impossible to defend myself. I looked like someone who truly needed help, and I couldn't promise it would never happen again. It happened every night.

I had no intention of quitting forever. To me, that just seemed too radical, too permanent and too boring. But I needed to do something to satisfy my family, so I agreed to talk to my doctor. Talking wasn't what my family had in mind but it was what I agreed to.

My doctor was no pushover and he wouldn't be easy to manipulate. He knew my father was a recovering alcoholic because they were both doctors in the same hospital. He knew my mother too, because she had been a nursing supervisor in the emergency room.

He was one of those Hemlock Society doctors who were all about choice and free will. He was featured on *60 Minutes* for helping one of his patients kill herself with barbiturates, so I figured he wasn't going to care if I did the same thing with beer.

He lectured me about family history, genetics and my father's battle with alcohol. I just nodded in agreement the whole time until he used the R-word... rehab. I acted astonished.

"Rehab for what?" I asked him. "I don't drink liquor [lie] and I don't do drugs [except pot]. I just like to have two or three [twenty or twenty-five] beers after [and during] work!"

He said, "You should know that your mother called last week. She understands this disease very well... more than me. She's very worried.

And she painted a much different picture of your drinking."

"Wait a minute," I said. "What about HIPAA and doctor-patient confidentiality?"

"Under HIPAA, I can't talk to your mom about your treatment," he said. "But she can talk all day, and if it pertains to the welfare of a patient, I will listen."

I'll never fault anyone for bending the rules a little bit for a good cause — especially when the good cause is aimed at keeping me alive — but my doctor caved in to my mother. It's hard to blame him. Neither him nor HIPAA were any match for my mother.

If my mother needed America's nuclear secrets to save my life, just give her an hour in the White House and she'd have Bill Clinton, George Bush and Barack Obama huddled around a microphone like the Beach Boys, singing the launch codes in perfect harmony.

I could tell she had my doctor singing. The day after I told him I'd be willing to discuss rehab options, she had a list of three or four options for me to choose from. Finally, I told her and my wife I was going to rehab but I wanted to handle it myself and I didn't want any more pressure.

I knew there was no reneging on that pledge. It would be easier to take back my recent vasectomy than a promise to my mother. I kept putting it off and pushing it further down the calendar until I inadvertently imposed a deadline on myself by saying I didn't want to check in until my birthday.

"That way I'll always remember my sober date," I told them, "and it will be symbolic of my rebirth," or something equally stupid and untrue.

The real reason I picked my birthday was because it was two weeks away instead of tomorrow. To everyone, even my mother, that sounded reasonable, and I thought I was a master procrastinator for delaying it for another whole month.

The problem is, my birthday actually came... and the answer is yes and no. Yes, I thought of trying to move it to my next birthday; and no, I didn't have the balls to even try.

Chapter Twelve

A Short Walk in the Park

I SHOWED UP TO MY FIRST REHAB DRUNK —not drunk by my standards but certainly by theirs. I blew a respectable .21 into their breathalyzer. Had I known they were going to breathalyze me, I wouldn't have had a twelve-pack before leaving, in which case I never would have gone in the first place.

Having alcohol slowly slip out of your system in a rehab is torture. Imagine the shittiest, most irritable mood you've ever been in and crossmatch it with your deepest depression. It's like that, with cold chills and a lot of shaking.

I woke up in a room with two other guys — one black, one Puerto Rican — who clearly hated each other's guts. So when I opened my eyes, their first order of business was trying to befriend me first so the other one would be the odd man out. It was as if they had postponed their daily fight until I woke up, and they were just sitting around waiting for my eyes to open.

They began yelling at each other but they were looking at me. I think they were watching for my reaction or something else that would indicate whose side I was on. The reality, of course, is that I had just woken up hungover in rehab, so I really didn't have a side.

They briefed me on the situation.

"That little bitch busted my [CD] player then dumped it in the motherfuckin' closet," the black guy yelled.

I was praying this was a dream.

The Puerto Rican guy rebounded with a stinging riposte in my other ear: "If he sees a bitch, he should smack that mother fuckin' bitch!"

After about a minute, the Puerto Rican guy scrunched his nose at me, like he was mad that it was taking me so long to take his side.

Welcome to sobriety. If there had been a gun, I would have shot all three of us.

Once that whole thing settled down, it was time to go out to the main lounge and meet the rest of the gang. I'll be honest; it was nothing like the brochures. Actually, I never saw any brochures. Whoever lied to me about this place did it right to my face. It was like a jail or a daycare, depending which room you were in.

A lot of these guys were waiting to be sentenced to prison. Some were out on conditional release. And the others were just upstanding addicts and alcoholics like me.

The building itself reminded me of the Mansfield Reformatory in *The Shawshank Redemption*. It wasn't a hell of a lot different on the inside.

The male population was divided into four units: A, B, C and D. They were separated from each other based on the severity of the patient's addiction, his temperament and any gang affiliation he might have. I'm sure there were other criteria but those are the ones that made me wonder how I got thrown into a room with two guys who clearly weren't running with the same gang.

Conifer Park is a drug and alcohol treatment facility but their philosophy seemed to be that, before there can be rehabilitation, first there must be discipline. They wanted you to follow the rules, and the rules were strict.

There was a point system and it was very simple: Points were bad. If you broke a rule, you got a point. If you got three points, they threw you out.

Making anything other than eye contact with a female patient was a quick and easy way to earn a point. The women were housed on the other side of the building, but there were a few common areas, like the hallways and the cafeteria.

They tried to stagger the eating times so men and women would never be in the cafeteria at the same time, but we routinely passed the women while walking in single-file lines to and from meals. Patients of both sexes were constantly earning points for saying "hey" or "sup" to each other, grabbing hands (or some other body part) and passing notes. If there were a hundred ways to get a point, eighty of them had to do with fraternization.

On the treatment side, we had group sessions and then more group sessions and then more group sessions. We had lectures and work sessions and group activities and private sessions with our counselors. Of the thirty or so guys in my unit, I was one of only three guys who was there because of alcohol. One of the other two was an Albany cop, although he went to extreme lengths to hide it.

We had never talked until he walked up to me one day and whispered "Am I the only one who's made you?"

At first, I thought he wanted to have sex. Turns out he was a cop and he thought I was too.

"Do any of these other guys know?" he asked.

"I'm not a cop," I said.

"Uh huh," he said.

In one of the group sessions, I must have slipped up and said something about working for the state and he assumed I was a State Trooper. I tried explaining my job to him but he kept saying, "Yep, yep, yep," as if I were feeding him a line of bullshit.

There were a lot of unstable people at Conifer Park. It was unsettling to know that a Sergeant from a large police department was one of them.

Anyway, he confided in me and I tried very hard to keep a good poker face while he told me his story. He was in a shitload of trouble. Apparently, while he was working and in uniform, he got drunk and caused a bad accident with his patrol car on an Albany expressway.

I remembered hearing the G-rated version of the incident on the news. Now, I was getting the uncut version. The Sergeant said that he was in the process of arresting the other driver when two other cops showed up and accused him of being drunk. That's when the shit hit the fan.

The mayor's office kept it out of the news. But even in Albany, where the police department and the mayor's office routinely cover each other's asses, there's no clean and easy way for something like this to go away.

He was demoted back to patrol officer and mandated to Conifer Park for a month. He got off easy, and now he wanted to be my rehab homie so he didn't have to talk to anyone else, like minorities — or, as he called them, "undesirables." As much as he tried to hide his identity as a cop, he did nothing to hide his feelings on race.

I kept him at arm's length because the other patients hated him, and despite his best efforts, they knew he was a cop the second he opened his big, fat arrogant mouth.

AFTER A WEEK AT CONIFER, I was actually starting to feel comfortable. A lot of that comfort came from the medications they were giving me, but I didn't realize that until I missed my noontime dose one day.

When I went up to get it, the med nurse was agitated. As soon as I walked up to the med window, he looked at me and said, "Oh come on! I'm filling orders," like I'm supposed to know what the fuck that means. "Okay," I said. "Thanks." And I just stayed there.

A minute later, he turned around and saw me still there and said, "You were five minutes late and now I'm filling orders so you're just gonna have to wait till later."

"I was with my counselor so..." I began to say.

In a mocking voice he said, "Then go tell your counselor that I'm filling orders."

That's when I realized he was being an asshole, so I tried to reason with him: "Stop acting like a little prick and get my medicine before I jump over this window and cram a bottle of pills down your fucking throat."

The med window wasn't really a window; it was one of those half doors with a shelf on top of the bottom half. My hands were on that shelf when he slammed the top half shut in my face. It closed just short of hitting me in the face and crushing my fingers.

I tried pushing my way in, but of course, it was locked. I went around to another door that led to the med room, and tried barging in that way but four nurses, all female, stood in my way, and as mad as I was, I've never been mad enough to cross that line.

So now I had a much bigger situation, and a team of administrators showed up to sort it all out.

I was told to go back to my room and wait. It was almost three pm, three hours after not taking whatever they were giving me to keep me calm. I must have really needed it because I was dizzy and shaking and sweating. It felt like I was back on the Million-Dollar Staircase, so I laid down in my room and tried to relax.

At some point, I lost consciousness and my roommate ran to the nurse's station, where they were still discussing my run-in with the med nurse. Apparently, having heard the med nurse's version of what happened, they were deliberating whether they should throw me out. They never heard my version, but that wouldn't have helped me anyway.

They were about to see the result of his laziness. My roommate later told me that about fifteen of them — some in nurse's uniforms, some in scrubs, some in suits — sprinted in herd formation down to the room. Trailing behind them was the med nurse with a cup of pills in one hand and a cup of splashing water in the other.

I was having a seizure… the kind of seizure the medication the med nurse wouldn't give me was prescribed to ward off. They said it lasted about two minutes and they somehow got the medications into my system while it was still happening. As soon as it was over, I fell asleep for three or four hours.

When I woke up, my first instinct was to use the incident as an excuse to leave. No one would blame me. But I was feeling pretty good about myself lately, and physically I'd never felt better, especially in the morning.

WHEN I REACHED my twenty-eight, there was a little graduation ceremony for me and another guy who was leaving that day. The counselors presented both of us with a "thirty-day coin." Then we took turns saying a few words about our recovery while sitting on a chair in the center of a large circle of about thirty guys.

Part of me wanted nothing to do with this clean and sober circle jerk. It's just not my style. But when it was over, at least for a minute or two, I was basking in a kind of pride I hadn't felt since winning my last tough wrestling match.

All along, I assumed that, for me, rehab was going to be a twenty-eight-day reprieve from drinking. Now I was starting to believe that I could make this "not drinking" thing work for longer than that — maybe forever.

THE ONLY WAY TO HUG ME is against my will. That's what several people tried to do on my first day back to work. To nip that awkwardness in the bud, I told everyone that, as much as I appreciated their sentiments, I didn't need to hear them… and I certainly didn't want to feel them by being squeezed. My real friends knew better.

Fortunately, the welcome home niceties were short-lived.

Thirty people were freaking out about the budget speech. Normally, I'd be almost done writing it by then, but in my absence, none of them had risen to the challenge of starting a draft. The Governor told the agency heads to be available 24/7 to answer any questions I might have.

"Fuck that," I told a friend in the Press Office. "I'll just make a lot of educated guesses, and if I guess wrong, the agency heads can speak up when we do a practice run the day before the speech."

"You're lying," she said.

"I've been doing it that way for years," I said. "It makes the whole process more efficient by chewing up time with substantive changes instead of stupid debates."

I was in my office getting started when I realized there was still a fridge filled with beer behind me. I was worried that just seeing a beer could tempt me, so I called a friend and asked if he could get rid of it.

"Oh, we already took care of that for you the day you left for rehab," he said. I opened the fridge and checked; they had cleaned me out.

I hadn't written anything without at least some alcohol in my system in years. Ironically, I remember everything about the seven State-of-the-State addresses I wrote drunk, but I don't remember a thing about the one I wrote sober.

In rehab, they said I shouldn't go back to work unless I was able to get to an Alcoholic Anonymous meeting every day. So every day, I'd leave work to attend a six pm meeting, then go right back when it was over. I wasn't sure how or if the meetings were helping me. My biggest problem with being sober was adjusting to work, and that wasn't something I wanted to talk about in an AA meeting.

Plus, because I was a newcomer to AA, people in the meetings were always coming up to me and saying things like, "Keep coming back and you can have what we've got." But I wasn't sure I wanted what they had.

There was a poster hanging at one of the meetings that said:

"Alcoholic Anonymous: We're not a glum lot." I wasn't so sure about that. To me, there was nothing more depressing than gathering in bingo halls and church basements and going to "sober sock hops" and potluck picnics.

But I kept going to the meetings, and as I began to feel better, I became a little less cynical.

The first thing I noticed was that I was more alert.

A week after leaving Conifer Park, I was looking for a store in the 1800 block of Central Avenue in Albany. When I pulled up to Central from Fuller Road, I wasn't sure if I should turn left or right to get to the 1800 block. In the past, I always guessed, then wound up doing a U-Turn a hundred yards down the road.

But this time, I noticed something I'd never seen before. There were little numbers and arrows at the bottom of the Central Avenue sign indicating the direction of the street numbers. By the end of the day, I discovered that all of the major streets in Albany were like that.

It occurred to me that the world might be easier to understand, and life might be easier to live, without alcohol. Maybe I never noticed the numbers because, even though I wasn't under the influence at the moment, alcohol was still in my system and obstructing the view.

My "awakening" on the corner of Fuller and Central Avenue wasn't the stuff of two roads diverging in a yellow wood. If it was an epiphany at all, it sure as hell didn't come with a pledge and a promise. For two months, I had been searching for a reason to stay sober, and this wasn't it.

At best, I was telling myself that, if I ever did quit forever, maybe it wouldn't be that bad. And that's what this experiment in sobriety was really about — quitting just long enough to see what it was like. Anything more than that — like committing to a life of sobriety in my thirties — was a sign of weakness. It was an admission that you couldn't discipline yourself and temper your impulses.

For now, I wasn't drinking, and according to one old-timer in AA, that was good enough. He was about eighty years old and he came up to me after a meeting, shook my hand and said, "Keep it simple, young man. Just don't drink and go to meetings."

After he left, I was talking to another guy and I asked him, "Do people really drink and then go to meetings?"

"Not very often," he said. "Why?"

"Because the other guy said, 'don't drink and go to meetings,'" I said.

The man laughed and said, "No, that's an AA expression for newcomers. Don't drink — period — Go to meetings — period."

"Oh, I think I can handle that."

I walked away before he had time to lecture me about connecting with a higher power. That wasn't going to happen, at least not when I was sober. When I was drunk enough, I'd connect to anything. On more than a few nights, I did.

For now, I wasn't even conceding that I was an alcoholic.

I was, however, faithful to the pledge I made during my little graduation ceremony at Conifer Park, which was to attend ninety AA meetings in ninety days. They call it a "90 in 90" and a lot of treatment programs want you to make that promise on your way out the door, so I did.

Chapter Thirteen

Crucible in the Church

I WAS DOING BETTER than that. I was on track to get one-hundred-and-eighty meetings in ninety days because I was going to two meetings a day. I didn't have a sponsor but I was introducing myself as an alcoholic and participating in the discussions.

I guess I was enjoying what the treatment community calls a "pink cloud." It's the euphoria some alcoholics experience after they get sober, even if the reality isn't so pink. Unfortunately, the kumbaya feeling doesn't last forever. Sooner or later, a cold reality check knocks on their door while knocking them clear off their pink cloud, and usually, right back to a drink.

Three months into my sober euphoria, I was at an AA meeting a few miles down the road from my house. It was an open discussion meeting, which is a format that allows people to share their thoughts and experiences with the rest of the group.

Halfway through the meeting, a middle-aged guy stood up and began talking about his friend.

"A lot of you know Dave because he's been going to meetings every day for five months," the man said. "He called me last week and said the days just drag on. He said he's always in a shitty mood and he hasn't felt like smiling for weeks…"

They like to keep things solution-oriented in AA, and this guy was definitely off-message. With just a few words, he managed to trigger my worst fear, which is that life without alcohol would be the worst kind of nightmare… a long, grey, depressing one. I didn't want that. I didn't want to throw in the towel at the age of thirty-seven and mope through the rest of my life like a defeated has-been.

The guy was still standing because, even though he stopped talking for a moment, he clearly had more to say. His face was turning red and his voice started to crack as he went on.

"And you know what," he said. "I've felt the same way and I've been getting by, but he couldn't… and last Tuesday he grabbed his hunting rifle and shot himself in the head."

I was sweating and my heart was racing so I stood up and pretended like I was going to get a cup of coffee. As I walked, my heart pounded even harder and I got scared, like I was losing control. So I headed for the door and out to the parking lot and began to pace.

Earlier in the day, I had filled a prescription for Klonopin and put it in the glove compartment. I grabbed the pills and headed back into the building. My doctor once told me that taking Klonopin with warm water speeds up the activation of the medicine.

I went to the sink in the kitchen — which was between the meeting room and the actual church — poured a glass of hot water and swallowed three pills. I took the bottle of pills and the water and went into the church to try and pray this feeling away, even though I had never really prayed for anything in my life… and I never got around to it this time either.

I sat in a pew, got on my knees and tried doing the breathing exercises that I learned at rehab. In through the nose, out through the mouth, in through the nose, out through the mouth.

That wasn't working and I was getting impatient waiting for the medicine to take effect, so I took three more pills. Then I sat and waited and waited for what seemed like an hour. I poured the bottle out onto the pew and took two more. That was when I noticed that my heart wasn't racing any more and I was shaking less and feeling calmer.

I was so afraid the feeling of death would come back, I took more pills, just to be sure. At some point after that, I remember thinking that maybe I had taken too many.

Every so often, I looked at the small print on the bottle trying to figure how many pills were in there to begin with. Then I would count the number of pills on the pew, but by the time I got done counting the pills that were left I had forgotten the other number. I went through that routine two or three times.

By then, I realized that I had taken too many pills and that it was probably enough to knock me out. That's not what I wanted and it's not what I was trying to do. I was so messed up I wasn't sure what I did or what to do next.

So, I did the one thing that's always been like a reflex for me when I was in trouble: I called Charles. When he heard my voice, he knew something was wrong.

"I think I made a mistake… a bad one," I said.

"Where are you," he asked.

"The Presbyterian Church on Western Avenue," I said. "That black Crown Vic is in the lot. Can you find a way to move it or hide it or take it home just so no one finds it?"

I didn't understand how I got confused enough to screw up this royally and I questioned myself about it out loud while kneeling at the pew. I wasn't praying because I don't do that.

I was in that agnostic position you see in church sometimes where a person's knees are on the kneeler but half of their butt is still on the pew. That's always been my way of being respectful enough to hold the cup without actually drinking the Kool-Aid. It's spiritually non-committal, like borrowing a yarmulke at the temple door.

I kept looking down at the nearly-empty bottle of pills in sheer disbelief. Even in a crisis, especially in a crisis, I wasn't going to pray… for the same reason I never slam on the brakes when I see a police car. The cop knows you weren't obeying the law and you're only hitting the brakes out of desperation.

If there's a God, He knows too, and if I ever stand before Him, I didn't want His first words to be, "You only come to me when you need something, you selfish little prick."

That's why I always capitalized His name in the Governor's speeches, even though, in a speech, no one can see punctuation. I did it out of respect.

The church just happened to be the next room over from the AA meeting so my being there had nothing to do with God. But since I was already there, I did say at least one thing out loud. I asked, to anyone who might be listening, "How did I get here?"

"IF HE DOESN'T FLINCH when the breathing tube goes in," I heard a woman's voice say, "it's not good." Then I felt something being pushed down my throat and I tried to flinch for her but I was just too tired.

I never saw anyone, including Charles, but I could swear I saw him pacing around above me dressed like LL Cool J in a baggy sweat top and a dark blue snow hat. I'm positive that what I imagined was exactly the way it was. To me it was as clear as day.

The last thing I heard was his voice. He wasn't yelling but he wasn't talking either. His voice was strong, deep and firm. It resonated like it was coming from the far end of a tunnel, and it was slow and deep, like a recording playing at half speed. All he said was "State Police."

THERE WAS NO BRIGHT LIGHT, no corridors lined with dead loved ones and no visions of Christ. I stopped breathing twice, but the EMTs in the church and ambulance were on the ball.

My mom flew in from Florida and joined my brother who drove in from Rochester and my aunt and uncle who came from Vermont. Even the brother-in-law I didn't like was there, presumably to give comfort to my wife. And of course, Charles was there.

I was on life support when they got there and I was still on life support when they were told to go back to their hotel. That's when I began to breathe on my own.

The first thought I remember having had something to do with my eyes. They were burning even though they were closed and I wanted to rub them and feel my face but I couldn't move my hands. So I just laid there and waited for the burning to go away so I could open my eyes.

My throat was throbbing and raw. It felt like I'd swallowed lava.

I waited for what seemed like a long time. Finally, I tried squinting my eyes while they were still closed to make the burning go away. Slowly, I tried to open one eye, just a little, to get a clue about where in the hell I was. It took several minutes for my one eye to adjust to the bright light shining directly down on my face.

I'd woken up in some fucked-up places before but this time I was genuinely clueless about where I was and what was happening. The ceiling was white and the walls were some sort of depressing variation of beige.

I laid there waiting for a clue — a sound or smell or recollection. Finally, I realized the bright light was attached to one of those extending hydraulic arms, and for a second or two, I thought I was in a dentist chair.

I turned my head a tiny bit and saw a nurse poking a book with a pen. She didn't see me see her, so I shut my eyes and tried to clear my mind and focus on remembering how I wound up in a hospital. At first I panicked... thinking maybe I got drunk, blacked out and plowed into some kids on a sidewalk with my car.

I opened both eyes slowly to get a better look at the room. This time the nurse was looking at me. As soon as she made eye contact, she said, "Don't move," rushed out the door, and returned with a handful of doctors and nurses.

They scrambled above me, rearranging tubes and wires and poking me with sharp things and playing with my eyelids. Then there were questions: What's your name? Do you know where you are? Do you know why you're here?

I didn't say anything; I just continued to look around the room, searching for clues and hoping to piece it all together. The place was a mess. There were blue gowns draped over surgical trays covered with bloody gauze pads, and there were monitors and medical tables shoved all over the room, and dirty surgical gloves on the counter.

On the tray closest to me, within reach, there was a prescription bottle laying on its side. It was my prescription bottle. I closed my eyes and pretended to fall asleep. There was a lot of mumbling that I couldn't understand. Then there was dead silence for about a half hour. The next thing I heard was a man's voice.

"Bring him to the ICU," he said.

A woman's voice responded. I didn't hear most of what she said, but I definitely heard the word "restraints."

These fuckers think I tried to kill myself!

For an hour, I fumed under the sheets, clenching my fists and my face and my teeth, struggling to keep my cool. The first time they all turned their backs, I snuck my "restrained" hand right onto the instrument tray and grabbed the bottle of Klonopin and tucked it in my underwear.

At this point, I didn't realize my family was there. I assumed Charles and my wife were the only ones who knew where I was.

I was venting to myself: *They think they can judge me, call me crazy, control me and tie me up? If I wanted to kill myself, I would have killed myself! I'll show them who's in control. I'll put myself right back in the fucked-up condition they just pulled me out of. I'll make them do it all over again and I'll do it right under their noses to prove I could've done it if I wanted to.*

As soon as they removed the restraints to put me on a clean gurney, I asked for water. Every time they weren't looking or couldn't see my hands, I counted out three pills under the sheets, then took a sip of water while swallowing three pills.

They didn't catch me until I dropped one, but by then I had already swallowed the last fifteen pills in the bottle. I was still disoriented enough from the night before to think that I had made my point.

Chapter Fourteen

And Ye Shall Be Judged

AS FAR AS MENTAL WARDS GO, mine was refreshingly homey. The staff was friendly and there were TVs and couches. The only thing I didn't like about it was that I couldn't leave.

Apparently, with some prodding from the Governor's Office, hospital officials put me here, at the Four Winds Psychiatric Center, instead of mandating me to the prison-like State Psychiatric Center.

Granted, it had all the comforts of home, including karaoke, electric shock therapy and a salad bar. I just couldn't fathom how in the fuck I would up here.

Getting me into a nice mental hospital was the closest the Governor's Office could muster towards feigning any sense of loyalty. From that day forward, I was never allowed to step foot in my office in the Capitol — and someone in the Governor's Office had the baffling thought to dispatch Charles to Four Winds to deliver the news.

You'd never know I was the same guy who had written nearly a thousand speeches for the Governor over the past eight years. I didn't feel like the loyal secret-keeper who sat through countless private meetings about political strategy, damage control and other sensitive issues.

I didn't even feel as worthy as other top aides whose drunk-driving accidents and awful performances were rewarded with high-paid agency jobs where shitty performance didn't matter.

While I was still on life support, the Governor's Office asserted itself strongly enough over Albany Medical Center to sidestep every privacy law on the books. At the direction of the Governor's Office, New York State's Deputy Commissioner of Health convinced someone at the hospital to divulge everything on my chart — what happened, my condition and the prognosis.

Apparently, the Governor was grossly misinformed about what happened.

The first and only time I spoke to him after the incident, he talked to me like I was standing on a ledge of a skyscraper, threatening to jump, and he was the crisis counselor they sent up there to talk me down. "You just take it easy for as long as you need to," he said. "I don't want you getting worked up about the stuff that happens around here."

I never heard from him again.

A couple days later, the Director of Four Winds got another call from the Governor's Office. The caller wanted to add a few details about the message Charles delivered. In addition to losing my job as the Governor's Chief Speechwriter and not being able to get back into my office, I was prohibited, once I got out of Four Winds, from getting within five-hundred feet of the Capitol.

The Governor had effectively banished me for overdosing on my prescription meds.

And yes, I'm crediting the Governor for that decision. He must have realized how shocked I would be to get this message. If he truly thought I was suicidal, why would he deliver the message two days after I tried to kill myself? What was the rush? I wasn't going anywhere.

When you get shocking, life-altering news like that, the worst place to be is in a mental health unit where they're evaluating your disposition.

The doctors didn't think I was crazy when I first got there. But now I was screaming stuff like, "I know things about rent control," and carrying on about the rigged 2000 Republican Convention in Philadelphia.

I learned that, even when you're trying to make a perfectly valid and innocent point about the exploitation of certain voting blocs, there's no right way to scream about "the Jews in Orange County" without sounding like an anti-Semite.

Now, they definitely weren't letting me out, although there was apparently nothing to rush back to.

Proving you're not crazy is like trying to prove you're not a racist. The harder you try, the worse you sound.

Meanwhile, I was getting a firsthand education on the behavior of people suffering from things like anorexia, schizophrenia and manic depression. There wasn't a single alcoholic or addict in there to talk shop with.

For the first few days at Four Winds, I wasn't just monitored, I was shadowed by someone around-the-clock as part of their suicide watch protocol. They watched me eat, shower, even sleep.

I spent a lot of time looking for flaws in their safety protocol, not because I wanted to hurt myself but to prove I could if I wanted to. Part of me — the same part that swallowed the rest of the Klonopin in the hospital — thought that pointing out how easily I could kill myself if I wanted to would prove I wasn't suicidal.

The first thing I noticed was that the electrical outlets were out in the open. All I'd have to do is jam something metal, like the prong of a belt buckle, into one of the holes and I'd be melba toast.

Of course, if I had a belt, I could hang myself. Didn't matter — anything metal would work, though. I opted against mentioning it to anyone. Making comments about suicide in a mental unit is like joking about plastic explosives while going through airport security. They will keep you.

I had no intention of killing myself in that church. I was there for an AA meeting. On the way to the meeting, I stopped at Ace Hardware and purchased a $119 chop saw to cut knotty pine at the lake house, which people rarely do an hour before they kill themselves.

Halfway through the meeting, I had some sort of mood spike — an intense feeling of doom and confusion. I got desperate and tried to chase it away with Klonopin, and as I got more desperate and more impatient and more confused, I lost track of what I was doing and kept swallowing pills until I passed out.

That's what happened, and it's perfectly consistent with the way I drank every night until I passed out.

I remember what I did, but I don't remember what I was thinking. I stopped breathing twice, so I guess technically I killed myself, which is against the law… but it was an accident. I can understand why so many people were skeptical. "Oops" isn't much of an explanation, but that's all I had because that's all there was.

Right before I drifted off in the church, I realized what was happening. On the front of the pew, there were little pencils and I used one to write a note inside a book on the pew next to me.

I wanted everyone to know how much I loved my kids, that I was happy with my life and that I made a mistake with the pills. No one ever saw it, which means that somewhere at the First Lutheran Church in Guilderland, there's a Bible or a church hymnal with my partially written *mea culpa*.

I'd like to think that, through the years, lots of parishioners have read my note and forgiven me.

Every day for three weeks, I sat in group therapy learning about mental illnesses I'd never heard of. One day, they gave us colored markers and told us to draw a picture of our disease. I drew a picture of Major Brock.

THEN, ONE DAY, WITHOUT ANY notice or parting advice, Four Winds just let me go. I didn't know what to do with myself. Up until now, I'd spent eighty percent of my time at the Capitol building. I couldn't go *there*.

Everywhere I did go, I had the paradoxical sensation of being scrutinized and ignored at the same time. I felt out of place, like a Saint Bernard on a balance beam. I didn't know where to step, what to do or where to go. And I sure as hell didn't know who to trust.

I felt like I was under surveillance, and I was… by my best friend. The Superintendent of the State Police, who I liked, put Charles in charge of monitoring me for the Governor.

The day I left Four Winds, I was in the passenger seat of Charles' state car when the Superintendent called to give Charles the head's up. "Wolfe's out [of his padded cell]," he announced, loud enough for me to hear. Charles just looked over at me and smiled. "Got it, sir," he said.

I wanted to drink, but I was afraid to. I was afraid to fall any further — even though, ironically, it was sobriety, not drunkenness that had led me here.

I spent a lot of time in the gym where everyone would ask, "Not working today?" and I was going to two AA meetings a day. In between those two activities, I didn't know what to do with myself.

At the gym, there was a personal trainer who I'd seen working out for a couple years. I didn't know her name; I just knew that, given my limited willpower, she was dangerously hot for me to be hanging out with. She would occasionally say hi to me, but other than that we didn't really talk. I was a little shy around girls I was attracted to, so I didn't say anything especially smooth when she walked up to me one day and struck up a conversation.

"So," she said, "I noticed you don't drive that black assassin's car any more."

"Ha, no... I changed jobs so they wanted that back," I said.

And that was the start of a half hour of small talk and white lies that ended with her saying that she had finished her last training for the day.

"You wanna do something?" she asked.

"Okay, uh... well, I umm..."

I probably would have continued to stammer like that but she interrupted me.

"Do you bowl? I'll drive. It'll be fun," she said.

There was an alley a few blocks down the road so we got in her car, and as quickly as I went from Chief Speechwriter to Crazy Eddie, I was bowling with a girl I'd been sneaking peeks at for two years.

After a few frames, she said, "Hang out for a second. I'll be right back."

I'd driven by this bowling alley hundreds of times, but this was my first time inside. A few lanes away, there was a birthday party for what looked like a ten-year-old kid. They were just getting started and he was the first one to bowl. The bumpers were up and all his friends were cheering him on. It looked like the ball stuck to his thumb a little bit when he tried to release it and it popped into the air before crashing to the lane. About halfway down, it hit the right bumper but I could tell from the bounce that it was going to hit the center pin at a great angle. His friends were cheering wildly as all ten pins fell.

"Here ya go," said the trainer. I turned around and she was holding two Coors Lights and handing me one of them.

I froze. I knew there was a bar behind us, but I thought she was in the bathroom.

"A beer, before five o'clock?" I said, very unconvincingly.

She began laughing. "I'm pretty sure I've seen you start earlier than that in the parking lot," she said.

I stood there staring at the bottle in my hand watching beads of water slide down the neck and over the silver label into the crevice between my hand and the bottle. The kids five lanes away were still celebrating the strike I predicted.

It's just a harmless Coors Light, I told myself, as I lifted the bottle to my mouth. *I'll drink one and tough it out for an hour until it's out of my system. It'll be uncomfortable for a little while but I can do it. It just takes willpower.*

But as soon as the first mouthful went down my throat, I could feel the alcohol flowing through my bloodstream, as if my body had been thirsting for it. At Conifer Park, they warned me this would happen. "For an alcoholic, it only takes one sip," they told me. For me, it was one beer and there was no turning back. I was off to the races.

I finished the first beer in less than a minute, then I went to the bar and stayed there for three hours drinking one after another. I picked up right where I left off. It was like I'd never gone to rehab or taken a three-month break. And now it was time to go home, but first I had to stop at Mobil Mart for a case of beer.

In treatment centers, they call it a relapse, but to me a relapse is when your cancer comes back. I had full control right up to the time the alcohol went down my throat. I fooled myself into thinking I would have any control after that. It was akin to pouring "just a little gas" on a lit match. That's all it takes to start a forest fire.

I never saw the personal trainer again. I barely remember the ride home or how I got my car back from the gym the next day. I remember putting zero effort into hiding my condition when I got home. There was a long period of silence between me and my wife after that.

At one point, I tried to reassure her that the three months I was sober was proof that I could stop at any time and that I wasn't an alcoholic. But now that I'd been to a rehab, a trauma unit and a mental institution — all in the past three months — my credibility was squat.

This was when all those AA sayings and slogans came back to haunt me. They have one for people who quit drinking but still think they can hang out in bars with their buddies and remain sober. The slogan goes, "Hang out in a barbershop long enough and sooner or later you're going to get a haircut."

Once I was comfortably drinking again, which took no time, I was willing to debate anyone who still insisted I had a problem.

"I did everything I was told to do," I'd say. "I went to rehab and I was going to AA meetings and after three months of sobriety I went to an AA meeting, went crazy, and overdosed on a narcotic. I wound up on life support, I was sent to a psych ward for a month and banned from the State Capitol. That's my sober record. None of that shit happened when I was drinking."

Another thing they say in AA is, "There's nothing worse than a belly full of booze and a head full of AA." It's like converting to Judaism then waking up with a swastika tattooed on your forehead.

Drinking after going to AA was a lonely combination of shame and fear — shame for obvious reasons, fear because the hundreds of horror stories you've heard are still fresh in your head.

A COUPLE MONTHS after being expelled from the Governor's Office, which was still paying me while figuring out what to do with me, I got a call from a close friend who was a top aide to the Governor. "Do you want to work for SUNY? I talked to King and he said the Board of Trustees will approve your nomination. It's $134k, the same as it was here."

The "King" he was referring to was Robert L. King, the former Monroe County Executive I wrote speeches for ten years earlier in Rochester. Now he was the Chancellor of SUNY.

I never even bothered to ask what I'd be doing because I knew what I'd be doing: nothing. But I'd be doing what they wanted me to do, which is collecting a disproportionately large salary and not being disgruntled enough to talk about my years with the Governor.

"Yeah, whatever," I said. "Do I actually have to go there?"

"Everybody's been asking about you. Everything okay?" he asked.

"Never better," I said, as I lined up shots of vodka to celebrate my new job.

I'll never forget my first day at SUNY because I didn't go. I should have been there at nine am but I woke up at seven am and started drinking instead.

I put off drinking long enough to make it there the following day though. My new office was in SUNY's headquarters at the foot of State Street in Albany, a gothic, medieval-looking building along the Hudson River.

If you stand somewhere in the center of the building, you can see straight up State Street to the top of the hill. From there, it looks like the majestic State Capitol Building is looking down on you, like an evil dictator looking down on his subjugated peasants. That was the view from my new office, although maybe I was reading into it too much.

They started work at nine o'clock in the Chancellor's Office. I got there at nine o'clock zero times. I was too bitter to show up on time. In fact, I was too bitter to show up at all. But I wanted to keep people happy and I found that occasionally popping into the office boosted the morale of the people who validated my timesheets.

I didn't have the shady connections at SUNY to get a beer fridge in my office, but I was a stone's throw from Coulson's News, which sold forty-ouncers, and I could sneak them back to my office four at a time. I usually got to work around ten o'clock in the morning and I tried to hold off drinking for at least two hours.

Around one o'clock, I'd walk across the street to Coulson's and buy some forty-ouncers. It was awkward. The guys working at Coulson's knew that I worked at SUNY because they could see me walking back and forth. And a lot of people from SUNY went to the same store for coffee and newspapers.

Every so often, a SUNY person would cross the street toward the store as I was walking up to the counter with an armful of forty-ouncers. I'd turn around and duck behind the magazine displays until they left.

When the coast was clear and I finally made it to the register, the guys who worked there would wrap them like Tiffany vases; they'd put each forty-ouncer in its own small paper bag, then put all the small bags of beer into one big bag. In other words, just like the bodega guys in New York City, they knew I wasn't taking them home for the ball game.

I never walked through the majestic hallways of SUNY's historic administration building chugging beer from a brown paper bag. Short of doing that, I put virtually no effort into hiding my drinking. I was positive everyone knew I was drinking at work but they also understood my relationship with the Chancellor and the Governor and were afraid to say anything about it.

I wasn't sure what they knew about my departure from the Governor's office. In particular, I wondered if anyone at SUNY knew what happened at the church — and if they did know, I wondered how embellished the story was by the time it oozed down the hill from the Capitol.

My social circle at SUNY was limited to two retired State Police investigators and Jen LoTurco, my closest friend from the Governor's Office. Jen worked a few floors below me in the SUNY tower, and we went to lunch together almost every day. She was on the receiving end of virtually every rant I delivered for a year following my expulsion from the Governor's Office.

John and Dave, the retired investigators, were on the Governor's security detail under the Colonel the entire time I was there. Now they were in charge of security at SUNY headquarters, and I hung out in their office when I wasn't working on something important, which was always.

With all that time on my hands, here's the thought that haunted and taunted me every minute of the day at SUNY:

When I was drinking, my career soared, from proofreader to Chief Speechwriter in just seven years. I'd written nearly a thousand speeches, many of them for national audiences, and even bronze plaques that will still hang in places like Grand Central Station long after I'm dead.

Perhaps the greatest testament to my talent was the magnitude of the shit I got away with. I did it all while I was drinking. Now, my reputation and my entire career were hanging in the balance because of something I did while I was sober.

That's what I thought about all day, from the time I woke up to the time I drank myself to sleep, which was increasingly becoming a simultaneous event.

Still, there was occasionally something gratifying and surreal about my paid incarceration at SUNY. I don't have a lot of vivid memories of my childhood, but I remember lying on a shag rug in the living room every evening while my father — a doctor and an alcoholic — watched TV and drank beer. I must have been nine or ten years old.

There's nothing important or memorable about it but I remember it anyway, especially those brown bottles of Genesee beer. I also remember — I have no idea why — my dad getting really pissed off at the man on the little black and white TV for several nights in a row. I don't remember why he was mad, but I always remembered who was making him mad. It was Garrick Utley, an NBC news journalist known for his reporting on the Vietnam War.

My ostensible job at SUNY was launching SUNY TV, a statewide TV network about life on the sixty-two state university campuses.

As part of that effort, I wrote a bunch of scripts for promotional spots that we filmed at SUNY's fully-equipped broadcast studio. But first, I went to the train station to pick up the narrator of these scripts. It was Garrick Utley. And as we were talking in the car, his distinct, deep voice brought me right back to the early '70s.

As he spoke, I imagined his voice on the little black and white TV, talking about Nixon and Vietnam, and I could feel my fingers in the shag rug and see the water droplets rolling down the side of the brown beer bottles.

This was my "Cats in the Cradle" moment.

I'm pretty sure Utley knew I'd been drinking because he never took his eyes off the road. If he didn't smell the beer on my breath, I'm sure he caught a whiff of the crushed beer cans and bottle of vodka under my seat.

It didn't matter. He knew who I was before we met. I'm sure someone told him the same old thing about me: "He drinks too much but we need his writing." Utley loved the scripts and didn't change a thing. Crazy or not, that was the one thing I could still guarantee every time.

But lately, no matter how much beer I poured down my throat, it was never enough. That menacing feeling in my chest kept coming back.

I was always able to drink it away with a heavy round of beer and vodka, then it wouldn't come back until the next time I was sober, which was usually the next day. Now, the feeling was creeping back up on me when I wasn't drinking fast enough. That was a bad sign, and I knew it. I was struggling through every day at SUNY, looking at the clock and trying to go as long as possible without another sixteen-ouncer, which I kept running out of.

Every two hours, I was running across the street to Coulson's. I knew how bad it looked. At the cash register, the same people were ringing me out every two hours for another bag of tallboys or six-packs. About half of the people working at SUNY Central had an office window facing the front door of Coulson's. I wasn't even sneaking around any more; I was just doing what I had to do without really caring who was watching or what they were seeing — and saying.

It was disabling... in more ways than I care to admit.

There was an extremely attractive intern who worked in Central Administration. As soon as I met her — I think it was on my first day at SUNY — it seemed like she already knew a lot about me, maybe too much.

I'm not sure what kind of file they had on me at SUNY but it seemed like my new intern friend had gone through it extensively. She was bubbly and she came off as sort of an airhead but she was very smart. She reminded me of Lonnie Anderson in her prime. She carried herself with extreme confidence, and she was always perfectly-dressed in provocative business attire.

On a daily basis, I was struggling and sweating and shaking and sneaking around every minute just to make it through the day. It wasn't like the Governor's Office. At SUNY, I had to run around a lot to drink. I was a sweaty wreck. And this girl knew I was struggling.

Almost every day, she'd see me through the window, walking across the street with my brown bag of big beer cans. Then she'd leave her desk to meet me in the hallway as I came through the door.

She'd glance down at the paper bag, then stare right into my eyes and say, "Hi John," then keep smiling and staring for an awkward length of time.

Then she'd step closer and say, "I'm glad you're here because I have something for you to sign. I'll bring it up to you in thirty minutes."

There was never a legitimate reason for this girl to be in my office, but she always found one. Every time there was interoffice mail, no matter how unimportant it was, she would hand deliver it to me. And then she would close the door and walk right into my two-foot bubble.

Staring directly into my eyes from about eight inches away, she would start throwing out lines that sounded like the verbal foreplay from a B-rated 1970s porn flick. It usually started with something horribly cheesy like, "I've been looking forward to bringing this to you all day."

The first time it happened, she walked in, closed the door, got within kissing distance and said, "Are you happy to see me?" It was such a dorky thing to say, I was sure it was a prank by my State Police buddies.

I just laughed and blushed and said, "Oh yeah, I'm very happy. Where's the camera?"

She didn't even react to the question. She just grabbed the back of my head and began kissing me. She was passionate about it... almost theatrical.

I didn't push her away, but I wasn't really participating either. I wasn't even enjoying it because I was shocked and self-conscious about my sweating and shaking. I kept wondering, *How could this gorgeous girl be enjoying this?*

She was melodramatic, gripping and stroking my back like I'd just returned from war. It would last for about a minute, then she'd stop abruptly and hug me like I was shoving off to war again. The whole thing came off like she was auditioning for the lead role in a school play. It was weird.

In fact, if I live for another thousand years, it will still be the most fucked-up thing that has ever happened to me. At any other point in my life, I would have been walking around with an erection, pinching myself to make sure I wasn't dreaming and probably bragging about it to anyone open-minded enough to believe it.

It took so much energy just to make it through the day, I didn't appreciate this whole situation for what it was — every middle-aged man's fantasy. Instead, it was just another thing interfering with my drinking. Every time she showed up at the door, my first thought was, *Let me drink in peace.*

It was the second time in a year that I'd attracted the attention of a temptress hunting at the back of the herd. The first one was the blonde trainer who co-sponsored my relapse. I'm not suggesting I was anyone's victim. I'm just saying these things never happened when I was in the condition to capitalize on them.

Many years later I was walking by a wall of TVs at Target when I saw a news report about the death of Garrick Utley. I wish I had told him about remembering his reports from the Vietnam War when I was a kid.

I never even got around to telling my dad about meeting and working with him.

I WASN'T PLANNING ANY FURTHER ahead than my next thirty-pack. I should have been more worried about my future than I was. The governor was serving his last term. Even though I was tucked away hidden at SUNY Central, I was still an appointee of the Governor.

I assumed the new Governor would be Eliot Spitzer, a Democrat, which meant that I'd be fired almost immediately after January 1, 2007.

I was doing nothing to prepare for that day. I met a thousand deadlines over the years — it was my great strength — but now I couldn't stay focused long enough to meet the biggest deadline of all: my own. I knew the clock was ticking on my career and I knew that I would be out of a job in a matter of months. I just didn't do anything about it.

Whenever reality made me too uncomfortable, I drank harder, while promising myself that I would confront the situation courageously when I got sober. Then the next day, I made the same promise, and then, et cetera. I promised myself I would deal with it before it was too late right up until the time when it was too late. For the next six months, I was never lucid long enough to understand what happened when I lost my job on New Year's Day.

AT THE SAME TIME, my fifteen-year marriage was about to turn into a five-year custody fight that will always be the most painful and regrettable period of my life. The break-up began several months after my relapse when my wife and I agreed to a temporary separation.

We were spending the weekend at the lake house when we made the final decision — it was more of a final straw in the form of an argument — so when she left with the kids on a Sunday, I just stayed at the lake. Before this latest fight, we had been discussing a two-week trial separation, but at the end of those two weeks, it was clear that our marriage was over.

There was a bitter divorce — I assume there's no other kind — and a custody battle that lasted five years. Unbelievable as it may sound, it had little bearing on my drinking. I didn't need an excuse to drink.

Once the trial was over, I promised myself to never get into the unsavory business of criticizing my ex-wife. All divorces suck, and although I'm positive mine sucked more than everyone else's, I'm also aware that it also sucked for her — and it especially sucked for Mallory and Jackson.

At first, custody wasn't an issue. My ex-wife was a good mother and they were living in a nice house on a cul-de-sac street and going to school in a good suburban school district. I never even contemplated the idea of moving them an hour into the mountains to live in an Adirondack lake house that was deserted during fall and winter. Not to mention, I was in no condition to raise the kids. I wasn't even sure if I could take care of myself.

For the first time in my life, I was living alone. And I sat on the front porch with a beer in my hand and watched as the family car disappeared over the top of the hill to the main road.

There was immediate guilt, but the flipside of guilt is supposed to be pleasure, and there was none of that. Now I could drink as much as I wanted — not that anything had stopped me from doing that before — but there was no one to hide the empty beer cans from. There was no one to tease, no one to chase, no one to play video games with, no one to jump out and scare, no one to argue with.

The more I drank, the lonelier I got; the lonelier I got, the more I drank.

I had dreaded this divorce for a hundred reasons. The only good thing about it was that I had my freedom. But winning your freedom is a pyrrhic victory when no one is looking for you. Suddenly, no one was.

My fortieth birthday was the ideal time to feel sorry for myself. There was no one around. Only a few people called. There was no party, no one calling me an old man or bringing me black balloons. Instead, as a demonstration of just how pathetic I was willing to be, I sat at my desk and listened to "The Wreck of the *Edmund Fitzgerald*," by Gordon Lightfoot.

The *Edmund Fitzgerald* sank on November 10, 1975, my tenth birthday. For some reason, news of the tragedy bothered me more than it should have bothered a ten-year-old kid. But even with all my drunken behavior over the years, spending my fortieth birthday wallowing in self-pity this way was one of my lamest moments as a human being. I can't believe I'm admitting it.

My mother called to remind me, as she does every year, that I was born in the dark. It's true. On November 10, 1965, there was a major electrical disruption in the northeast that left thirty million people without power. I don't think my mom ever appreciated the ill-fated irony that I came into this world in a blackout. Every year for at least twenty years, I commemorated the day accordingly.

Chapter Fifteen

"Since No One Objects"

THE LAKE HOUSE IS ONE OF FIVE seasonal homes on a dirt road that runs from the main road down to the lake. My house is the one closest to the lake and it overlooks a beach and a dock I share with a few other families. This was the place of my dreams, a place I fell in love with as a kid while camping and climbing the high peaks of the Adirondacks every summer.

From my second story deck, I have a perfect view of my little corner of the Adirondacks and I know and love every square inch of it.

Most of the homes on Loon Lake are seasonal, so I usually had all that beauty for myself. On an average November day, I wouldn't see or hear another person from the time I woke up till the time I went to bed.

On an August day, our dirt road was buzzing with golf carts and ATVs. There were dogs and kids running all over the place with sticks in their mouths and fishing poles in their hands. The picnic tables on the beach had tablecloths covered with everything from wine bottles and juice boxes to hamburgers and shrimp cocktail.

On our beach, and the one next to it, people were swimming and pulling canoes and kayaks in and out of the water.

Dads stood on the edge of the dock with their daughters staring at their bobbers. Friends drank wine on the beach and made margaritas with blenders plugged into cars and ATVs. There were always kids playing "King of the Hill" on floating docks to a chorus of moms yelling, "Watch your head on the edge of the dock," and dads shouting, "Come on, Kyle, blitz him!"

A hundred feet from the shore, dads were trying to teach their kids to waterski for the first time, a wonderful thing to watch, a sadistic guilty pleasure that never gets old because, like a NASA rocket launch, it never goes as planned.

Dads sat in the water behind their kids, telling them to hold on tight to the rope and keep the tips of their skis out of the water. From the back of the boat, another adult yelled, "bend your knees and let the boat pull you up."

On the first try, the kid would invariably do none of that, fall face forward, then hold on to the rope too long and get dragged through the water for a few feet like a surface lure. But on the third or fourth try, they always gave you a reason to applaud as they stayed up long enough to disappear around the bend.

Around dinner time, there were fires and fireworks on the beach. We all walked in and out of each other's yards and houses like they were our own. And on any given summer day, the same thing was happening twenty miles down Route 9 in Lake George.

But now it was August of 2006 and I knew that two bad things were about to happen.

First, all that summer happiness was about to make a giant sucking sound as it disappeared down the Northway after Labor Day. Once that happened, my little corner of the Adirondacks would start looking less like the Beach Boys' Endless Summer and more like a double feature of *The Shining* and *Deliverance*.

And second, my gubernatorial appointment was about to expire which meant that my days of using SUNY as a frat house were numbered. My salary was going to change from $135,000 per year to $0 per year, and my only plan was to come up with a plan to sit down and make a plan.

And as much as I loved the Adirondacks, I knew the silence and isolation of the fall and winter months was going to be an issue for me. So I worked with what I had.

At night, I turned on all the lights and TVs and appliances and music like there was a big party going on. I'd set up a "quarters table" and play by myself. In the game of Quarters, which has been replaced with Beer Pong, you have to bounce a quarter off a table into a glass that's filled with beer or liquor. If you get it in, you get to choose who has to drink the contents of the cup.

If you're like me, and you like drinking more than games, you play to lose.

People always used to say to me, "For as much as you drink, it's amazing how much you suck at this game?"

Then they'd sink the quarter in the glass and scream, "Drink up, Wolfe!"

And I'd say, "Oh drumsticks! Me again? Stop the insanity before I get drunk!"

Of course, now that I was playing alone, it didn't matter whether I made the shot or not. I had to drink every time, but without the playacting, it just wasn't the same.

After quarters, I'd do a couple rounds of something called the "Platypus." It's a drinking maneuver, more of a performance really, that I invented while hanging out with Boz, Mike West and a few other friends — probably the best group of friends I've ever had.

It was 1992 on a warm Saturday afternoon and we were in a beachside-type restaurant near Charlotte Beach on Lake Ontario.

When the waitress brought a round of beers to our table, Boz said, "These glasses are the perfect size for chugging."

In an attempt to be entertaining, I leaned over and pushed my face against the top of the glass of beer, with my lips and mouth inside the rim, and sucked hard enough to make the glass stick to my face like a suction cup. Then, without using my hands, I tilted my head back, balanced the beer upside down over my mouth, and let all the beer fall directly down my throat.

It was a messy first performance, but it was the greatest thing the rest of the group had seen since high school.

Over the next few hours, days, weeks and even years, I perfected the maneuver until I could do it without spilling a drop. We'd go to bars and my friends would ask the bartender, "If my friend can drink an entire glass of beer without ever touching the glass with his hands, will you give us a free pitcher?" They'd take the bet and we won every time.

Alone at the lake house, after two hours of drinking beer the usual way, I'd go to the cupboard, get my only pint glass and try to recapture some of that old spirit. I'd fill it with beer, place it strategically on the desk and go through my little routine, starting with a ceremonial sip off the top.

It was important to take a deep breath and exhale thoroughly, before shaking off my hands and executing a full-blown platypus. And when I was done, even though no one was there, I'd do my trademark wiping of the mouth with my wrist and smile to acknowledge the praise.

I realized, even as I was doing it, that it was unusual, but that's why I did it… so I could laugh at myself when there was nothing else to laugh at, and so I had something to look back on and pity when I got better. I did the platypus in an empty living room for the same reason Mr Bojangles danced in a jail cell. It was the most fun I could have under the circumstances.

EVERY SO OFTEN, I took little vacations for myself… and by myself. Usually I'd get a hotel room in Queensbury, which is about twenty minutes south of the lake house. I'd get a room just so I'd be near other people, within walking distance of a few things so I could be in public places without driving drunk to get there.

There were two perfectly-placed hotels — one right across from the entrance to the Aviation Mall and another one around the corner. The second one had a nice pool and it was across the street from a giant Wal-Mart.

I think people underestimate how much fun it is to get wasted and wander around a Wal-Mart. I'd do that for a couple hours, go back to my hotel room, take a bath (because I could) and steal towels, lotion and other stuff from the maid's closet. Then I'd go back to Wal-Mart and wander around a different section of the store.

When you're shitfaced and easily-amused, like I typically was, you can convince yourself that something fun is also clever and useful. I'd steal a ton of big white hotel towels, buy clothing dye at Wal-Mart, fill up the tub with warm water, throw in a package of red, green or blue dye, and let the whole thing sit for a couple of hours. A few hours later, I'd wring them dry and hang them up overnight to dry.

The way I saw it, the money I spent on the room was really an investment. I was going home with fifteen $10 towels, so I made $150 by going to a motel. It was fuzzy math and I didn't need the towels, but at the time, it made perfect sense to me and I showcased my colorful towels in both bathrooms of the lake house.

MALLORY WAS CALLING ME every night recently, usually upset about things I had no control over. She'd call late at night after everyone else in the house had gone to bed. And as she told me things, I'd write them down on index cards so I could look at them in the morning and make a clear decision about what I could do to help her.

I knew from experience — tons of it — that reacting to situations while intoxicated was a guaranteed way to wind up in front of a judge.

When my ex-wife's boyfriend told Jackson, "I'm not here to kiss your ass like your father" then proved it by treating him like garbage, I tried calling him to discuss the issue. He wouldn't pick up the phone so I left him a message, posing the hypothetical question, "How would you like it if I treated your son like that?"

Except that's not how I said it. His son was a wide receiver for the Dallas Cowboys, so the message I left was more along the lines of, "Leave my son the fuck alone or I swear to God I will hunt you down and take out your teeth and then find your son and break his fucking catching arm."

I didn't realize how bad it sounded until a few weeks later when the judge read it out loud to me in open court.

I got arrested for that. They granted the boyfriend an Order of Protection, and I spent a year in court — eight appearances before a judge — before the DA agreed to an Adjournment in Contemplation Of Dismissal (ACOD). I wasn't even drunk when I made that call. I was perfectly sober, driving with both kids in the car when one of them told me about how the boyfriend talks to them.

I got mad and left the message without thinking, or caring, about how much trouble I would get into. That's the kind of sober person I was becoming — impulsive, miserably serious and short-tempered. I never would have made that call if I was drunk. At the very least, I would have tried something else first.

I made my safest decisions when I was lightly inebriated, after seven or eight beers. That was enough to calm my nerves and eliminate cravings without impairing things I needed to be civil, like motor skills, particularly the ones that control the tongue.

To get *that* wasted, I would have to drink an entire case quickly, which, for me, was about two hours. I could do that easily, but it was rare for me to drink that way. I spaced out my drinks like a slow narcotic drip to keep me steadily buzzed throughout the day. Then, about two hours before going to bed, I would pick up the pace and drink hard until I passed out.

I used the index cards to remember what I said but also to temper what I knew my sober reaction would be in the morning. It wasn't a foolproof strategy. One night, after talking to Mallory about her mother's boyfriend, I left myself an index card for the morning that read, "Tell that asshole that if he keeps talking shit to the kids, no order of protection will stop me from smashing his face in."

The next morning, I looked at the card, thought about it for a minute, then picked up the phone and read the card verbatim into the boyfriend's voicemail. A few weeks later, at my arraignment, the same judge that read my last message to me in open court read this one and asked, "Do you have a drinking problem?"

"Maybe," I said. "But I was sober when I left these messages."

Chapter Sixteen

Sober Reign of Terror

MEANWHILE, IN STATE SUPREME COURT, where my custody battle was spinning out of control, my ex-wife's lawyer was, understandably, painting me as an unstable and violent alcoholic. Not by coincidence, I began getting unscheduled visits from Mallory's law guardian even though I didn't have custody of the kids.

Late one afternoon, on an unusually hot day in early Spring, the law guardian dropped by unannounced. I saw his car at the top of the hill so I had plenty of time to hide all my beer and brush my teeth.

Four months earlier, in February, my mom had been visiting during a snowstorm and I had gone outside to drink a twelve pack while pretending to shovel the driveway. I'd hidden the empties by cramming them into a giant snow pile in front of the house.

Now, many months later, I watched from the window as the law guardian walked up to the driveway. He stopped for a second, looked down and raised his sunglasses to get a better look at something. This was the day that it got hot enough to melt all that snow covering the beer cans. As soon as I realized what he was looking at, I ran out to greet him, looked down at the empties and said, "Damn teenagers!"

AFTER A COURT APPEARANCE where my drinking was identified as a major issue, my lawyer and I met afterwards to discuss things. In a casual tone, and with a straight face, she said, "Listen, they're going to call you an alcoholic every time they file a motion, so until the trial is over, you need to not drink at all."

I just laughed.

"That's funny?" she asked.

"It's hilarious. You really think they're going to stop calling me an alcoholic if I quit drinking now? If I can't quit, which is a very real possibility, it'll look twice as bad."

"Then just stop and we won't say anything for a while," she instructed.

"All of the shit they're throwing in our faces is stuff that happened when I was sober, not drunk.".

"Wait a minute… you're an alcoholic," she said.

"It's just a word. Doesn't bother me. I've accomplished a lot of things I'm proud of," I said.

"Then you need to get help or I can't represent you," she said.

"Okay."

"You'll get help?" she asked.

"No, I'll get another lawyer," I said.

I wasn't trying to be difficult, but for me, not drinking wasn't an option. It's not that I refused to give up the fun of drinking because drinking stopped being fun a long time ago. I just couldn't function sober. Without alcohol, my entire demeanor changed and I became irritable, impatient, and in too many cases, dangerously violent.

When I didn't drink, I got into fights, I got arrested, I overdosed, I wound up in psych wards, I lost my career, and I felt like I was going to die. The consequences of not drinking were a lot worse than the consequences of drinking heavily every day.

That's not just the way I saw it; that's the way it was. All anyone had to do was look at the record. I didn't tell my lawyer that, of course. But it's what I was thinking as I stood firm.

We swept our last conversation under the rug. "Fine," she said. "Just be careful and don't drink and drive, okay?" And that was the end of it.

Now, I was going to have to put off drinking until the end of the day, every day, no matter what. I had no idea when the law guardian was going to show up at the house or when the judge would summon me and my lawyer to his chambers.

So I imposed a new rule on myself: no drinking until after five o'clock. But my first week of forced (daytime) sobriety seemed to backfire. I kept getting pissed off at my lawyer, I threatened a local plumber and I was swearing at the TV for playing too many commercials.

IT WAS A BAD TIME for Mallory's bus driver to start acting like a dick. For weeks, he had been "punishing" her for minor transgressions like leaving papers on the bus. Mallory said he was a big guy, about six-foot-three-inches and heavyset with a roaring voice. He was constantly swearing in front of her, ridiculing her and making her sit at the front of the bus where he could, in his own words, "Keep an eye on you."

At first, my ex-wife wanted to keep me out of it.

"Let me go to the school and talk to the supervisor at the bus garage," I told her.

"No," she said. "Let's try diplomacy first... no offense."

Finally, my ex-wife went to the bus loop and confronted the bus driver face to face. The bus driver ridiculed her right in front of the kids. He made a derogatory comment about Mallory — something about the apple not falling far from the tree — then laughed at her, and told her to get away from his bus.

Now, she was calling me so livid she could barely talk because she had just gotten off the phone with the principal who told her there was nothing he could do.

"Okay," she said to me. "Now it's time for you to step in."

The timing was perfect. It was one o'clock and I still hadn't had a drink. It took an hour and fifteen minutes to get to the school, and the bus pulled into the loop every day at two-thirty. I was on my way out the door when I remembered to test my state of mind by calling Charles.

I could have called from the road, but from experience, I knew that once I was on my way, I was on my way. Charles was the only person with the influence to cut me off at the pass.

I had already told him about the situation a few days earlier, so I just filled him in on the rest. Then I asked him, "What would you do?"

"Are you asking Charles the cop or Charles your friend?" he said.

"What would you do if it was Jasmine?" I asked.

"I'd be on the way down there," he said.

That was all I needed to hear.

As I raced past the median turnarounds where troopers tended to hang out, I rehearsed what I would say if I got pulled over. I would have been honest, too, because I thought that protecting my daughter was a valid reason to speed.

The line of buses hadn't pulled into the loop yet so I parked my car in the teacher's lot and just stood like a sore thumb in the center of the loop.

I had about ten minutes to kill so I went to the main office and asked for the principal who wouldn't return my calls. They said he was in a meeting, but they were aware of the problem with the bus driver. They said the bus drivers were employed by a private company, not the school district, and they were waiting to hear back from the driver's supervisor.

"This guy is swearing at my ten-year-old daughter and telling her mother to go to hell... and you guys are waiting for what?" I said. "It's been two weeks and no one is even returning our calls."

The principal finally came out and admitted that the school had received several other complaints about the driver but he couldn't... blah, blah, blah. That was when I saw the buses pulling into the loop. The last thing I heard as I sailed out the door was the principal screaming, "Wait, no! Let us try to..."

I was looking for bus number 19. About four or five other buses pulled up and the drivers were eyeballing me. I didn't know it at the time, but the school officials inside alerted the bus garage. And all the drivers knew why I was there. Finally, bus 19 pulled into the loop but instead of parking in his spot next to the other buses. He just kept circling the lot. After two or three laps, I walked in front of the bus with my hands up and he stopped. When I ran to the bus door, he opened it just a crack.

"What in the hell do you want?" he asked.

I didn't say anything. He knew who I was and what I wanted.

As soon as I looked at him, the scene materialized in my mind. His left hand was hanging out of the driver's side window. That's where I was going to ram the back of his head after taking the clear shot I had to his throat. Then it would just be a matter of holding him there and letting him decide how it was going to end.

"Are you Dave Sullivan?" I asked. I knew it was him because he was a big, loud asshole just like Mallory said he was.

"No, but I'll get him," he said while laughing and pulling the door closed. I wedged my fingers between the doors and started pulling one side open. He was pulling back with a red lever on the other side.

Just as I pried it open enough to force one arm through, voices behind me were yelling "stop" and "let go." Since I was surrounded by cops, I decided to stop... and then let go. I had no idea how five cops snuck up on me. I never heard a siren or saw a single police car.

Turns out their cars were scattered in between other cars all over the parking lot. They had been hiding and waiting for something to happen.

It made no sense to me why they were hiding. They could have just told me to leave before the bus got there and I'd have left. Two of the cops got in between me and the bus then another cop motioned for the dirt-bag driver to take off, which he did, without any kids on board.

"Okay, he's gone and he's not driving the bus home today," said the officer who looked like he was in charge. "I've heard part of this situation but why don't you tell me what's going on."

Just then a group of four or five school administrators walked out of the school and stood about ten feet away from me and the cops, as if they were overseeing the situation. I never gave them the chance to get comfortable. I walked right past the cops and straight into the face of the principal who had been deflecting my calls.

"Whose principal are you?" I yelled. "When some three-hundred-pound guy is scaring and swearing at little kids, you're supposed to protect the kids, not the scumbag adult."

He didn't respond. He just looked back and forth between me and the police officers. I think he was waiting for the officers to do something to extricate him from the situation, like arresting me. Instead, they watched on, intently, almost as if they were waiting for him to answer my question. I unloaded a verbal nightmare on the principal for ignoring parents' complaints about the bus driver's abusive behavior.

I carried on for several minutes until I ran out of stuff to say. All the other bus drivers had been standing outside of buses watching the whole thing. That's when I realized that the kids had never come out of the school when the bell rang about fifteen minutes earlier.

The school was in lockdown. Students were confined to the classroom and they couldn't go home until my tirade was over. I thought it was odd that the school went to such extremes to protect the kids from me but did nothing to protect them from an abusive bus driver.

Mallory later told me that all the kids in class rooms facing the bus loop were watching the whole thing from their classroom windows. I'll never forget what she said later that night when she called me at the lake house. "Dad, you locked down my school… But I love you." It's not the conventional way to show a child you love them, but Mallory always took it that way.

Turns out, one of the cops was dating a close friend of mine from the Governor's Office. She called me the next day and told me why the cops hid in the parking lot until the shit hit the fan. Many of the complaints about the bus driver had come to them, but there wasn't much they could do without the cooperation of the school, and they weren't getting it. They knew I was going to confront the principal and they wanted to hear what he had to say for himself.

Aside from the school being locked down, this incident, in my mind, was so minor it's barely worth recounting. The cops were there. I never got a hand on the guy. And I didn't get arrested. There's really no story.

Still, I expected to hear about it in court from my ex-wife's lawyer, who was constantly arguing that my history of violence and drinking made me an unfit father.

A week after the bus incident, while still struggling to stay sober during the day, I helped him make the case against me… right in front of the judge.

It all started when my ex-wife's lawyer refused to adjourn a court appearance. The appearance was just a formality. In fact, I insisted on appearing without my lawyer.

"No way," she said. "You'll say something and freak everyone out; you can't help yourself."

"It's fine," I assured her. "I'll just smile and not talk."

She finally agreed to it, but asked, "How did you write speeches for the Governor for so long? Every time you talk, motions start flying."

"I won't say a word," I promised.

A few hours before the appearance, I injured my hand with a table saw. I didn't tell my lawyer; I just called the court directly and requested an adjournment. The judge said he would grant the adjournment if my ex-wife's lawyer agreed to it. He didn't.

I was mad as hell, and with each sober second that passed during the hour-long drive to Albany, I got madder. I showed up to court with my bloody hand in a red cup of snow.

The cops at the security gate didn't want to let me in. "You need to get that hand to the emergency room," they said.

"No," I told them. "The court knows all about it and they want to see me."

It was a large courtroom with three or four private consultation rooms built into the back wall. They all had glass doors so you could see who was in them; you just couldn't hear anything.

The court was in session and there were about thirty people and a handful of cops in there. As soon as I walked into the courtroom, I saw my ex-wife's lawyer in one of the glass rooms.

He saw me coming and grabbed the door handle with both hands trying to prevent me from getting in, but I yanked it open and pinned him against the back wall, using my good hand to shove my bloody hand into his face.

The cops were pulling me back into the courtroom, and the judge was banging his gavel and the lawyer was running in circles waving an Order of Protection yelling, "I want him arrested! I want him arrested."

The next thing that happened was totally unintentional, something I would never purposely do no matter how angry I was. A cop grabbed me from behind and I turned and instinctively shoved him off. I should have known it was a cop. He went flying over a courtroom bench and landed on his back. As soon as he hit the floor I ran over to help him up and apologized profusely. I even apologized to the other officers while they handcuffed me.

The judge called everyone into his chambers (except me, obviously) while the three cops held me in one of the glass rooms.

I knew that any minute my lawyer would call and say, "Just calling to make sure everything went smoothly."

Maybe I'd break the news with something lighthearted like, "I kept my promise and never talked."

While we waited, I told an officer that the divorce had made me crazy. After about ten minutes, another officer came into the glass room. He had just left the judge's chambers. He said, "Do you realize what you could be charged with? You assaulted a lawyer and a cop in front of a judge."

The first officer told the second officer, "He said his divorce is making him crazy."

"That's what his wife's lawyer is telling the judge," the first cop said.

"Not permanently crazy," I said. "I just need to…"

"What you need to do is shut up and pray," he said. "They're on the phone conferring with your lawyer right now and if you're lucky, they'll bulldoze this whole thing under the rug."

God must have a soft spot for me because, incredibly, that's exactly what they did. Apparently, they conferenced in my lawyer, who had a long, contentious, love-hate history with the other lawyer. I think she had to make a deal with the devil.

All she said to me was, "No one wants to pull the trigger on you but you're becoming very unlikeable, and that's when people are going to stop wanting to help you."

Before I left the courthouse, one of the officers came up to me in the hall. "The judge wants you to get that hand taken care of. He said to consider it an order," he said. "You should also talk to someone. You're no good to your children in this frame of mind."

"I'm trying," I said.

With a firm smile, he said, "Try something else."

I never should have walked into that courtroom the way I did… sober, that is. As I was speeding down to Albany that day, my heart was racing and I was sweating and I wanted to pull off the Northway and grab a few forty-ouncers to take off the edge.

If I had done that, I never would have attacked the lawyer. Instead, I would have sat in my car for ten minutes before going into the courtroom, taking nice long gulps of cold beer.

And the beer would flow down my throat and caress the inside of my chest, like a cooling agent, soothing my heart and sending a calming sensation throughout my body. I was planning on doing that after my court appearance, but I should have done it before. Ironically, the best way to conceal my drinking from the court was to never let them see me sober. I was now convinced that I needed alcohol to hide my true self and whatever disorder I had.

I LEFT THE COURTHOUSE and started driving to the house in Guilderland until I remembered I didn't live there any more. There was no place to do a U-turn, so I took a detour behind the 20 Mall in Guilderland.

After a long, sober and near-felonious day in court, the last thing I needed was to be called out by a porky, six-foot-three-ish, white-gangster-wannabe with a sideways cap, a big silver crucifix and sagging pants.

I slowed down for a speed bump right next to a group of about seven or eight guys who looked like they were taking a smoke break. As I drove by, the only white guy in the group, a family-sized Eminem who was showing off for his black buddies, walked up to the side of my car with his arms spread, palms up and fingers extended. It was a glaring "What's Up Bitch?" gesture.

I was still sweating from my altercation in court but I was also still sober and mad. I ignored the guy at first — until I looked in my rear-view mirror and he was standing on top of the speed bump like he just scared me away. I should have looked away but I could hear him yelling, "That's right!" as if I were running away.

It was stupid; I should have just kept driving. But once the thought of attacking him ran through my head, I was out of the car, walking straight toward him and hoping he'd back down before I got to him. He didn't. In fact, he stepped up the taunting.

"Sup, yo? Sup, yo?" he yelled as I got closer to him.

I hit him as hard as I could in the throat with my right forearm and elbow. The back of his head was the first thing to hit the pavement. His buddies went ballistic — but not ballistic enough to help him. They stayed back, about twenty feet away. Two of them were calling 911.

I was on top of Big Eminem with my hand around his throat and I told his friends to get off their phones or I would kill him. When I could almost touch my fingers behind his trachea, I caught myself. *This is not okay*, I thought. *It's time to leave.*

I jumped up, looked down at him and said, "We're cool, right?" He was only moving a little and his hand was over his face.

I ran back to my car and took off with my window down to listen for sirens. I heard them, but I didn't think it had anything to do with me because they were coming from both directions of Western Avenue.

Instead of trying to get onto Western Ave, I pulled in-between some parked cars in front of a grocery store, then ducked down and did what I always did: I called Charles. He was at the command center at the Governor's Mansion. I told him everything and he said "hang tight."

He looked at a local police wire and said, "They're looking for someone who looks like you and drives a car that looks like yours."

"Looks like me? What are you…"

That's when I remembered he was on a recorded line and couldn't say anything. The last thing I wanted to do was get my best friend in trouble so I just ended the call and turned off my phone. Now I had to get out of it myself, which wasn't one of my talents.

I was still bent over with my face against the passenger seat and my heart was racing. I was reasonably sure they didn't have my plate number because I didn't see any of Big Eminem's friends get close enough to read it. I peeked out of the side window. The coast was clear so I walked into the grocery store. On the way in, I saw a Guilderland Police car zip behind the mall.

After hanging out for a few minutes in the produce section, I began to worry that I was giving the police too much time to notice my car in the parking lot.

It was time to make a run for it, but I had to blend in with the other shoppers so I couldn't walk out of the store empty-handed. I put two eighteen-packs of Miller Lite into a shopping cart, checked out and walked to the car with my head down, like I was studying the receipt.

By the time I got to the car, I was sweating and lightheaded and I couldn't stop shaking. I threw the beer, my keys and myself in the backseat and began sucking down beers from the fetal position, while methodically crushing the cans and putting them in a plastic bag.

I knew it was the worst possible time and place to start pounding down beer — and I should have stopped after three — but I couldn't. I was convinced that the more I drank, the less likely I was to get caught because I handled situations like this better with alcohol in my body.

Besides, I told myself, *If they find me, I'm in trouble anyway, so it doesn't really matter if I'm drinking. That's just an open container violation which is nothing compared to whatever I'll get charged with for attacking Big Eminem. Plus, with a bunch of beer in my system, I'd do a much better job of executing the next part of my getaway plan.*

When I finally got the courage, eight beer's worth, I squirmed up to the front seat without leaving the car, drove out of the rear mall entrance and took a hundred backstreets to get to the Northway heading back to Chestertown. Along the way, every ski rack in my rear-view mirror looked like police lights.

I wanted to call Charles back but I was already feeling guilty. I had to remember that, even though he was my closest friend who would (and always did) help me out of any predicament, he was still a cop, and a high-ranking one at that. I needed to be a good friend back and stop putting him in these conflicting positions.

One thing was certain: On this day, I had had way too much interaction with the police. Like the Albany cop said, I needed to try something different or I was going to wind up in prison. If it weren't for sheer luck and Charles, I'd already be there.

I tried to piece together the events of the day. The thing with the bus driver a week earlier had to be done, but maybe I would have done it better if I wasn't craving alcohol. Maybe I could have done it like other parents, without forcing Mallory's school into lockdown.

The other two incidents, in court and behind the mall, were different.

These mood spikes were like bolts of lightning and they were going to get me killed or incarcerated. They'd come out of nowhere, wreak havoc, then disappear. They'd fire an extreme thought into my head and before I could contemplate the thought rationally, I was acting on it. One second I had no intention of doing anything, the next second I was doing it, and a second later I was thinking, "Why in the hell did I do that?"

But again, it only happened when I was sober. It made no sense. I wondered if my drinking was masking something. I worried that maybe it meant I had a screw loose.

All I knew for sure was that my mood spikes, these radical impulses, weren't normal. Alcohol was the only thing that controlled them and that wasn't normal either.

I was almost home when Charles called.

"You're good, right?" he asked.

"I'm past Lake George," I said. "But…"

"What?" he said.

"I'm not out of control, am I?" I asked. "Everyone keeps saying I need help. I'm okay, right?"

I was positive he was going to give me the assurance I was looking for and say that everything was fine and I was just being me.

But he didn't say anything for a long time and I could tell he was looking for the right words. I didn't wait for him to find them.

"Wait, really?" I asked. "You think I've got some sort of mental..."

"It's me, Charles," he interrupted. "I'm on your side."

"What does that mean?" I asked.

"It means you can trust what I'm saying. You've always done your thing without caring what other people think, but now you're doing stuff that even you don't want to do. Maybe you should talk to someone."

"Fuck that," I said. "This is just me being me."

As soon as those words left my mouth, I felt guilty for prying advice out of Charles only to reject it helter-skelter... so I lied.

"Just kidding," I said. "You're right, I'm going to consider that."

I TRIED TO GROUND MYSELF with something other than alcohol. I got the idea after posting an ad on Craigslist for my Italian scooter. I had bought it a few years earlier thinking it was the best way to avoid getting a DWI, short of not drinking and driving. My theory was that no self-respecting cop would want to be seen pulling over a scooter, and I was right.

But I couldn't drive it very well drunk. I kept running into curbs and parking meters. Twice, I got off the thing and walked away without putting the kickstand down, and nothing says drunk like dumping a scooter on the sidewalk in front of an Irish bar.

A guy responded to my ad and we agreed to meet at a random parking lot in Queensbury. He drove it and said, "I can give you $500. That's all I have in cash."

"Why would you show up with $500 when you knew the price was $800?" I asked.

"Because I was supposed to pick up more cash in Ballston Spa but the guy didn't show up. Maybe we could make a... You're not a cop, right?" he asked.

"I'm not a cop," I told him. "What is it?"

He went to his car and came back with a duffel bag, then pulled out the biggest bag of marijuana I'd ever seen. It looked like a head of lettuce.

"I can put this up," he said. "I'd usually sell it for a lot more than $300."

Anything mind-altering was hard to resist so I didn't. My first thought was that it would mellow me out when I couldn't drink. At Conifer Park, they called it the "Marijuana Maintenance Program." It's when you try to kick a serious addiction by staying high on pot throughout the withdrawal process.

I knew that replacing alcohol with pot wasn't the best idea, but it was the best idea I had. Besides, I figured I was no different from the millions of other people who were using marijuana for medicinal purposes.

That night, after about fifteen beers, I grabbed the bag and pulled out a big bud, but I didn't have anything to smoke it with. I thought about just eating the thing since I didn't own a pipe or a bong and I sure as hell didn't know how to roll a joint. I never smoked cigarettes, but in college we smoked a variety of things with an empty beer can, and I had plenty of those.

As soon as I got the can in my hands, it all came back to me. I caved in one end of the can, poked tiny holes in the dent with a little nail and punched a carb hole in the side.

I didn't have matches so I fired it up with a small blow torch and sucked on the end of the can while watching the bud catch fire and turn bright orange. I took in too much… way too much. It felt like I swallowed a cup of lava but I tried holding it in anyway until it all came out — along with my lungs and kidney — in one explosive cough that made my throat sore for a week.

When the coughing stopped, I laid down and stared at a picture of a bear cub for about an hour without thinking of beer once. I thought I was cured.

For a while, the Marijuana Maintenance Program seemed to be working. I was drinking less at night than I used to, but mostly because smoking pot and drinking just don't mix. The more you do of one, the less you can do of the other. When I simultaneously did excessive amounts of both, I turned into a wandering vegetable, blobbing around the house without a clue in the world.

On more than a few nights, I'd wander off into the woods and just lay down on top of branches and rocks and listen to the snakes slithering over the leaves... or what I thought were snakes slithering over leaves.

And one time, I wandered over to a friend's house, which is about two hundred feet from mine. On the way home, after drinking and smoking pot for two hours, I lay down to look at the moon and ended up staring at it for so long I forgot where I was. I was so drunk and high I could barely see. Suddenly I was lost.

Remembering what I learned at summer camp, I stayed in place and made a lot of noise. My friend called out to me from his porch when he heard me yelling, "SOS" and "mayday."

"What in the hell are you yelling about?"

"I'm really, really lost," I cried. "Can you come get me?"

"Lost?" he screamed. "I can see you and I can see *Law and Order* playing on your damn TV — and I can see both of those things at the same time. How in the flaming fuck can you be lost?" It was no use, and he ended up getting in his truck and driving me fifty feet to my house. Apparently, it was really good pot.

My experience with drugs didn't go much further than that. I tried cocaine in college and I've been petrified of it ever since. I enjoyed the Vicodin my dentist gave me but not enough to go looking for it. For me, there was no substitute for alcohol.

AS FOR POT, it was fun and it gave me my appetite back, but I gave it up as soon as I learned there was a motion in front of the judge in my custody case to test me, not just for alcohol, but for everything.

I wasn't worried at first because drinking alcohol is legal and no test could satisfy the court's real concern, which was how much I drank. But I panicked when my lawyer told me that the judge might order a "five-panel test" screen, which detects marijuana, cocaine, PCP, amphetamines and opiates.

I tried to flush the marijuana out of my system with an Omega Flush kit. It's a sixteen-ounce drink that you drink a half hour before a drug test to cleanse the toxins from your urine, and it works — unless they go for the whole enchilada and administer a hair follicle test. He ordered both, which meant they'd know about everything I'd done for the last sixty days.

I freaked out on my lawyer. "What does he think I'm doing, meth and heroin?"

"You're not, so why do you even care?" she asked.

"I don't," I said, "but don't those tests come back positive even if you just, like, walked through a house where people were smoking pot?"

"Oh, here we go!" she said.

She knew alcohol was going to be a thorny issue in my custody trial so the last thing she wanted to hear about now was drugs. I assured her that drugs weren't an issue.

"Listen," I blithely told her, "Yes, I drink a little — a little in the morning and a little more in the afternoon and night. But I don't use drugs, and I may have inadvertently walked through some secondhand marijuana smoke, but it's okay because I ordered a detox shampoo kit online that will eliminate all traces of it from my hair follicles."

"We have a bad connection and I didn't hear a word of that," she said. "And now I'm hanging up."

I got the point, but just for fun I sent her an email asking, "How could you have a bad connection when we were both on landline phones?"

A few days later, I got a letter from the court, directing me to report to the Center for Recovery for a hair follicle test. When I got there, a lady in a lab coat led me into a big white room that looked like a forensic lab. She had me sit on a stool then she began inspecting the top of my head like it was a dead guinea pig.

She circled over me, gawking at different parts of my head with her chained glasses parked halfway down her nose. Then she'd poke my head with two fingers and say, "Your hair's not very long, is it?"

I didn't know how to respond to that so I didn't.

"Is it?" she said again.

"No," I said. "My hair's not very, umm, long. Nope."

"Did ya cut it last night or something?" She asked.

This time I caught her drift. She thought I chopped off my hair to avoid a hair follicle test.

"No, I didn't cut it last night and I'm not some rapist on probation," I said. "I'm just a father trying to get custody of his kids so lose the condescending attitude, lady."

She just stared at me with her shriveled face.

"If your hair's not a half inch long, we won't do the test," she said. "And then you'll have to answer to the judge."

"So you're going to make me sit here until it grows?" I asked.

She just glared at me.

"There are other places," I added, while peering down into my shorts. "Just say the word."

Suddenly, she decided the hair on my head was long enough. Thank God. The last thing I needed was this wicked witch waving her scalpel around down there.

Chapter Seventeen

The Best of Impaired Intentions

ME AND MY SHAMPOOED HAIR FOLLICLES passed the test, but the fact that I even had to take one made me question what I was fighting for and why. Both kids said they wanted to live with me, so I fought to get them. But as much as I loved them, I thought they were better off living with their mother in Guilderland.

Privately, I thought everyone responsible for giving me custody of Mallory and Jackson should lose their law licenses. I knew I would eventually pay the price for my behavior, but how did a Supreme Court Judge, a couple lawyers and a handful of social workers allow themselves to get duped by someone who was always drunk, right in front of them?

I did everything I could for Mallory and Jackson short of not drinking. Most times, I thought that being around them sober was the worst thing I could do to them. When I was a little kid, I was afraid of my father when he wasn't drinking. When I got a little older, I wasn't afraid of him any more; I just didn't like him. Without alcohol in him, he was pissy and miserable.

Drinking aside, I taught Mallory and Jackson how to laugh, how to have fun and how to listen — and I did it without ever having to spank them, or wanting to. I've only even raised my voice at the kids a few times, and it was at Mallory every time.

But at the end of the day, Mallory and Jackson needed a Dr Huxtable-type father (the character, not the actor) who would watch his language in front of them and make corny little quips like, "Hi, Hungry. I'm Dad." They needed a father who'd know where to find the Band-Aids, or a father who would at least *look* for Band-Aids before using duct tape.

And they needed a real neighborhood. The lake house was on a dirt road next to a lake surrounded by seasonal houses that are empty for nine months out of the year. There was no cul-de-sac, no neighborhood kids, no slumber parties — none of the stuff most kids grow up with, none of the stuff they had back in Guilderland.

I looked for every opportunity to make the lake house more like a traditional home, but some things were beyond my control... at least I thought they were.

I confided in my mother about all this one day and she quickly corrected my thinking. "Address the drinking and they'll be too happy to care about cul-de-sacs and slumber parties."

IT WAS THE FIRST DAY of the dreaded month of October and no matter how many lights and TVs and appliances I turned on in the lake house, I couldn't fool myself. I knew I was alone.

Both kids were with their mom for the weekend, and I hadn't left Chestertown in a while, so I packed some clothes in a bag and began driving down the Northway assuming I'd know where I was going when I got there. It was a short adventure — I never made it out of Warren County — because after twenty minutes, I got impatient and pulled over so I could start drinking.

I got a room at the Quality Inn in Queensbury, which is directly across the street from the Aviation Mall and a 99 Restaurant & Pub with a bar that's perfect for "extended stays" — big TVs, endless pitchers of beer and the smell of charbroiled steak, even though I would never compromise the effect of alcohol by eating one.

Some people go to the South of France; I was content with the South of Warren County. This was my way of spoiling myself — icy cold draft beer in a pint glass, filled right to the top with less than a millimeter of foamy head, poured perfectly by an attentive bartender who stayed close by because he knew why I was there.

I could hear the faint sound of barking puppies coming from the mall pet store, which was about a hundred feet away. After four or five pitchers at the bar, I told the bartender to keep one on ice for me while I went to play with the dogs.

A woman sitting at the bar turned to me and said, "Those puppies come from puppy mills where they breed dogs in awful conditions."

"I know," I said. "They need to shut those mills down and prosecute the owners and anyone who does business with them."

"Yeah, like the pet store you're going to," she said. "When I go by there, I turn my head. I won't even look at them."

"They're still dogs," I said. "You won't pet them? That makes no sense."

Fortunately, she didn't want to advance the discussion any further than that. I had the perfect beer buzz going and she ruined it with her stupidity. It's like refusing to talk to Jews because you're opposed to antisemitism.

In the only cage big enough to hold him, there was a giant German Shepherd puppy attacking his metal water bowl with his big paws, creating a disproportionately loud racket akin to bullets hitting a cymbal.

After a few minutes of pouncing on it from every conceivable angle, his little rampage ended abruptly and he came to a dead halt. He froze mid-pounce and looked straight at me with one jowl hung up on his lower fang. He glared at me like I just said something vile about his mother. I glared back at him until he went back to his routine.

For about a half hour, I just stood there watching him until the clerk finally walked up and asked if I wanted to play with him in one of their visiting rooms.

"No," I said. "He seems to be having plenty of fun by himself." I decided to leave before doing anything stupid in the heat of an intoxicated moment. There was a free pitcher of beer waiting for me when I returned to my place at the bar.

"This was a mistake," the bartender said, pointing to a full pitcher. "A guy wanted Heineken and I poured Coors, so it's yours if you want it." He assumed I'd drink a pitcher of beer I didn't really like. I guess I give off that vibe.

"Oh, thank you," I said. "I think I have a little room left."

"I thought you'd be coming back here with a puppy," he said.

"The last thing I need right now is a German Shepard," I told him.

"I said puppy," he smirked. "I didn't say anything about a German Shepard."

I changed the subject and stayed at the bar until closing, walked back to the hotel and drank for another hour until I passed out.

The next morning, I spent a lot of time wondering what would happen to that rowdy puppy when he outgrew his cage,

It worried me a little because he was already too big to be in a pet store and I had a hard time believing that anyone capable of raising a German Shepard would be dumb enough to shop for one at the mall. It's not the kind of thing you pick up on your way to get a neon vibrator at Spencer Gifts.

Quality Inn offered me another night's stay at half price, so I went back to the 99 Bar for a couple hours. That led me right back to the German Shepard puppy and his water bowl.

I don't know if it was because he recognized me, but he stared directly at me as soon as I walked in the store even though there were other people walking in at the same time.

I played with him in the visiting room for about ten minutes. Every time I stood up like I was preparing to leave, he froze and looked at me with an expression that said, "You can't leave without me." It was compelling enough to convince me that he was right. I needed this dog in my life.

Mallory's birthday was coming up, which was the perfect pretext for buying myself a German Shepard. Jackson and I named him "Bam," after Bam Margera, a cast member on the *Jackass* series.

So, Mallory's birthday present was the satisfaction of seeing the men in her life happy.

Bam was an expensive puppy. My family thought I was irresponsible to pay $1,300 for a dog, no matter how pure his breed was. But Bam quickly became a priceless companion.

Years later, there were nights when I'd wake up in severe alcohol withdrawal, frozen in fear and confusion. Bam never left my side. I would literally squeeze his paw and he'd lick my forehead until I got my bearings. The puppy with the bowl turned out to be everything I needed him to be: a guard dog, a guide dog, a rescue dog, a therapy dog and always a best friend.

Chapter Eighteen

A Lifelong Dread

ALTHOUGH MALLORY WAS LIVING at the lake with me, Jackson was still with his mom in Guilderland. I was on my way to pick him up one Friday when I made the mistake that sent me driving straight into the worst moment of my existence as a father.

On this day, I was picking Jackson up from his school. It takes about an hour to get there and along the way, as always, I drank just enough to control the symptoms of not drinking.

It was a calculated routine. For the total round trip, I would tide myself over with seven beers in two-and-a-half hours. "Tiding myself over" meant drinking just enough to prevent myself from slipping into my most dangerous state: sobriety.

Five of the beers were in a duffel bag on the floor of the backseat, which made it easy to reach back and discard an empty can while grabbing a new one. I didn't guzzle the beer like I normally did. I drank in slow measured sips, allowing myself to drink one beer every fifteen miles. Based on my math, that would put my blood alcohol content at .08 by the time I got Guilderland.

I got to Jackson's school early so I decided to park the car and wait for him in the school lobby. As I was standing there, the principal of the school, who I had spoken to in the past, walked up to me and started a conversation.

After a few minutes, she said goodbye and walked away. About a minute later, the school resource officer — a local cop assigned to the school — walked up to me and asked me how I was doing. Then he asked me if I had been drinking. I said that I had a couple of beers at a local bar before coming to pick up my son but I was fine to drive.

After a minute or two, the conversation turned less conversational and suddenly, for the first time in thirty years, I was back in the principal's office. Two other officers rolled up to the bus loop with a breathalyzer.

This was my worst nightmare. I blinked my eyes hard a few times praying I'd open them and see the knotty pine ceiling of my bedroom. It was happening. The horror I had worked so hard to avoid was happening, and it was happening in the principal's office of my son's school.

The legal limit in New York is .08. I passed the breathalyzer test the first time by blowing a .07, but they did it two more times and both times I blew a .08.

They read me my rights, arrested me and led me out the front door, past my son and hundreds of his peers, and into the back of the police car. I stared straight ahead the entire time, purposely keeping my eyes wide open without blinking so they would glaze over and blind me to everything that was happening.

When I got to the back of the police car, I closed my eyes tight then opened them, hoping to interrupt this God-awful night terror.

At the police station, I tried to imagine what would be going through my mind at Jackson's age. Would I be mostly sad or mostly embarrassed? Would I be worried about my father or mad at him? What would I tell my friends?

Even as they took my prints and my photo, I just looked straight ahead trying to figure out what must be going through Jackson's mind. Thank God Mallory was with her mother this weekend.

When I first got to the station, they sat me at a desk and handcuffed me to a big metal ring. But then another officer came along and said, "This doesn't seem necessary," and unhooked the cuffs. I never moved or said a word. I just sat there, staring at the metal ring and thinking about a million things.

I needed a drink so badly that I almost admitted it to one of the officers. I was going to tell him that without alcohol I would go into a seizure. Luckily, I thought twice about doing it, and the second time I realized how dumb it would be to confide in the people who arrested me. Finally, I asked one of the officers if I was going to end up in a cell.

"No, it's a violation," he said. "You'll be released with an appearance ticket."

"A violation?" I asked.

"Yeah, a .08 is just a violation, not even a misdemeanor," he said. "But now you have a new relationship with the DMV, and you're not going to like it."

They gave me my appearance ticket, my duffel bag (minus the empty beer cans, which they kept for "evidence," as if they needed any more), and a little card that told me where I could pay two hundred dollars to get my car back. They asked if I wanted to use the phone.

"No," I said. "A friend is picking me up."

"How is that possible?" he asked. "You haven't had access to a phone in over two hours."

I lied because I had no one to call and nowhere to go, and I didn't want them giving me another ride in a police car.

I walked out of the police station and straight to the grocery store next door where I bought an eighteen-pack of beer. I put it in my duffel bag and tried thinking of a place to drink it. I knew everything would be fine if I could just find a way to get the beer out of the can and into my mouth. Vodka would have been better but there wasn't a liquor store within walking distance.

I went from the checkout line to the restroom and brought my bag into the stall. While cracking open a beer, I coughed loudly, just like I did a hundred times before in a hundred other bathroom stalls during a hundred other moments of distress.

The first beer went down quickly and so did the second, third, fourth and fifth one.

After about twenty minutes, I realized I'd been in there too long and needed to get out before someone started wondering why. I dumped the crushed empties into the trash, zipped up my bag and walked back into the store.

It probably looked like I was shoplifting, especially with the duffel bag. I was genuinely thrilled that no one accused me of that because my only defense would have been to show them that I was just a raging alcoholic.

I sat on the bench in front of the checkout lines to figure out what I was going to do next.

It was about fifteen degrees outside with the wind whipping in every direction. I couldn't pick up my car until the next morning. Even if the impound lot was open, I sure as hell wouldn't try to pick it up now. After drinking half of an eighteen-pack in less than a half hour, I predicted my blood alcohol was .17, the threshold for aggravated DUI in New York.

Years earlier, my trooper friends would occasionally bring a breathalyzer to my office so I could get a feel for what I'd blow if I got pulled over. At home one night, I blew a .31, and that was while I was in the middle of writing a speech.

My calculations were generally very accurate. Alcohol content + time + body weight + number of drinks = blood alcohol content. Even when I got arrested, my estimate was spot on. What my formula lacked was an equation of common sense because when you're picking your child up at school, blowing the legal limit is hardly a virtue.

That's why I walked passively through the entire process — from the school through the courts — without asking for leniency or issuing so much as a word in my defense. Even the judge questioned why I wasn't seeking a reduced charge of a moving violation.

I knew what I was. Everyone else knew what I was. I didn't want the added stigma of being a blamer and an excuse-maker.

I NEEDED A PLACE to spend the night. I was an hour from the lake house and a quarter mile from my former residence where my ex-wife and my kids were, which I crossed off my list of options right off the bat. I wasn't sure where the closest hotel was, but I started walking because this was Route 20 in Guilderland... How far could it be?

As it turns out, two miles.

When I woke up the next morning, I lay in bed, stared at the ceiling and fantasized about various things crashing into my hotel and blowing it to smithereens — a fuel truck, an airplane, a cruise missile... anything that would shift everyone's attention away from me and towards something else, like the incredible news of Guilderland getting hit with cruise missiles.

I walked to the place that was holding my car. It was a Saturday and they were closed for the weekend so I kept calling the number on the door. A guy finally called me back, thoroughly annoyed that I was bothering him on a Saturday.

I handed him the money.

As he handed me the keys, he said, "I should get another $20 for coming out here for this shit."

"I left your tip in the trunk next to my tire iron," I said.

"Easy, pal, aren't you in enough trouble?" he said.

"Fortunately for you, I am," I said.

I drove off the lot, paranoid, with both hands on the wheel. I was shaking… itching to get the hell out of Guilderland so I could pull over and get drunk somewhere. I'd worry about how to get home later.

I headed for the "Across the Street Pub," which was two miles down the road in Albany.

All I could think about was sitting in front of a big pitcher of beer. I could almost feel the beer flowing down my throat and splashing into my chest, calming and cooling my heart and making everything seem a little better, one pitcher at a time.

When I felt this shitty, I didn't waste time worrying about what I was going to do after that. First, I needed to drink those pitchers, then I would be in the right frame of mind to plan my next move, like getting back to the lake house.

I knew I wouldn't get drunk and jump in the car — never again — but that's all I knew.

At the last second, instead of pulling into the bar, I turned onto the on-ramp to the Northway and headed home. Every time I passed an exit, I had to convince myself that I could make it to the next exit without pulling over to drink.

When I got to Chestertown, I picked up beer and vodka, thanked the neighbor who took care of Bam overnight and took the phone off the hook. For the next few hours, I sat on the floor with Bam and drank until I passed out.

When I woke up the next morning, I drank what I had left and called a guy in town who had been nagging me to sell him my ATV and trailer.

"You've got a deal," I told him. "But only if you can be here in the next hour with the money, a bottle of vodka and two thirty-packs of beer."

He got the better end of deal, but once I knew he was coming with money and booze, I didn't care about the ATV. I never drove it sober anyways, and now I'd be too scared to drive it drunk.

Obviously, I was embarrassed — beyond embarrassed — about being arrested while picking up Jackson at school. It wasn't like the other bad things I had done.

There was no way to spin it into something honorable. It wasn't like going after Mallory's bus driver and sending her school into lockdown. At least Mallory could say, "Hey, my dad was standing up for me."

But Jackson, especially at that age, must have been mortified, and I was heartbroken that I had created what was probably the worst moment of his young life. I was worried about how it would affect him. I knew he wouldn't outwardly hold it against me and that's what concerned me the most; it would be easier if he did. At least then I could see and hear the damage I had caused so I could try to repair it.

My fear was that this would affect him in a deep and unknowable way that wouldn't present itself until it was too late. I was afraid of him turning into me. I was afraid of seeing him struggle down the wrong path because now I wouldn't have the credibility to set him straight.

I was worried that his apparent apathy and acceptance of my behavior might be a sign that I had lowered the bar of expectations right to the ground. I wanted him to be afraid to turn out like me. But if that's all I could teach him, what good was I as a father? Truth is, I did want him to be like me. I just didn't want him to be an alcoholic like me.

At this point, the only remotely honorable and productive thing I could do for Mallory and Jackson was show them that I was accountable. I would condemn my indefensible behavior, I would not make excuses, and I would prevent it from happening again. I promised myself I would never test the law again by trying to drink and drive at the legal limit.

And I began to openly acknowledge that I was an alcoholic, but I acknowledged it the way some people acknowledge an unsightly birthmark, like it was just the unfortunate genetic curse that I was born with and there was nothing I could do about it.

Still, I had to show a good faith effort. I had to show Mallory and Jackson and my mom that I was at least trying, so I checked into the detox unit at St Peter's Hospital in Albany… again.

Chapter Nineteen

It's Just the Insanity Talking

FOR ME, THE ST. PETER'S DETOX UNIT was an asylum from whatever shitty situation I had gotten myself into. In the arcade game *Asteroids*, if your spaceship is about to get crushed by oncoming space rocks, as a last resort you can push the Hyperspace button and it'll make your ship disappear from your shitty place and reappear someplace else.

Whenever I got desperate enough to check into the St. Peter's Detox Unit, I was basically hitting the Hyperspace button.

It was a vanishing act, a way to avoid shame and ridicule in a place where I was protected by hospital walls and HIPAA laws, while ostensibly seeking treatment.

The problem with the Hyperspace button is that sometimes you land in a place that's even shittier than the shitty place you started… and it doesn't get any worse than the St. Peter's Detox Unit. It's where I developed a phobia for institutional white walls and hallways.

A detox unit isn't a full blown, twenty-eight-day rehab center. It's a medical unit, usually in a hospital, where they monitor and medicate you through your withdrawal from drugs or alcohol or whatever else you're killing yourself with. It's like a nursing home for addicts and alcoholics, and they won't even take you unless you're a hot mess when you walk through the door, which was never a problem for me.

I'd been to this detox unit once before, about a year earlier. That time, I was medicated and detoxed for five days. As soon as I was released, I walked across the street to Andy's Sports Bar.

This time, the detox wouldn't even take me because I was too dehydrated and my blood pressure was through the roof.

They treated me in the Emergency Room for two days then admitted me into the hospital on a floor with mostly terminally ill people.

I couldn't move because they had IVs running into each arm.

On the bed underneath my butt there was an alarm cushion that would sound off if I tried to get up.

There was no TV and the nurse only came by once every two hours. I just laid there and stared at the ceiling. I couldn't even sit on the edge of the bed and rock back and forth to ease the alcohol withdrawal symptoms.

After a full day of laying still and sober, I began looking for a way out. I purposely moved around to set off the alarm cushion, forcing the nurses to come running into my room twice. I told them I must have been moving in my sleep.

After I set it off the second time, I asked, "Do I really need this? It keeps waking me up." The nurse agreed, undoubtedly to make her life easier, not mine.

As soon as she left, I knew it would be a long time before anyone came back to check on me. I peeled the tape off the IVs, pulled the needles out of my arm and taped the IVs to the bed rail.

I got up slowly, walked over to my duffle bag and got dressed. When the coast was clear in the hallway, I grabbed my duffel bag and made my way to an elevator and took it down to the ground floor.

I went out the side door, through the parking lot and across New Scotland Road to a CVS Pharmacy.

I knew CVS sold beer and I was sure an eighteen-pack would fit perfectly into my duffel bag. It did, so I zipped it up, headed back across the street to the hospital and prepared for re-entry.

I conceded, in advance, that I was going to get busted on the way back in. I'd never get the IVs back into my arms without screwing something up. My goal was simply to get my duffel somewhere on the floor, like a bathroom or in a linen closet.

Surprisingly, I made it all the way back to my room and I was in the process of fiddling with the IVs when a nurse casually walked in and said, "I need your blue bag."

"That one?" I asked, pointing to the only blue bag in the hospital.

"Yeah, this one," she said as she unzipped it. She looked at the beer, then looked back at me and said, "So, what's going on with you?"

"Oh, the beer?" I said. "Yeah, I wasn't sure… is that allowed on this floor?"

"A doctor saw you get off the elevator and walk across the street," she said as she was cramming — yes cramming — the IVs back into my arm.

"You can have your beer back when you leave," she said.

"Then I want to leave now," I said, as I pulled out the IVs she had just put in. "I don't want to be here."

Another nurse showed up and walked away with my duffel bag. I knew they weren't going to let me leave so I watched the second nurse to see where she was going with my beer.

"You're on a seventy-two-hour hold," the first nurse said.

"Oh, like I haven't heard that a million times," I said. "Why? Who am I a danger to?"

She ignored all of that and just gently pushed my shoulders down to the bed while adjusting the mattress.

"I'm going to take your vital signs again and talk to the doctor," she said. "Just hold on and I'll be back with something to make you feel better."

I knew what that meant. She was going to use prescription narcotics to shut me up. After about an hour, she came back with a generous dose of Librium.

"I can only take that with Ativan [a stronger narcotic]," I said.

"And maybe you'd like to wash it down with a beer," she said. "Just try to relax. The doc wrote you a good prescription for this. You'll be fine."

"Can you just check my chart?" I asked. "I just want to see the HIPAA releases I signed."

"I won't tell your family about your trip to CVS," she said. "But can I ask you something?"

"Anything," I said.

"You were out of the hospital and you had the beer…" she said. "Why did you come back here to drink it?"

"I… feel the Librium kicking in," I said. "I'm gonna try to sleep."

Chapter Twenty

A Fight Out on the Town

THE PANTHER MOUNTAIN INN is the only bar in Chestertown. It's not a redneck joint, but you'll hear some Skynyrd in there and the regulars know their way around an engine block.

I didn't go there much, mostly because drinking in a bar wasn't a cost-effective way to get drunk. For the same cost of getting drunk one night in a bar, I could get drunk four nights at home and still have a few left over in the morning.

A week after leaving St. Peter's Detox, I was passing the Panther around seven pm one Tuesday night and I decided to go in. I don't know why.

There were only a few people sitting at the bar — three guys huddled up at one end and a middle-aged woman at the other. The woman was kind of attractive but looked like she had her fifteen minutes of fame about ten years earlier, probably right there on the same bar stool. It sounded like there were also a few guys hanging out in the back.

I took a seat in the middle of the bar and ordered two Coors Lights and a shot of Goldschlager. One of the guys at the end of the bar was kind of loud but I couldn't really hear what he was saying. It must have been funny because the other two guys were laughing obnoxiously.

I glanced over at them a few times, just casually trying to hone in on what was so funny. Each time I looked over, all three of them stopped laughing for a second, then started snickering.

The guy doing most of the talking was bald and stocky. That's about all I remember. I heard him say something like, "He has his daughter living with him." That caught my attention because... well, because I had my daughter living with me.

When I looked over, all three of them looked back and started laughing.

It seemed like they were going out of their way to get my attention, but I pretended not to notice so they would try a little harder. That's when one of them said "Mallory" in a drawn-out voice like they were calling her for dinner. It's not a common name and there's only one Mallory in Chestertown so I looked and stood up.

My body language wasn't confrontational; it was more along the lines of, "Oh hey, I have a daughter named Mallory. Do you know her?" They were too young to have kids her age, and they didn't look like fathers, so it was unlikely they did.

As soon as I stood up, all three of them jumped to their feet. One of them shot up so fast his bar chair fell against the wall. Then they just walked towards me in a single file line.

That's when I knew they didn't want to swap cheesecake recipes. I forgot when I remembered this, but when I first ordered my drinks, the bartender said, "Don't you have kids at North Warren?" I must have mentioned her name loud enough for these guys to hear it, and now they were just being assholes.

If I ever have to fight three guys again, I hope they line up just like these three did. The guy at the front grabbed the neck of my shirt and tried pulling me down, but the shirt ripped instead.

I punched him in the side of the face and he went down and never got up. The second guy went for my neck with both hands. I hit him under the chin, just hard enough to stop him. He went down to his knees. When I leaned over and told him to stay down, he started swinging up at me so I hit him again, a lot harder. He fell backwards, taking part of my shirt with him. I may have knocked him out.

The third one just disappeared. I could hear him yelling to whoever was in the back room. I figured he was probably coming back with reinforcements but I'd met enough of his friends for one night so I decided to pay my bar tab and make a run for it.

The bartender was screaming at the top of his lungs, "What did you do? What did you do?" It was sort of a high-pitched, shrieking sound, totally unacceptable coming from the mouth of a male.

I threw a handful of money on the bar and told the screeching bartender to keep the change. I took one last look before heading for the door.

There was yelling coming from the back room but I couldn't see anyone. Both guys were still on the ground. One was moving, one wasn't. They were surrounded by a pool of blood. Part of me wanted to make sure they were okay but a bigger part of me wanted to get the fuck out of there before the cops came.

The bartender was looking down at them describing the scene to what I assumed was a 911 operator. The Warren County Sheriff and the State Police share the same barracks a few blocks away so I knew it was going to be hard to get away.

On the way out the door, with all the screaming and chaos behind me, a neon Bud Light sign caught my attention. It was hanging in the window.

I can't fully explain a lot of things I've done in my life, but I usually have at least an inkling of what triggered my various transgressions. That said, I can honestly proclaim the following: If I live to be a thousand years old, I will never understand why I stopped running and took the time to stand on the window sill, unhook a fragile neon sign that I didn't even want, and carefully carry it to my car when I could hear police cars coming to arrest me.

Just as I was turning on to the main road, I could see police lights reflecting off my rear-view mirror as they turned into the Panther Inn. I had a clear shot home, but the cops in that area wouldn't have to Google my address. They knew where I lived so when I pulled up to the lake house, I half expected to see them waiting for me, but they weren't.

Mallory was home so, as soon as I ran in, I told her that some guys tried to beat me up in town and I had to defend myself and not to worry when the cops showed up. I grabbed an empty bottle of vodka and put it on my desk, essentially making any sobriety test they were planning to give me meaningless.

I could hear the sirens, and even though I knew what to do this time, out of habit, I called Charles anyway.

On the way in the house, I must have run right past Bam without noticing him. Now he was standing in front of the police cars going nuts. They didn't want any part of him. They stayed in their cars, blowing their air horn sirens to get me out of the house. I went out to get Bam, and once he was safely tucked away in my bedroom, a Warren County Sheriff came inside.

"Okay, first things first," he said. "Where is that German Shepard right now?"

"Bam's in my room," I said. "He can't get out."

Then Mallory's head popped out of nowhere from behind the stairway wall. "He was just defending himself," she said, then disappeared back up the stairs.

"That answers my next question," he said. "I assume you know why we're here."

"I have a pretty good idea," I said.

Another officer came in with a breathalyzer.

"You must have driven here pretty fast after drinking at the bar," he said. "I'm gonna need you to blow into this."

I grabbed the vodka bottle on the desk, waved it at him and said, "I guzzled this as soon as I got home to calm me down, so…"

He knew I was lying but it didn't seem like he wanted to give me a hard time about it.

"Why, you were traumatized by all of their bleeding?"

"I just stopped in for a beer, and they were looking for a…"."

"Whatever," he said, "You left quite a mess back there."

"It was three against one. Look at this," I said, pointing to my torn T-shirt.

"Your shirt?" he snapped. "The gash on the guy's face goes from the corner of his eye to his nose. The other one has a broken nose and maybe a broken jaw. They were still on the ground being looked at when I left. There's blood all over the floor… and you expect me to be outraged about your torn shirt?"

They could have handcuffed me as soon as they got there but they never did. It almost seemed like they were helping me get my story straight. They didn't write anything down. They seemed empathetic. When I told them about how they used my daughter's name to provoke a fight, they nodded like they had already heard that part of the story from someone else.

Maybe the woman at the end of the bar confirmed my story.

"These guys are going to need medical attention," the officer said. "You better hope they have health insurance."

"I didn't go in there looking for a fight. I was by myself and minding my own business."

"We'll be back," he said. "Don't go to bed."

The same officer came back a couple hours later by himself, without all the lights. He said all three guys claimed I was the aggressor and they wanted to press charges.

The bartender and the woman both said that the other three guys provoked the fight, and had a reputation for doing that, but thought I started punching too early.

"I told them I wasn't going to take their statement until they were sober so there aren't going to be any charges tonight," the officer said. "I'll talk to them in the morning and come back here."

The next morning, the officer came back to the house with good news. "It's just like I thought," he said. "They woke up in a different frame of mind. Their insurance covered everything at the hospital and they're not pressing charges."

"Thanks for anything you may have done to help them come to that decision."

"That's okay," he said. "But listen, you can't go back to the Panther Inn. They don't ever want to see you again. Just hang tight at home for a while and lay low, okay?"

I promised him I would. For the most part, I kept that promise but staying at home and staying out of trouble weren't mutually exclusive. Either way, I was almost guaranteed to hurt someone who probably deserved it, but now the deserving victim was me.

It's a matter of science. Every major study concludes that home accidents are the number one cause of injuries for older adults. That number is multiplied infinitely when the adult is me with a beer in my hand, which was always. The number skyrockets further into oblivion when you throw guns and fire into the equation. All these factors contributed to a string of preventable "mishaps" in the months following the Panther Inn incident.

Every week, I had to build large bonfires in my giant backyard fire pit to incinerate garbage. I'd chop down tall thin trees, cut the stalks into twenty-feet lengths and use them to construct a tall teepee using a screw gun and twine to keep everything together. Then I'd pack the inside with dry wood, about eight feet high.

Depending on my blood alcohol content, I'd ignite it with either a match, a molotov cocktail or a flaming arrow. A couple hours later, I'd place all the garbage on the bed of bright red glowing coals, and it would just incinerate on contact.

Sometimes, to break up the boredom, I would throw something on the coals to make a loud noise, usually something with a label that read, "Warning: Extremely flammable. Contents under pressure, blah, blah, blah."

One night, I threw a can of spray paint in the pit but it rolled off the bed of red coals and landed on the edge of the fire, not exploding. I knew trying to retrieve it would be a bad idea, so I came up with an even worse one: I shot it at point blank range. When it exploded, the "contents under pressure" shot straight back at me and set my left arm on fire.

The scene was toxic in more ways than one. Jackson and my nephew saw the whole thing. In fact, they both rushed over to help extinguish my arm before I raced into the house and doused it with cold water from the bathtub.

The smell of my burning flesh was disconcerting and so was the pain, but since I was, well, playing with fire, I didn't even think of complaining. I underwent several weeks of burn therapy, which included an unpleasant procedure every few days where they scrape off the top layer of crusted-up, burnt skin.

They put me on a heavy dose of Vicodin, an opioid narcotic that a lot of people in the rehabs I'd been to were hooked on. It took away my pain, but I must not have the opioid gene because that's all it did for me.

My body was loyal to alcohol. Anything that delayed or altered the effect of alcohol got kicked to the curb.

My bandaged arm was hard to hide and impossible to explain. I tried to keep the whole thing a secret, but the story got relayed to my entire family. There was really no way to sugarcoat the incident because there's no good reason to shoot a can of spray paint in a bonfire.

If I said I shot the can so it wouldn't explode, the logical follow-up question would be, "Why was the can in the fire and why were you standing there with a gun?"

Even in my forties, after buying four homes and raising two children,

I was very answerable to my mother. She was keyed in to my drinking and I was committed to keeping her reassured and unworried.

She had her ways of getting to the truth. After the can shooting, she started asking people questions and managed to unearth another secret having to do with guns.

About a month earlier, I was holding a .243 caliber rifle while sitting at my desk in the living room of the lake house. What I did next — and I don't remember what prompted it — was probably the most potentially-deadly stunt I've ever pulled while drinking.

I fired once into the passageway of a staircase going up and down. The shot went through the first step of the staircase, then passed through two more walls and into a screened-in porch where it tore a hole through an empty propane tank. The tank next to it was full.

If the bullet had hit that one, the explosion would have taken out the stairway and the bedroom it leads to, where my daughter was hanging out with two friends.

It was hard to deny the incident. There was an obvious bullet hole in the staircase and it wasn't hard to follow the path of the bullet back to the chair I fired it from.

I was always afraid that, after stuff like this, the most important people in my life would give up on me unless I did something to show that I knew I had a problem.

So, I'd take it upon myself to check myself into a program, any program, to appease my family. Sometimes it was the detox unit at St. Peter's, which was easy to get into for me because all you had to do was show up perilously intoxicated.

I preferred Four Winds because I was comfortable there (having been mandated there following my overdose). It was, first and foremost, a psychiatric facility. That didn't bother me because, at this point in my life, I couldn't stigmatize myself any more than I already had.

Since Four Winds wasn't a rehab, they wouldn't admit people solely for addiction or alcoholism. They'd evaluate you first and admit you if they could assign you a dual diagnosis, which meant that, in addition to having a mental illness, you were addicted to drugs or alcohol.

The first time I went to Four Winds, after I overdosed on Klonopin in 2003 while still working in the Governor's Office, I didn't have a choice. It was either Four Winds or the State Psychiatric Center. So, I guess I did have a choice, just not much of one.

This time, they wouldn't admit me because I couldn't make it past their breathalyzer. Two days in a row, I tried to check in around ten o'clock in the morning. Both times, their breathalyzer picked up the remnants of alcohol from the night before.

After the second time, they told me they wouldn't admit me unless I completed the detox program at St. Peter's Hospital.

"I don't think they [St. Peter's] want to see me again," I told the intake nurse.

"Why," she asked.

"Because the last time I was there," I told her, "they stuck me on a bed with wires and alarms and I couldn't sit still so I disconnected everything and went across the street for an eighteen-pack of beer."

"Right," she said. "But seriously, they have a nice program at St. Peter's and you should at least go there to check it out."

"I told you," I said, "I was just there and… okay, I'll check it out."

Chapter Twenty-one

A Match Made In-Toxicated

I DECIDED TO JUST STAY AT HOME and work on disciplining myself. I needed a distraction, a pretty one. After seven years of being single in a small town in the Adirondacks, entertaining myself with drinking games lost its effect, and loneliness got the best of me.

I missed the feeling of being missed. Except for the police and several town courts, no one was ever looking for me. I even thought it would be nice if someone would scold me for spilling something in the kitchen. Right now, I could set the kitchen on fire and no one would give a shit.

I didn't want to search for a serious relationship because I always believed that things like that happen naturally.

In the past couple of years, I had a handful of encounters that all ended abruptly, usually after a long day of heavy drinking. I scared most women off in the first seventy-two hours.

I had a two-week relationship that came to a screeching halt after an intimate evening at her place. When the intimacy was over, I casually and convincingly told her that I was living proof that HIV wasn't a death sentence.

It's not a funny joke, but for a nanosecond that night, I must have thought it was. These nanoseconds — these sudden, radical thoughts that, too often, were turning into words or actions — were destroying my life. The drinking wasn't helping much either.

I tried apologizing a hundred different ways, but she wasn't even considering forgiveness. She was looking for the quickest way to get me out of her house and out of her life forever.

Any relationship I got into had a shelf life of about two weeks, so this one was about to expire anyway. But I liked this woman and she really liked me. I spent the next few days asking myself, "What in the fuck is wrong with you?"

PROBABLY THE BIGGEST complaint from users of Match.com is that people lie on their profile. Either they exaggerate about their lifestyle or post old pictures of themselves, at the peak of their physical charisma, before they stopped taking care of themselves and got fat.

I didn't lie about any of that stuff. But Match's questionnaire is pretty thorough. It asks all the sensitive questions that, conceivably, could make or break a relationship — everything from your political and religious views to the details of your lifestyle habits.

They even ask what kind of drinker you are. You had a few categories to choose from, ranging from "I never drink" to "heavy drinker." I didn't feel like any of the categories applied specifically to me, so I checked the box that said, "social drinker" — a detail that couldn't survive one hour, much less one date.

Late at night, I'd scroll through the profiles on Match and send out a few messages before passing out or going to bed. In the morning, I'd sift through the responses I got to the messages I don't remember writing.

First, I'd read whatever message I sent to them. That was always good for a cringe and a laugh. Then I'd read their response, which was usually positive. If it was too positive, I didn't write back. In my drunk and arbitrary and possibly bipolar world, I was petrified of a commitment. I just wanted a little company.

It's not that hard to intrigue me late at night because I was always bombed. But given my ever-changing mood and personality, the odds of intriguing me two nights in a row are virtually nil. You'd have a better chance of killing two bats with a boomerang.

For me to sit down and look through profiles on Match, I had to be more than just drunk. I had to be "late-night-mussel-run" drunk. That's when I was drunk and hungry enough to go diving into the lake at night digging through the muck for mussels to boil and dip into butter for a late-night snack. If I was drunk enough to do that, chances are I'd also be drunk enough to go digging through the muck on Match.com looking for love.

There was only one profile that stuck in my mind, night after drunken night. It belonged to Lisa O'Donnell. She had a black and white profile picture and she was beautiful in a wholesome, "That Girl" sort of way.

Through many blurry nights, her face remained clear in my mind.

I sent her a note one night and she wrote back. We emailed back and forth for quite a while before we talked on the phone. I really liked her. There was no small talk. We were talking about important stuff, personal stuff, and when we weren't doing that we were laughing at each other.

For the first time in about two decades, I was picking my words carefully — not to hide my thoughts but to make sure my words reflected how much I cared about her.

I told her about my divorce and my kids and everything else that was happening in my life except for my drinking, which, of course, was everything that was happening in my life. It certainly dictated everything that was happening in my life.

I knew that my drinking was going to be the deal breaker. It had to be. But I didn't want to lose her — at least not right away — and part of me wanted to keep our platonic, electronic relationship going the way it was into perpetuity. That way, she could love me for who I was and not how I drank.

Finally, I found someone I actually connected with, in a strong way. I knew that when we met face-to-face, I was going to have to say something about my drinking. I couldn't just invite her over and start emptying a thirty-pack in front of her.

I never found the courage to do that. But even in the beginning of our relationship, Lisa was patient, protective and fiercely loyal. She came to the lake house every weekend.

Most nights we would order out, and when it was time to drive into town to pick up the food, I made sure her car was blocking mine so I didn't have to drive.

It was no big deal because we never drove more than a few miles together. But after a while, I felt comfortable enough to be partially honest. Instead of blaming the way the cars were parked, I'd say, "Maybe you should drive; I've had a couple beers."

As time went on, I got more honest and dishonest at the same time. I told her that my custody trial had driven me to drinking, but it was just a phase and I would get over it.

As it turned out, my drinking didn't affect our relationship as much as I thought it would. After six months, not only were we still together, we were starting to say things like "I love you" and "Let me pop that zit."

It didn't make any sense to me. She was attractive, smart, successful and wealthy — everything that I used to be. Why was she standing by a man who was drinking himself to an early death?

I even asked her that question one night (without the part about me being a washed-up drunk). She answered, "Because you're a great father with a big heart who loves his dog, loves his kids and likes being with me."

It was nice to hear, but she left out "loves to drink."

Late one Friday afternoon, I wound up back at the Panther, even though they had banned me for life for fighting less than a year earlier. A bartender I knew let me in after I promised to stay in one spot and not to talk to anyone.

After a couple of beers, my only ride home told me it was time to leave. I told him I'd get a ride with "those guys over there" as I pointed towards a place where there were no guys.

I didn't want to leave. I forgot how fun it was to drink with other people. And the bartender said he'd keep giving me free drinks if I continued to behave.

The problem, which I didn't realize was a problem at the time, is that I didn't have a phone and I didn't tell Lisa I was leaving the lake house for the night.

As pathetic as that sounds, I always made a point of telling Lisa when I wasn't going to be reachable — not because she had trained me that way but because, for good reason, she worried when she couldn't get in touch with me.

She cared, and I wasn't about to exploit that. But one night, even though it wasn't on purpose, I kinda did.

I knew a lot of people at the Panther that night and I was being unusually chatty. Maybe I blacked out for a few hours then blacked back in, if that's possible, but the next four or five hours sailed by.

I didn't realize that Lisa had been trying for hours to get in touch with me. It's in her nature to worry quietly, without telling me to stop doing the things that made her anxious (which makes her the polar opposite of my mother).

Lisa knew that my drinking tended to get me in trouble — especially when I was in public — so when I suddenly dropped off the grid, she panicked.

I was hanging out in the center of the bar, surrounded by people, talking to the mother of one of Mallory's friends. She was being what Jerry Seinfeld called a "close-talker." The more she drank, the closer she got.

Suddenly, a bunch of people by the door made the "Ohhhh" noise you hear in restaurants when a waiter dumps a tray of dishes. I turned and saw Lisa walking straight at me with a blank look on her face.

She looked so out of place... an attractive, serious, professionally dressed woman walking into a small-town redneck bar. She marched right up to me without saying a word, then looked me up and down like she was inspecting door dings on a used car lot. She didn't even look at the girl I was talking to.

It was perfectly innocent but I could see why it didn't look that way to Lisa. It took me by surprise and I started stammering in a drunken panic. "I, I, I... Arr, arr, arr..." I said, sounding like a stuttering sea lion.

The whole thing drew a lot of attention. There was a cross section of the town in the bar at the time and most of them knew I wasn't supposed to be there.

It didn't help that the woman I had been talking to was loudly proclaiming the innocence of our relationship, shouting and slurring, "I love your boyfriend like a b-b-brother. He loves me like a s-s-sister," which, in Chestertown, exonerates no one.

As Lisa was walking back to her car, I followed behind, trying to explain why I hadn't called. She seemed more confused than mad. Her twelve-year-old son, Michael, was sitting in the backseat with a seatbelt on.

She had driven forty minutes from South Glens Falls because she couldn't get in touch with me. She was worried that I'd gotten arrested or passed out in the woods somewhere or set myself on fire again.

Every irrational-sounding fear Lisa had about me was perfectly rational.

One day, Lisa and I were just hanging out watching *Law and Order*.

"I'll be right back," I told her as I walked out the front door. Thirty seconds later, I was bruised and bloodied in the middle of the road. It was just a simple trip, but because I was drunk and made no effort to break my fall, I somersaulted forty feet down the hill, hitting trees and rocks along the way.

Outside the Panther, having seen that I was okay, Lisa's fears were allayed and now she could go home. She didn't yell; she didn't lecture; she didn't even tell me to stay away from the drunk chick. She just made sure I was safe so she could go to bed with peace of mind.

I DIDN'T KNOW FOR SURE, but I suspected my mom was talking to Lisa about my drinking. I couldn't ask Lisa because that was something only an alcoholic would do. Subtle interrogation was my mom's MO. She connected with the people around me — neighbors, friends, co-workers, even doctors and nurses — and built a comfortable relationship with them so she'd have eyes and ears on the ground.

The following week, my mom was in Vermont visiting my aunt and uncle and the three of them came to the lake house for the weekend. Relatives or not, I did my best to discourage visitors to the lake house unless they planned on showing up with beer — the good kind of beer — which is the kind they don't take with them when they leave.

This particular trio was problematic for me. I think the Latin term is *intoxicus interruptus*. I always "stage-managed" the house the day before they showed up, stashing various alcohol containers in a thousand different hiding places — in the car, in my bed, in snowbanks, trash cans, even in Bam's sleeping cubby.

This time, my mom broached the subject of alcohol within the first hour of getting there. The last time I visited her in Florida, I ran out of alcohol one night and drank all my stepfather's Beefeater's Gin.

He always kept his gin in the freezer, presumably because it was better that way (I thought so) and apparently gin doesn't freeze. But the water I replaced it with does.

My poor stepdad was probably looking forward to a relaxing gin and tonic one night, but then he had to settle for an icicle flavored with my backwash.

I knew my mom. Broaching this subject right off the bat was her way of announcing her agenda for the visit. Now I was edgy and defensive because I dreaded conversations about drinking, especially when I was outnumbered three to one, just like I was twenty-five years earlier when I got triple-teamed by my mom, my dad and my dad's AA sponsor.

The four of us sat in the living room and exchanged pleasantries while my mom just sat and listened, staring out the window with a contemplative look that was scaring the shit out of me and making sweat hemorrhage from my forehead so fast it was streaming down my face.

I told my aunt and uncle about a series of editorials I had just published in a bunch of newspapers around New York. Then I told them about my efforts to control the spread of milfoil in Loon Lake. I knew my mom could hear me but I also hoped she was listening. That was the point.

I used to do the same thing in high school. Whenever I got called to the principal's office, which was often, I'd sweet-talk his secretary while waiting for the principal to open the door and call me in. I'd loudly tell her about all the honorable things I did after school, hoping my voice would carry into his office and mitigate the terrible things I did during school.

As we sat in the living room with the TV off, I knew I was being evaluated. The minutes were going by painfully slow. Each moment of silence was an opportunity for them to bring up my drinking, so I struggled to come up with new things to talk about. Every time one of them changed expressions or adjusted the way they were sitting, I thought they were going to spring something on me.

When I went outside to get Bam, I swore they were comparing notes about my drinking and all the alcoholic Freudian slips I was making. I heard a car coming down the hill, and I thought it was more people coming for the intervention. I could feel it coming any second, and I was ready to run into the woods and stay there until they left. The thought of being pushed out of the lake house into another rehab — against my will — was driving me nuts.

I couldn't take it any more. In a panic, I just blurted it out: "So, I was thinking about going back to rehab."

It was like a missile just came through the roof. Even Bam was shocked. He must have sensed the sudden change in demeanor from everyone else because his ears shot straight up.

My mother pretended not to be surprised and overjoyed even though I knew she was. "Oh, well that's good news," she said. "That's certainly something we all support."

I was so relieved. Suddenly everyone liked me again.

But here's the thing: They weren't planning an intervention or anything else. I could tell from their reaction and our subsequent conversation. My imagination got me all worked up, then I panicked and stupidly volunteered to incarcerate myself for another twenty-eight days in a hospital rehab.

Still, I felt a giant sense of relief because, at least for the moment, I had restored everyone's faith in me by admitting I had a problem and needed help.

I felt like a giant burden had been lifted off my shoulders, although I still didn't think I could make it through another treatment program.

Even if I could, I was positive I couldn't stay sober. Look what happened last time: Sober + AA + Church ÷ Overdose = Mental Ward. Fuck that. Not again.

Chapter Twenty-two

The Nirvana of Rehabs

THERE WERE TWO TIMES in the past when I announced I was going to rehab but never went. In both cases, I made the premature promise because I couldn't stand the vibes of guilt and disappointment I was getting from my family, especially my mother.

I'd get drunk, defensive, vulnerable and compliant — in that order — then agree to go to a rehab.

This time, I caved in to my own paranoia and a growing constituency of influential people in my life that now included Lisa. I still believed I could drink the way I did and function well — even though I was functioning like shit — but I had to send a message to Mallory and Jackson that that wasn't okay. I had to show them that I cared enough about the concerns of others to at least make the effort.

I wasn't dumb, which is to say, I wasn't *that* dumb. I knew I had a drinking problem. I couldn't go more than a couple hours without a drink, and I could barely think straight without alcohol in my bloodstream.

Clearly, that was a problem. But it was a problem I had come to accept. I accepted it as an inconvenience, a defect I was born with. I'd heard experts call it a disease, and that is how I accepted it, as a disease like cancer for which there are treatments but no cure.

And like a lot of cancer patients, I thought the treatment (which, for me, was rehab) was worse than the disease. I just adjusted my life so I could live with the disease conveniently and comfortably until it killed me.

I didn't know how long I could pull it off, but if the only alternative was being sober and miserable and violent and confused, I was prepared to stay drunk forever.

After all, I kept reminding myself, it was sobriety, not alcohol, that sent my life into a downward spiral. As they say, that's what happens when you go off your meds. All of this made perfect sense to me.

Even though I was only going to rehab to satisfy others, I did see one benefit to me. I thought a month of sobriety would cleanse my body, reset my tolerance for alcohol and turn the clock back on its progression. I figured that if I got sober for a month when I was forty-five, I could backdate the problem to the way it was when I was, say, forty... maybe even thirty-eight.

Of course, the list of rehabs vying for the challenge of treating me was getting shorter. But there was at least one that didn't have a choice, and within hours, my mother had its program director on speed dial.

So now I was off to St. Mary's Hospital rehab center in Amsterdam, New York. It was the only full-blown rehab I had checked into since Conifer Park in 2003. In between, there were a handful of stays in detox and Four Winds, but never for more than fifteen days.

At least this time I didn't have to pretend to be mentally ill to get in.

The hospital admitted me through the emergency room. For the first two days, I stayed in a hospital bed, on Librium, until my vital signs were stable enough to go to the rehab unit. Unfortunately, I couldn't take the narcotic drip with me. As soon as they pulled that out of my arm, I was too jittery to talk.

For the first two days in the rehab unit, I tried to avoid any kind of interaction with anyone. There were a couple of other guys going through the same thing — early withdrawal — so we sat together at mealtime, looking down at our food and not talking.

Other than that, there was nothing to do but sit on the edge of my bed and "do the rattle."

That's an expression I learned from a young addict. When you're going through severe withdrawal, an automatic response to the symptoms is sitting on the edge of your bed with your elbows on your knees, rocking back and forth. Some meth head saw me doing it and said, "Don't worry, bud, it won't last forever."

A few days later, when I was feeling better, he said, "Oh man, you look good. The other day you were hurting in your room, doing the rattle for hours."

"Doing the rattle, yeah," I said.

"Yeah," he said, "the rattle, because when you shake a..."

"Oh, I get it," I chimed in. "A rattle goes back and forth, like a million other things. You came up with that?"

"Noooo," he said, as if it were preposterous to suggest that he could have given birth to such a clever phrase. "I got that from a dude at Conifer Park."

"Conifer Park," I said. "I've been there and now I'm here. See, a lot of things go back and forth."

"What do you mean?" he asked.

A counselor who'd been listening to all of this said, "Where you are is more important than where you were."

More cleverness. It was going to be a long twenty-eight days.

I'm not sure why rocking back and forth helps. I never did it consciously. It was more of a reflexive action because, when withdrawal is really bad, you're in a constant state of panicky helplessness — like being attacked by a swarm of angry bees that keep coming back no matter how many times you swat one away. Rocking back and forth took away some of that agitation.

There were also the persistent fantasies of alcohol coming to the rescue in a medical emergency. At St. Mary's, I had the same one I used to have while stuck in FDR traffic driving out of Manhattan.

Over and over again, I could see my heart quivering and beating dangerously out of rhythm. Then a waterfall of aquamarine-colored alcohol would rain down into my chest, drenching my dry, spazzing heart muscle like cold water on a hot, cracked desert floor.

So most times, as I was rocking back and forth, over and over, I was thinking of ways to get out and drench my heart. It's not as easy to get out of a hospital rehab as it seems, at least not without causing chaos.

Hospital rehabs are usually one long hall with a nurse's station and med window in the middle, and an eating and meeting room at one end.

Everything is white. The halls are white. The ceilings and floors and counters are white. Even the patients who were black looked white. The doors at both ends of the hall had alarms that made a God-awful piercing noise if you opened one without swiping a card.

And that's what dissuaded me the most because, while withdrawing from alcohol, there were two things I wanted to avoid at all costs: a debate where facts mattered and a physical confrontation. In both cases,

I knew I'd lose the moment a hospital official showed up using phrases like "Seventy-two-Hour Hold" and "5150."

Once they start talking like that, you're not going anywhere and a lot of times the police will show up to prove it. Both phrases are numeric shorthand for "this guy is crazy and he's a danger to himself or others." It gives them the right to hold you against your will even if you've broken no laws.

Being told that you're too unstable to be trusted with yourself is worse than being arrested, and the only thing you can do about it is sit on the edge of the bed and rock back and forth.

There were about fifteen other patients. Most of them were in their twenties and not nearly as miserable as they should have been.

They were playing board games, laughing and defying Conifer Park's zero tolerance for drug glamorization by singing "Semi-Charmed Life" right in the faces of the oblivious counselors. They were the problem children of the narcotic nineties, the last generation of the twentieth century, the last generation that actually gave a shit about September eleventh.

I liked their slang, their Nirvana and Soundgarden and Pearl Jam, their shitty clothes, their grungy rebel spirit. And I spent a lot of time with them, at Conifer Park, St. Peter's, Four Winds and now at St. Mary's.

Their generation came of age just in time to discover the nastiest drugs ever to hit the suburban streets of America: heroin, crystal meth and ecstasy, just to name the worst three. 999

Most of them started with pot and alcohol before experimenting with benzodiazepines and opioids. Unfortunately, a lot of them graduated downward, to heroin and crystal meth.

I was twenty years older than these guys, but they were already confronting the same problems it took my drinking thirty years to create. They were bound to snort or inject their way to rock bottom a lot quicker than me. Some of them already had.

There's something truly sad and unnatural about a good-looking, clean-cut, all-American young man with perfectly straight teeth that are disintegrated from meth. But for now, these guys were in high spirits.

They were riding the pink cloud, enjoying the euphoria and irrational happiness that comes from being clean for the first time.

These guys had a chance. They said all the right things in group sessions, and most of them acted like they had had enough. Most of them, God willing, would run the course of their addiction in a matter of years, not decades like me.

They would hit rock bottom in their twenties, seek treatment in their twenties, and move on with their lives in their twenties. Either that or they would die in their twenties.

About two weeks into the program, there was a "Family Workshop Day" where the spouses of patients came in for a few hours and participated in special groups. Lisa came and I was a little embarrassed about it. We had only been together for a few months, and already I had driven her into group therapy.

At first, I didn't know what to make of her steadfast loyalty. Why was she standing by her man like we had a house full of kids together? Why didn't she just cut and run?

I knew she couldn't be using me for anything because I didn't have anything left except my house and what was left of my sense of humor. And yet, bewilderingly, she was there, notepad in hand, ready to learn all about the dysfunctional relationship she'd gotten herself into.

ON DAY TWENTY-ONE, I completed the first phase of the program, and the treatment team at St. Mary's recommended me for another ten days, followed by an aftercare program.

"Thanks for the recommendation," I told my counselor, "but I feel great and I'm ready to leave."

"You're done with your initial treatment," she said, "but you really aren't able to leave."

I could tell she was about to say something that would make me explode, so I braced myself and calmly asked, "Aren't able?"

"If you left, it would be AMA [Against Medical Advice] and technically they could opt to place you on a seventy-two-hour hold," she said.

There it was again. In a way, the phrase is a self-fulfilling prophecy because it always made me act like a paranoid lunatic.

"A seventy-two-hour hold for what?" I yelled. "I've been here for three weeks!"

"It just means…" she began to say.

"Oh, trust me, I know what it means," I ranted. "I'm not drunk, so it means they think I'm crazy. If I try to leave, how are they going to keep me here?"

Almost as if on cue, another hospital official came in to answer my question.

"No one is calling you crazy," he said. "But you're only three weeks into this and even you must admit that you're not in the right frame of mind yet."

"What does that mean," I asked.

"It means, stick around and get right, okay?" he said.

"Get right?" I yelled. "Discharge me because I'm leaving."

Legally, they couldn't keep me so they discharged me with papers stamped "AMA."

Obviously, I didn't share that with Lisa or my mother, and they couldn't find out on their own because I didn't put their names on the HIPAA release.

I told them I completed the program with honors and the counselors said that if alcohol continued to be a problem, I should check into a more comprehensive long-term program.

Lisa believed it, but my mother said, "No one told you that."

"Well," I said, "they told me that if I… you're right, they never said that."

When Lisa brought me back to the lake house, I was trembling and sweating and couldn't think straight. I loved her and I wished she could stay, but I needed her to leave. It felt like I was going to die. There was no way I was going to make it through the night like this, and in my mind, life was too short to feel like death while I was still alive.

SOMEWHERE ALONG THE LINE, I was told, "There's nothing worse than a belly full of booze and a head full of rehab." If I had known how brutally true that statement was prior to going to rehab, I never would have gone into it with a cavalier attitude. I would have waited until I truly believed I could quit drinking, instead of simply checking into a hospital rehab to placate the people in my life.

Once it's been drilled into your head that alcohol will destroy you, and once you realize that taking a single drink can bring down your entire world, it's a fiendishly difficult task to kick back with a case of beer without feeling like you're banging another nail into your coffin.

Drinking with a head full of other people's horror stories is like watching someone deteriorate from AIDS, then injecting yourself with the HIV virus. But for me, it was still better than trying to claw through the suicidal symptoms of trying to stay sober. I just couldn't do it.

Two months after leaving St. Mary's, I was drinking more than ever, but no one was calling to lecture me about it anymore. I wasn't sure what bothered me more — their lecturing or their silence.

Chapter Twenty-three

An Official Disaster

I WAS DESPERATELY LOOKING for a way to take the focus off my drinking, but I knew that, until I found a way to change the subject, that was going to be impossible.

Before I left for St. Mary's, I got a call from Patricia, the Town of Chester's Deputy Zoning Administrator, who had just been elected Town Clerk. During her campaign, I had given her advice and other support and she wanted me to take the job she was leaving behind.

"With your experience, the Town Board would appoint you in a second," she said.

"I was a speechwriter, Patricia. That's a completely useless skill to have in a zoning office."

"You can write letters telling these people to get their shit together," she laughed. "They ignore *our* letters so maybe you can scare them with all your big words."

I didn't want to be a town official because I knew it would be accompanied by small-town scrutiny. My drinking had outgrown my ability to be discreet. I couldn't stop drinking for an hour or two anymore. Sneaking sips here and there wasn't going to cut it. Just to get through the day, I'd be running around trying to hide thirty-packs and vodka bottles.

A few days later, Patricia called and said, "You've been nominated for the job and next Tuesday night at six o'clock you're scheduled to appear before the Town Board at the Town Board meeting."

I hadn't been sober at six o'clock in years.

"Wait... what?" I yelled. "I'm not sure I can..."

"It's too late," she said. "They'll be expecting you."

"Okay," I said. As soon as I hung up, I started calling friends for a ride.

When I showed up that night, I was probably the only person in Warren County wearing a suit and tie.

With at least twenty beers flowing through my bloodstream, I did what came very easily to me: I pretended to be smart and stone sober. By the time I was done taking questions from the Town Board, I was craving another beer and a shot of vodka, both of which were on my person in the same suit pockets that served me so well in the Governor's Office.

The Board voted unanimously to approve my nomination. Now I was going to have to figure out how I was going to show up sober to work every morning at eight o'clock and stay that way until it was time to leave five hours later.

My boss was Walter Tennyson, the Zoning Administrator, a hard-nosed, seventy-four-year-old mustang of a guy who said exactly what he thought. He didn't care who you were. He treated everybody with equal bureaucratic indifference. Normally, that would be an insult but with Walt, it was a virtue. His palm was non-greasable. Every so often, a homeowner's lawyer would walk into the zoning office to intimidate Walt into bending the rules, a stunt that invariably backfired in the direction of the homeowner. The only way to impress Walt was with a perfectly- scaled floor plan on grid paper.

Everything about him, from his appearance to his personality, was a spitting image of Colonel Potter on *M*A*S*H*.

Me reporting to Walt was a combination of karma and Murphy's Law. Even before I started working there, he caught me off-guard with a firm admonition on alcohol use.

"The one thing I can never put up with is someone who goes out all night drinking then shows up to work the next day hungover or smelling like booze," he said. "I won't stand for it."

At first, I thought he was giving me a preemptive warning because of something he'd heard in town. If he knew I was a problem drinker, why did he twist my arm to take the job... so he could rehabilitate me with a cranky lecture?

I could have said, "How are you going to know if I'm hungover in the morning when you didn't know I was drunk at the interview?"

But my recent custody trial taught me the virtues of not talking, so I just mumbled something boneheaded and indecipherable like, "Yeah...

drinking is a thing that… can't happen… lots of times."

The timing was perfect. My mom had been pressuring me to come see her in Florida. Now I could visit her and tell Walt that I could start work when I got back — and me and my mom would have something other than drinking to talk about.

If the subject turned to drinking, I could just say something like, "Those days are over because I'll be out in the community now instead of isolating at home."

Every piece of that plan fell flat on the floor before I even got on the plane.

I WAS AT THE SOUTHWEST GATE in a line of about forty passengers waiting to board the flight to Tampa. I was using my duffel bag as a carry-on, and it was loaded with Coors Light and a handful of vodka nips. Back at the airport bar, I inhaled five pints and two kamikazes, then ducked into the men's room and sucked down another two beers from my duffle bag.

It was the same old routine for me: Flush the toilet to drown out the sound of the can opening, guzzle the beer, and cough loudly while crushing the can flat with two hands.

In the past, this had gone horribly wrong, mostly due to poor planning, bad timing or — as was the case in the airport — counterproductive technology.

Toilets with sensor flushing mess up the whole routine because there's no flush handle, which is easy to push with an elbow or foot. Instead, you have to twist your entire body around and try reaching a small flush button by the small of your back while simultaneously crushing the can between your free hand and knee.

Drinking surreptitiously at an airport, or any place where people are watching for suspicious behavior, is next to impossible. It's almost better to get caught sneaking drinks so they don't think you're sneaking explosives.

This time, something went horribly wrong but I wasn't sure what. Three TSA agents were hovering around the line at the gate, just pacing in circles staring at… well, I swore they were staring at me. I thought maybe I was just being paranoid so I looked down at my ticket and squinted my eyes like I was having trouble reading it.

Then one of them got right in my face and said, "Do you mind stepping over here for a moment and talking with us sir?" (I put a question mark at the end of that sentence, but it wasn't really a question.)

"Oh yeah sure," I said. "What's up?"

"We're concerned about how much you've been drinking," he said.

"So is my mother," I joked. "But I'm going to start soon."

Now there were three or four agents in front of me with dead blank expressions on their faces. The serious silence was killing me.

"Listen," I said, "I just hate flying so I had a few drinks to calm me down."

There was a little back and forth between us. I don't remember exactly how the whole thing went down. They said some things. I said some things. I was hoping we could all just agree to disagree and go our separate ways. Nope.

I was surprised to learn that airports had jails, and I was twice as surprised to find myself inside of one. They conceded that I hadn't broken any laws. I asked them how they would justify restraining me if I tried to leave, even though I knew what they were going to say.

"A doctor will be by in the next hour to check you out," an agent said. "Until then, we..."

Stay calm, I told myself. *He's getting ready to pull a seventy-two-hour hold out of that holster.*

"We have the authority," he declared, "to hold you if we think..."

"Yeah, I know the rest," I said. "Fine."

This time, I was smart and drunk enough to keep my mouth shut. If I had been sober, I'd have made the national news.

They put me in one of six holding rooms. It was like a hospital examination room, with a gurney bed, a chair and nothing else.

"If you promise you won't try to leave, I can leave this door open," an agent said. "Otherwise, I'll have to lock it shut."

I laid down, closed my eyes and tried to sleep it off, but there was yelling coming from a girl in the room across the hall.

She was about twenty years old and she kept opening the door, making sexually explicit sounds to get the attention of an officer at the end of the hall. I couldn't tell if she was drunk or on acid.

Every so often, the guard she was summoning came down to talk to her. This went on for about two hours and I had a front row seat for the whole thing. I was laying on my stomach on the gurney bed with my chin on my fist enjoying the show.

She was trying to seduce him but she was struggling to hold a thought for the duration of her sentences.

She'd say something provocative like, "So I was peeking around the corner and looking at you and I was imagining you coming into my room and closing the door and..." Then she'd stop mid-sentence and look in the air. She was wired to a machine but was still able to walk around.

My entertainment ended abruptly when she got pissed off and began ripping out the wires.

She opened the door, stepped into the hall and yelled, "I was gonna give all you fucking airport cops a blow job and you fucked it up! Are you all faggots?"

Two officers and a female doctor went into her room and closed the door and it got silent. One officer stood outside the door. He looked at me and shrugged.

"Can I borrow your TSA hat for fifteen minutes?" I joked. "Maybe a blow job will sober me up."

He just stared at me with a smirk and shook his head. "That proves you're not in your right frame of mind."

Meanwhile, my mom and stepfather were at the Tampa airport trying to figure out why I didn't get off the plane.

They knew Lisa dropped me off at the Albany airport, so they began calling around to see what happened after that. As they were doing that, there were cops and other emergency personnel scrambling around them.

According to news reports, which they could see on the airport TVs, a guy around my age was killed at the Tampa Airport, close to where they were supposed to pick me up.

Apparently, as he walked through an elevator door, he didn't notice that the actual elevator car wasn't there and he fell to his death at the bottom of the shaft. He was intoxicated. He was carrying the same prescription meds as me. And his last name was Wolfe.

So, obviously, when I finally made it to Tampa two days later, the first topic of conversation wasn't my new job in the town zoning office.

I didn't want to discuss the topic that was currently trending in my family circle — my rampant drinking and unmanageable life — but I knew it was inevitable, so I did it on my terms.

As soon as I saw my mom, I said, "So, while I was here I was hoping we could look at some of those renowned treatment centers like Betty Ford and Hazelden. Could we do that?"

That warded off whatever lecture she had planned, but only briefly — very briefly. I had no choice but to follow through with an actual conversation about treatment centers.

After a couple hours of me being very agreeable to pretty much anything, we decided that the world-renowned Caron Foundation in Pennsylvania was the best option.

The Caron Foundation wasn't just another rehab; it was the place to go after everything else failed. I was determined to do it and I thought that my new zoning job could prepare me for it by helping me drink a little less.

At first, admittedly, I didn't put much pressure on myself. I assumed that being busy for the first four hours of every day would help me drink less, but I couldn't rule out drinking at work. For the first week, I tried to make it till noon with no alcohol at all. But I was struggling right off the bat.

I was confused and trembling too much to fill out forms or handle paperwork. I couldn't concentrate enough to remember property "lot numbers" and dates without second-guessing myself like a panicky switch-flipper with OCD. I was too agitated to get anything done.

The next day, I started to see black things crawling on the white walls. Walt saw me taking pictures of the office wall and said, "Is there something wrong with our walls?"

I couldn't tell him about the black turtles. They looked so real I wanted photographic evidence.

"Just testing the zoom," I said.

When I made a conscious effort to not look at the walls, I could feel them closing in on me.

After two hours, I ran out to the car, grabbed four beers from the trunk and drank them in the front seat — straight down, in about five minutes. The instant sensation of relief was its own high, like escaping a close call with death. I went back inside and I was fine for another two hours.

I knew I'd have to find another drinking spot because the parking lot was visible to several offices, including the one occupied by the Town Judge.

From then on, I carried beer into the office in a thermos bag, drank backstage in the school auditorium, then crushed the cans flat and shoved them under the stage. Then I'd go to the courtroom kitchenette and cover my breath with a mixture of flavored coffee and Listerine strips. This became my daily routine for the next year.

Turned out, I later learned, Walt's temperance lecture wasn't inspired by any rumors he'd heard about my drinking. It was personal.

He quit drinking about forty years earlier after he got drunk and caused a fatal car accident. The surviving family still lived in Chestertown, so it was hard to escape the reminders.

One day, the sister of the guy who was killed in the accident came into our office. As soon as she walked into the office, Walt stood up and greeted her at the counter to take care of her zoning issue.

He was friendly, helpful and confident. It was clear that he had long since taken responsibility for his role in the tragedy, and now he understood the magnitude of his mistake. I admired that about him.

All the time I spent deciphering legal and government jargon in the Governor's Office paid off in the Zoning Office.

After a week of drinking and breezing through a thousand pages of local and state regulations, I could tell you anything you ever wanted to know about the state and local laws governing lakes, rivers, barns, stores, houses, sheds, docks, moorings, signs, setbacks and subdivisions in the Adirondack region.

I had long since accepted that my writing career was over… that I had drunk it away.

Even if I got sober someday, I'd never be able to write the way I used to write because I used to write drunk.

It was time to leave writing and all the places it led me to — Ground Zero, the First Presbyterian Church, the Million-Dollar Staircase. All along, I had to drink to write, so maybe it was the writing that got me into so much trouble.

Now I could just be the guy everyone hated for making them move their fence another three feet from the road.

Chapter Twenty-four

A Greyer Shade of Pale

THE OTHER HALF OF MY CRASH COURSE entailed hours of driving around with Walt, wandering through old buildings in the mountainous, backwoods region of the southern Adirondack Park.

One day, after a morning of poking around an old hotel that looked like a Transylvanian spook house, I surprised myself by making it till noon without a drink.

On the way back to the office, where there was beer waiting for me in my trunk, I was cursing Walt out in my head for driving too slow. As soon as we got back, I went straight to my car and popped the trunk. But then Walt yelled out to me from the office window, "You've got messages from your brother."

I thought that was weird. My brother Greg and I got along and we weren't fighting, but we didn't call each other to chit chat either. Greg served in combat in Panama and Iraq with the 82nd Airborne Division.

He was in Iraq for a long time, and I've always wondered what part of him he left there. He was always the toughest guy in any room, but you would never know it because he had the innocence and social finesse of Richie Cunningham.

Some guys mistook his bashful boyishness for weakness. The ones who tried to make my brother their victim didn't just get beat up; they got tenderized, quickly and severely.

He seemed fine when he returned from the invasion of Panama. But the Richie Cunningham side of my brother never came back from Iraq. My mother did some digging.

He and his unit disappeared from Fort Bragg for a long time in the 80s. She thinks that part of his Airborne unit spent time training or fighting with rebels during or after the Iran-Contra affair. I don't know. I asked him once when both of us were drunk and he didn't tell me.

A few years after he returned from Iraq, Greg stopped drinking altogether... I think. He had a problem with it, too, but the alcoholic gene hit him sideways instead of head on.

When he drank, he got drunk quickly and it always ended with some form of ugly. But then he could go another two weeks without drinking at all. In rehab, they call that a "binge drinker," a part-timer.

He was calling because my dad had been in a car accident after having a minor stroke behind the wheel. He was in the hospital, but he was supposed to make a full recovery.

My parents got divorced soon after I graduated from college. My brother was the last relative my dad had left in Rochester, and he was doing all the things my father couldn't do for himself. I was in Chestertown, providing zero assistance.

Writing was really the only strong connection I had with my father. He had been an English major in college and he wanted to be a writer himself before he went to med school and became a doctor.

As a teenager, my father would sit in his mahogany library and drink Genesee beer while reading selected works from his beloved book collection.

After a few beers, he would get chatty and ask me how my writing was coming along, and I would pick something from my writing folder and ask him if he wanted to read it. He always said yes. He'd read it intently — a lot slower than I knew he could read — and he gave helpful feedback, but it was always encouraging. My dad was smarter than I'll ever be.

In 2010, I wrote something about the design of the proposed mosque at Ground Zero and it was published in the *New York Times*. I'm pretty sure that's the last thing of mine my father ever had a chance to read.

When I was a kid, I used to imagine my dad sitting in the den of our house reading a book written by me.

He was socially awkward, but my dad always found ways to connect with me on certain things.

The only music he ever listened to was classical until he heard the constant sound of The Who coming from my room when I was a teen. He went on to develop an almost obsessive love for the group's two rock operas, Tommy and Quadrophenia. I never heard him listen to classical music again.

Instead, he developed rock and roll tastes of his own, gravitating toward groups with names that were as eccentric as he was: Jethro Tull, Procol Harum and Mothers of Invention.

A few weeks after my dad's car accident, my mom called and told me that he had died. I remember getting the phone call and I remember thinking, *What the fuck? I thought everything was supposed to be fine!*

That's about all I remember about my dad's death. I assume I was drunk when I got the news, but I don't remember how drunk I was. The next day, I doubt I even remembered he had died.

My dad had his peculiarities, but he didn't try to cover them up. He either didn't know about them or didn't care. It was probably the latter, since he wasn't much of a people pleaser. He wasn't good at it.

When it came to family, he was an excellent provider. Everything else was up to us. He wasn't sentimental or loving. When he tried to be either one of those things, like when my brother shipped off for Iraq during Desert Storm, it was awkward, weird and wincey.

It all worked out just fine for me and my cantankerous brother. Dad never gave us hugs and we never wanted them, from him or anyone else. But it was… unrewarding — and I'm being charitable there — for my mother.

And I try not to be a hypocrite. My father was an alcoholic, but I drank more in a day than he drank in a week. His mode of drinking wasn't even in the same galaxy as mine.

I didn't go to my father's funeral because I couldn't stop drinking long enough to make the trip. Using any other excuse would have been beyond the pale, even for me.

My father did the best he could while struggling with the disease of alcoholism and now I was doing the same thing.

Some people think that my dad wasn't even trying. The same people, if they're honest, would have to say the same thing about me. That's my real connection to my father. Sadly, I get it.

My throat still gets sore when I hear his favorite song, "A Whiter Shade Pale," with its melancholy organ chords befitting his funeral, which was attended only by my brother.

My mother has earned the right to voice whatever opinion she wants on my father since she had to deal with both of us. She'll defend me to my grave. She defended my father until 1988. That's when she found out he was cheating on her with his longtime nurse.

Nonetheless, a mother's loyalty to her son is a million times stronger than her loyalty to her husband. She'll say her son's defects were inherited from the father. Of course, her husband's defects were inherited too, but after enough screw ups, he can go fuck himself.

AFTER ABOUT A YEAR in the Zoning Office, Walt felt comfortable enough to disappear for more than a month and leave me in charge of eighty-six thousand square miles of the Adirondacks. That became my first legitimate excuse to postpone going to the Caron Foundation.

Before he left, Walt told me, "Just keep things nice and quiet. When they start fighting and backstabbing each other on Friends Lake, send them a letter and smooth it over. Just take calls, issue permits and do whatever it takes to keep the peace till I get back."

This was the perfect time to raise holy hell — to knock my drinking problem off everyone's radar screen by replacing it with something more newsworthy. This wasn't even something I did subconsciously; I planned it.

Walt was probably still stowing his carry-ons when I was threatening to repossess a horse from the woman who was neglecting it.

We had received several complaints from people who said the horse had no place to seek shelter from snow, rain, sleet. One neighbor sent us a picture showing the horse's tail encased in ice.

Weeks before Walt left, I went there and took pictures and sent her a letter telling her the horse needed a place to shelter. She ignored the letter and I complained to Walt about it the day before he left and he said I could always send her another letter. Screw that.

This form of animal abuse is actually covered under a zoning law on farm structures, and now I was reading that law in its entirety to the woman over the phone as she cursed me out mercilessly.

I knew the woman, but just enough to say hi. She was good looking with a drop-dead body — proof that I place a higher premium on the welfare of animals than my own primal desires.

By statute, the Zoning Office was authorized to write court

appearance tickets. When I first started working there, I asked Walt if he had ever issued one. "Oh God, no," he said. "A strong official shouldn't have to."

But the strong official wasn't there, so I dusted off a box of unopened tickets. A local cop showed me how to fill one out, then said, "If this backfires on you, keep my name out of it."

I sent triplicates to the Town Court and the Town Clerk, which are in the same building as the Zoning Office, then drove to the woman's house and taped her copy to the door.

A couple days later, the town judge walked into the zoning office with the ticket in his hand and said, "I don't want to have an *ex parte* conversation about a pending case, but what the heck is this?"

"A ticket for failure to provide shelter for farm animals," I said. "It's covered under our zoning laws."

"At least give me something so I know what's going on when this woman shows up for court," he said.

I gave him a copy of the law on "structures and non-domesticated animals" and he scanned it and said, "Yeah, okay," and left.

I tried calling Walt to give him a head's up about the situation, since it was probably the most controversial thing the Zoning Office had ever done and he wasn't there to see it. But the number he gave me went to dead silence every time.

It's not like I woke up that morning and decided to go after the horse lady. I made the decision over the course of several intoxicated nights, then abided by the decision in the morning.

A lot of people check themselves the other way around. But I always stood by my drunk decisions, even the bad ones, because they reflected my true feelings.

AFTER ANOTHER FEW NIGHTS of irrevocable ruminating and plotting, I acted on a handful of complaints in and around Schroon Lake whose southern end, the source of the complaints, is in Chester's zoning jurisdiction.

The complaints were about something in the water, not on land, so technically they should have been investigated by the state Department of Environmental Conservation (DEC) — an agency I'm well acquainted with from my years with the Governor.

But now that I was writing tickets for horses instead of speeches for a Governor, I couldn't resist the opportunity to assert the little power I had.

One afternoon, I went to Schroon Lake and had a boat drop me off about fifty yards from the shore. I waded toward the Word of Life's sewage plant with a camera, a knapsack filled with beer and vodka and a notepad. The notepad served no purpose.

About ten yards from shore, I snapped a dozen photos of what was clearly floating feces. I picked some up to smell it, then I threw up. I don't know what I expected it to smell like, so I guess I got what I deserved.

From there, I followed an intake pipe directly to the plant, then slipped into the space between the security fence and a line of tall shrub trees designed to camouflage the plant's ugliness. I sat down and started drinking the beer and vodka, occasionally pausing to take photos of the plant. I didn't actually need any photos of the plant, just the ones of the poop in the water. Mostly I went behind the shrubs to get drunk.

While I was drafting an official letter to the Word of Life about what I found, a few area newspapers got a hold of one of the photos I took. I can't imagine how, except that I gave it to them.

The next day, the headline was: "Chester Town Official Finds Word of Life Sewage Leak on Schroon Lake."

As the week went on, other newspapers picked up the story. A Word of Life official and one of their attorneys showed up in the Zoning Office a few mornings later.

As soon as I realized they were trying to intimidate me with the power of their money, I told them to get the fuck out, a sentiment I repeated over and over as I walked behind them all the way to the parking lot.

Newspapers were talking to Adirondack environmental groups and they were questioning my tactics and tone, but also criticizing DEC for not getting there before I did.

The DEC was questioning why I didn't take samples of the feces for testing, providing me with an easy rebuttal: Because poop in the water is what DEC is supposed to investigate; I just took pictures of the poop while wading towards the sewage plant.

Chester's Town Supervisor, Fred Monroe, stood by me, saying the photos spoke for themselves. The Word of Life defended itself by saying that the suspicious floating matter was "matted algae."

My response to the papers was, "If it looks like poop, floats like poop and smells like poop, it's not matted algae."

Plucking poop from a lake and sniffing it was a vast departure from discussing the unrest in Kosovo with Henry Kissinger and the Governor. I may have been drunk, but I wasn't oblivious. I knew that my dreams had taken a backseat to my drinking. But for the first time in years, I was having fun.

Walt finally called the day before he was scheduled to come back.

"Quiet up there?" he asked.

"Oh, yeah," I said, "Just a couple things we can go over when you get back."

"Right, about the Word of Life? Too late," he barked. "The Word of Life is down here too, and I read all about it in the local newspaper. I'll bet you can't imagine how surprised I was."

"Oh that," I gulped. "Did they say anything about a horse?"

"What horse?" he yelled. "Wait, there's more?"

"Not really," I stammered. "It's just… remember that box of court appearance tickets?"

"You planned all of this! What would have happened if you acted like this in the Governor's Office?"

I *did* act like that in the Governor's Office. Turns out he was referring to my drinking, not the other stuff.

He walked into the office a couple days later with a firmer-than-usual scowl on his face.

"Welcome home," I said. "How was the flight?"

"Before you even started working here," he said, "I talked to you about drinking… and now, I've gotta be honest, a lot of people in this town are saying you're out of control. People are talking and I can't have that."

"I know."

"Listen, if you need help, get it," he said. "I've been there. Do what you have to do to get better and I'll be waiting for you when you get back."

It wasn't the first time someone scolded me for my drinking, but it was the first time I was speechless afterwards — speechless, and at this point in the game, defenseless. I didn't even search for something to say because I knew there was nothing.

I couldn't just stand there, letting the sweat on my forehead confirm the rumors. He knew.

"Sorry," I said. "You're right. It won't happen again." But even that was a lie, unless I was prepared to quit right then and there (quit the job, that is; there was no way I could quit drinking. I was too far gone).

I cared enough about the whole thing to piece it back together in my mind. Walt was smart. My guess is that Walt knew about my past at the Panther, but never said anything until it was affecting my work in the Zoning Office.

So when he left me in charge only to come back and find me prosecuting a case in town court and attacking a Bible institute in the newspapers, he surmised that my drinking was clouding my judgment.

It took me about a week to set aside my ego and summon the courage to tell Walt I couldn't limit my drinking to eighteen hours a day. The worst part is, that wasn't even true. I had enough control to not drink for five hours; I just couldn't control my mouth, my demeanor or my temper when I was sober and craving alcohol.

I called him one night at home and said everything I wanted to say in one long sentence so there wouldn't be any silent gaps where he might feel compelled to say something back.

"I've been thinking about what you said the other day and you're right, so I'm going to disappear for a while and go someplace where they can work with me to get all the alcohol out of my system and I blah, blah, blah...."

When I was done, he just said, "I've been there, and I support you, so just go because if you keep doing what you're doing, you'll die."

MY RECURRING NIGHTMARE went something like this: I'd be sitting on a couch — sober — surrounded by friends and family members who took turns crying and giving me long, melodramatic speeches about my drinking while passing the tissue box.

The thought of an intervention scared me so much, I preemptively checked myself into Four Winds twice when I thought my family was planning one.

This time, instead of checking into Four Winds to avoid an intervention, I did it to avoid going to the Caron Foundation. I was afraid of the Caron Foundation because failing there would mean failing once and for all, and I wanted to put that off for as long as I could because I didn't think I was capable of succeeding.

I chose Four Winds because it wasn't a rehab — it was a psych center — but I always pitched it off as a rehab to my family. The distressing thing isn't how many times I went to Four Winds Psychiatric Center; it's that they kept letting me in.

From the outside, the Ferndell Unit of Four Winds looks like a cozy ranch home. It's set up like a college dorm hall, with two living rooms and a kitchen and about twenty rooms of varying size. And scattered all over the place, there are crazy people.

Some are really crazy, some are a little crazy, some are severely depressed, some are anorexic and some are there to get shock treatment. Yes, they still do that, but they call it electroconvulsive therapy, or ECT.

The real reason Four Winds kept taking me back is because I still had a lot of street cred after being mandated there ten years earlier. But reputation alone wasn't always enough to get me in the door.

At some point during the initial evaluation, I'd have to raise a little red flag. Usually I did it right off the bat, when they asked, "Are you a danger to yourself or others?" With my history, all I had to do was start my answer with a "Um," and I knew they'd be making a bed for me.

My guess is that anyone could get into a mental institution if they articulated their occasional crazy little thoughts to a psychiatrist. That's all I was doing with the intake counselors at Four Winds. I just didn't want to tell them too much and get branded with an official diagnosis.

This was my third visit. God only knows what they had already written on my chart.

I did tell them about the mood spikes, though. I figured, even though I was just there to dodge a trip to the Caron Foundation, while I was there, maybe I could get something out of the visit. I told the doctors at Four Winds about the mood spikes when I was there in 2004. The good news is that they understood exactly what I was talking about, although they referred to them as "dissociative episodes brought on by post-acute-withdrawal syndrome."

The bad news is that they put me on the Mother of All crazy meds — lithium — and I hated it.

This time, the cuckoo roster at the Ferndell Unit consisted of four men and seven women, most of whom were suffering from depression and undergoing ECT (shock) treatments... not an especially fun bunch to be around. The rest were there for eating disorders or because they'd been contemplating suicide.

There was one of my peeps, an alcoholic, who went too far and got "wet brain," a form of dementia God uses to punish people who drink too much. Some people call it "drinking yourself dumb."

People with wet brain come off as mildly retarded. It's a result of drinking too much for too long, and it's permanent.

For obvious reasons, I wanted to know more about the guy with wet brain so I grilled a counselor I knew from my previous visits.

"If he's just an alcoholic," I asked, "why's he in a psych ward?"

"I'm sure he has a dual diagnosis just like you," she said.

"I don't have a dual anything," I said. "I'm just here for alcohol."

"Are you sure?" she asked, in sort of a patronizing, therapeutic tone.

"I've got dual exhaust on my new Chevy Impala," I said, "and that's it."

I wasn't going to tell her, but I looked at my chart one day when the doctor left the room. Under diagnosis, it read: "Alcoholism and NOS." NOS means "Not Otherwise Specified," which is just a clinical way of saying I drink too much and they had an open bed.

In the group sessions, I had to fit in with the crowd and talk about something deeper than drinking. Everyone needs the cobwebs chased out of their attic now and then, so I participated by talking about my mood spikes. I described it as a problem with impulse control.

If I could somehow quit drinking for a year, maybe my sober behavior wouldn't be so awful. Maybe... but since I couldn't stop drinking, I had to find a different way to suppress the sudden and uncontrollable urge to attack lawyers, run from hospitals and overdose on prescription meds.

The person who did those things — and a lot of other things that are worse — wasn't me and it wasn't alcohol. It was me needing alcohol.

I didn't think it was alcohol withdrawal, per se; I just knew the problem went away when I drank. I still wanted to keep that detail to myself, because I knew how bad it sounded.

A part of me still believed that the only solution to my problem was to ensure I always had alcohol either in my system, or close by. Still, I was hoping Four Winds could send me home with a mood stabilizer — but not lithium again —to help me through the inevitable dry times.

I steered clear of the guy with wet brain. I didn't want to think it could happen to me. I can't imagine how awful it would be to wake up one day from a twenty-five-year drunken binge and realize you'd drunk your way into a permanent state of stupid.

Parents used to tell their little kids not to make silly faces because their faces might stay that way. When those kids got older, they were warned that if they masturbated too much they'd go blind. That's a myth because, back in college, Eric Jackson had 20/20 vision.

Maybe it's time for the folks at DARE to parade a guy with wet brain around the school auditorium when they're lecturing kids about alcohol. That'll make them think. It was making me think.

I WAS IN A GROUP SESSION in another building when my counselor came looking for me one day. He told me an important call came for me and said I should return it in his office. I knew it was something bad.

There were two calls — one from my lawyer and one from my mom, who was staying at the lake house with Jackson till I got back from Four Winds.

The judge who presided over my ongoing five-year custody dispute ordered Jackson back home to his mother pending a further decision from the court when I returned home. Mallory stayed up at the lake with a friend.

I still had custody of both children, having miraculously hidden the extent of my drinking problem from a State Supreme Court judge. There were times when I stood in his court drunk while my lawyer rebuffed my ex-wife's claims that I had a drinking problem.

Now, I was hoping to ask the children what they wanted me to do, but I couldn't do it from Four Winds. I would deal with it when I got home.

A shrink at Four Winds said that, most likely, five years ago, Mallory and Jackson told the judge they chose to live with me because they were worried about me living alone — worried that I would either drink myself to death or die of loneliness.

I don't know if that's true or not, but I wish I could have died without ever having heard the theory. Both of them would deny it, or minimize the impact of my drinking on their lives the same way I brushed off my father's drinking on mine.

The difference is that my father's problem wasn't the drinking so much as the chronic bad moods related to the drinking. I figured that out about him, but not me.

I try not to think about that too much because, well, it makes me feel like vanishing from Earth. There are times when I've had to literally shout and slap the thought out of my head.

The Wolfe men don't do well with guilt. But we're not big on dishing it out either. As sure and as rampant as alcohol runs in the roots of the Wolfe family tree, so too does the ability to own the blame, forgo the whining and roll with the punches.

My dad did it all his life, and so far, Mallory and Jackson have done it for all of theirs. Their strength in the face of adversity will be a virtue for them so long as there is someone there to ensure they aren't suffering in silence or quietly killing themselves. My mother did it for me, but so long as she was still doing it for me, there would be no one to do it for Mallory and Jackson.

All along, I vowed to prove everyone wrong. I insisted that I could drink the way I did — the way I thought I had to — and still fulfill all the functions of life. But now, I realized that even if I could fool the judge yet again, I could no longer fool Mallory and Jackson.

The first thing I had to do is extricate Mallory and Jackson from the mess I had gotten myself into.

The day after I was released from Four Winds, I directed my attorney to file a final motion with the court conceding that both kids were better off with their mother.

My father struggled in his role as a dad. The worst decision of my life was thinking that I could drink ten times as much as he did and still do a better job as a father.

ONCE THEY WERE BACK in Guilderland with their mother, I realized how sick I was going to get. I left Four Winds after twelve days. While I was there, they managed my alcohol withdrawal with Librium, and they based the dosage on my vital signs. My blood pressure and heart rate were consistently through the roof, so they were pretty generous with the drugs.

They gave me one more dose for the road, and that was it. I had a prescription for Klonopin, which is also a benzodiazepine, but I wasn't sure if my doctor was going to refill it after all the calls he'd been getting from rehabs.

I was never honest with him about my drinking. I used to pound beer in his parking lot before walking in to see him. Now he knew about my drinking, but he still had no idea how bad it was.

He gave me a prescription for one more month and told me how to wean myself off the drug over the course of four weeks. At the time, I didn't know about the synergy between Klonopin and alcohol.

Klonopin is a powerful narcotic that intensifies the effects of alcohol. Naturally, it also suppresses the urge to drink, which means that my tolerance for alcohol was even higher than I thought.

Even while taking Klonopin, I was drinking an average of forty-five drinks a day. Without the drug, God only knows how much I would have to drink to get the same effect.

The first morning I woke up after I ran out, I didn't know what hit me. It was just like being in withdrawal in the detox unit at St. Peter's, but a hundred times worse. I was sweating and shaking. When I tried to stand up, the room was spinning and I saw little lights floating all around me like fireflies. At first, I tried swatting them away because they looked so real.

I went to the refrigerator and stood there with the door still open, drinking as fast as I could. Normally, it only took a few drinks to take away the morning shakes. This time, I didn't feel the slightest bit of relief until I had finished all ten beers in the fridge. Now I was way over the legal limit to drive, and I was out of alcohol.

I didn't have a choice so I drove into town. Fortunately, it was after eight o'clock in the morning so I went straight to the liquor store.

My credit card was $78 away from being maxed out. I needed to get the most alcohol for my dollars, so instead of wasting money on eighty-proof vodka, I grabbed a bottle of Bacardi 151. Before heading home, I stopped at the usual place for a thirty-pack to wash it down.

The Bacardi hit me harder than I thought it would. After an hour on the couch taking sips straight from the bottle, and washing each sip down with half a beer, I stood up to go to the bathroom and was surprised to discover I was hammered.

Amazingly, I was still shaking. It still took a full two hours of drinking until I finally felt "normal." And it was only noon.

Even if my body survived that amount of alcohol, logistically it seemed impossible to do the same thing every day. I did it anyway, for about a week, until I ran out of money and energy. I called my mother and Lisa and said, "Okay, I'm ready to go."

Chapter Twenty-five

The Last Best Hope

I HAD ALREADY CHANGED my mind about going to the Caron Foundation a dozen times before boarding the plane for Philadelphia. In the days following my desperate Bacardi binge, my condition got better — not a lot, just enough to make me wonder if I could make alcohol work again.

I was still drinking around-the-clock, but after a few drinks in the morning, I was at least able to function — to the extent that sending dishonest emails, playing with Bam and driving six miles a day is functioning. I even had several hours of relative peace and comfort.

The day before I was scheduled to leave, I scrambled for a face-saving way to renege on my promise. I realized, though, that I had no face to save, nothing to fall back on except my face.

My best hope to avoid what I agreed to in a moment of desperation was to get thrown off my flight again by TSA agents. It was a far cry from saving face, but it was all I had.

I was sufficiently drunk by the time I got to the airport and I drank as much as they would serve me on the flight, which was nothing. But I had vodka nips, and for the hour-long flight those helped to raise my spirits about Caron.

Maybe I would like it, I thought. After all, it was just a matter of time before I wound up at the Caron Foundation. It worked for Steven Tyler of Aerosmith and Liza Minnelli of, whatever, so maybe this was the place that could save me from myself.

As soon as I landed, I grabbed my suitcase and found the bar closest to the spot where the guy from the Caron Foundation was supposed to pick me up. There were four guys holding up signs near the baggage claim. Without looking to see if my name was on any of the signs, I walked right past all four guys on my way to the bar.

Now my mind was changing yet again. It was probably too late to find a way out, but I continued to look for one as I drank and ignored the sign guys.

My only plan was a weak one. I thought I could sit at the bar until I ran out of money and claim the guy from Caron never showed up. But I didn't plan much further than that because I was in Philadelphia with no phone, very little money, and nowhere else to go.

This time, I couldn't even call Charles. Even *he* thought my days were numbered. I later learned that my mom had been pressuring him to pressure me.

That should have been a losing battle for my mother because my bond with Charles included a loyalty oath, which meant that neither of us would ever go against the wishes of the other, even if the wishes were misguided.

My determined, furiously loyal mom got to him. She just couldn't get to me.

But since I had a tentative plan for the next hour, I ordered two beers and a shot of vodka from the bartender. I glanced back at the sign-holding guys, just out of curiosity, but I didn't see my name anywhere.

There was only one guy left and his sign said "Wolf." That could be anybody, I told myself. It's possible that he could be looking for me but I really had no way of knowing that. I wasn't going to just walk up to him and start a conversation.

I ordered another round of drinks and waited for him to leave. Instead, I watched him talking on the phone, then our eyes met. I turned away quickly, but I could feel him walking towards me.

When he got to my barstool, he held up his sign right in front of me.

"Oh, there you are!" I yelled.

"Yes, I'm waiting for you and it looks like you're ready," he said with a smirk on his face that I wanted to slap into the metal detectors.

"Oh, good… I didn't see you over there, and you spelled my name wrong," I declared. "Do you want to sit down so we can discuss the program and decide if the Caron Foundation is right for me?"

"No, you'll do that when we get there. I'm just a driver, but I can see that the Caron Foundation is right for you."

Everything was fine for about a half hour. That was when the alcohol began to wear off. By then, we were on a commercial road passing strip malls and listening to one of the most depressing things on Earth — AM radio.

He talked about his son's Little League batting average while I considered the pros and cons of grabbing the wheel and steering us into an oncoming tractor trailer.

They breathalyzed me as soon as I got there. All I heard the nurse say was, "He's above three." That meant my blood alcohol level was over .30 percent, which is another way of saying "shitfaced."

They put me in a room with a bed, an Alcoholics Anonymous Book and nothing else for the next twenty-four hours.

This time, there was no Librium or Ativan. I was on my own. I stood, I sat, I paced, I laid down, I sat on the edge of the bed and rocked back and forth. I was sweating, shaking, shivering, groaning and clawing at my head... for the rest of that day, through most of the night, right into the afternoon.

The next day, they breathalyzed me again, then it was time to go to the unit.

I couldn't muster small talk or even a polite smile for two or three days, and I had a roommate who wouldn't shut up. They gave me a schedule packed with classes, appointments and groups I had to attend the next day. They were scattered in different buildings all around a giant campus.

I didn't even know the name of the building I was *in* so I sure as hell didn't know how to get to the "Chit Chat auditorium," which was the location of my first three hour class. The name alone made me want to drink hand sanitizer and the thought of sitting there for three hours made me want to find a rope and hang myself from the nearest tree. I just wanted to lay on the bed and rock myself to sleep just like I always drank myself into a blackout. Then I didn't have to worry about anything until I woke up.

They put my luggage in the room but I was shaking too much to open it. I gave up after one try and laid back down on the bed. Within fifteen minutes, some obnoxious, clipboard-carrying staff person in a bright yellow shirt with the word "asshole" printed on the front knocked on the door and began saying loud things to me.

I kept thinking the same thing: *I should have jumped out of that fucking minivan on the way here*. Getting out of this place wasn't going to be easy, but it quickly became my top priority.

The campus was about the size of a small college and it was surrounded by thirty miles of farmland in every direction. I was in Alcatraz. Even if I muscled my way out, I was a long way from a drink.

My roommate, Matt, was an excessively Italian twenty-four-year-old guy from Philadelphia, and his parallels to Rocky Balboa didn't end there.

He was surprisingly muscular and athletic for a heroin addict, and he was well-respected in all the wrong circles but all the right ones too.

He had a reputation as a badass on the streets of West Philadelphia — according to other guys at Caron who knew who he was — but he was also adored by Father Bill, the nationally renowned priest and patriarch of the Caron Foundation.

I liked him. He was a perfect example of how drugs can destroy an otherwise good person — not that Matt was destroyed... at least not yet. He was awaiting trial while he was at Caron, and his lawyer called him almost every day to update him on the plea negotiations.

Every night, we'd turn off the lights and lay down to sleep, and that's when he wanted to fill me in on everything that was going on. He looked up to me for some reason. I never told him much about my background.

It's the golden rule in rehabs: don't tell anyone anything personal. Adhering to that rule with Matt and his million probing questions was no easy task. For some unfathomable reason, he was convinced I had a history he would admire. Even if he knew what a speechwriter was, I doubt he'd believe that I was one.

At night, while lying in our beds in the dark, he wanted to know what I thought about the DA's latest offer. This poor kid (to me he was a kid) was facing a minimum sentence of eight years in prison if he accepted a plea agreement. If he went to trial and lost, he would serve a minimum of thirteen years.

He used heroin, but he wasn't really at Caron for treatment; he was there hoping to impress the DA, which he said stood for "Dumb Ass," but it apparently wasn't working.

He got arrested carrying eighty bags of heroin in the trunk of his car.

The door prize in Pennsylvania for getting caught with that much heroin is bad enough but it's a hell of a lot worse when you're passing through a school zone, and he was.

"I was nowhere near a school," he told me. "Wouldn't you think a school zone is where they have the flashing light telling you to slow the fuck down?"

"Yeah," I concurred. "Why, It's not?"

"Not according to the D-fucking-A," he roared.

With Matt, there was a "fuck" in every sentence, even if he had to shoehorn it into the middle of a word.

I thought he should go to trial, but he was constantly playing devil's advocate... poorly I might add.

"Dude, if I took the deal," he griped, "I'd be out when I'm fucking thirty, and that's seventeen years younger than what you are right now — and dude, I wouldn't go out of my way to fuck with you."

"I have no idea what that means or why it makes you feel good," I said.

"Hey, tomorrow I'll cut your hair okay," he'd say. "I got those badass fuckin' clippers I told you about. You psyched?"

That was why I liked Matt. Whenever he detected a little disagreement in your voice, he changed the subject.

"Yeah, I'm psyched," I told him. "Short on the sides and a little longer on top?"

He looked at head and beamed.

"Skin on the side and turf up top, fuck yeah."

RICK FROM KENTUCKY had a thick southern drawl, the kind that was so deep and slow and twangy that, for me, making fun of it whenever he spoke wasn't a choice; it was a reflex.

One day we were all sitting around debating sports. Rick knew all about sports and it didn't take him long to silence the group with a debate-winning statistic. Clearly proud of himself for his superior sports knowledge, he stood up, looked at everyone and bellowed, "How 'bout them peaches?"

My immediate thought was, *I'm going to repeat that line every time he opens his mouth for the rest of the time I'm here.* I did, and no one loved it more than Rick himself.

"How 'bout them peaches?" became my punchline for everything at the Caron Foundation, and it never got old because each time I did it, I said it slower, louder, deeper and dumber.

Kentucky Rick will never know it, but ultimately, he would get the last laugh. Turns out, his drawl wasn't just funny; it was enough to drive a guy out of Pennsylvania. More on that later.

At the beginning of the third week, it was my turn to sit in the middle of a circle surrounded by everyone in my group for an intervention-style exercise. Yay.

My counselor got written impact statements from Mallory, Jackson, Lisa and my mom. I wasn't allowed to read the statements before the exercise, but I could see the names of who wrote each one on the back of the paper. Then I had to select a different patient to read the statements aloud while I sat in the middle of the circle, hearing it for the first time.

When the whole thing was over, I'd get all the statements to read privately for an hour, but then I'd have to give them back to my counselor. I guess they wanted the patient to get the point, but they didn't want us to obsess over it.

For the actual group exercise, I was allowed to excuse myself if I needed privacy. That almost happened during the first statement, from Mallory, which was read aloud by an earthy, twenty-three-year-old female heroin addict from Boston who I closely identified with.

Mallory wrote about what it was like living alone with me at the lake house. "I was never afraid of my dad, but I was always afraid for him and that was worse because I never knew what he was going to do to himself next."

I used every mind trick I could think of to avoid crying in front of these people, but I could see Mallory sitting in the grass somewhere writing those words and my heart was breaking. I wanted to say I'd rather read the rest of the statements alone in my room but I couldn't talk. So they pressed on with the next statement.

I was praying it would be my mother's statement because I knew she wouldn't want to shame me while I was in rehab. Besides, I'd already heard her stump speech on alcohol every week for the past twenty years.

I was still choked up from Mallory's statement and I really wasn't ready to hear Jackson's yet.

I had given Jackson's statement to Matt because he knew how sensitive I was on the issue of my kids, and I assumed he'd take it easy on me by reading it straight, without drama and voice inflections.

I assumed wrong. Before he started reading, he cleared his throat like the President gearing up for a big speech. Then he read it sadistically slow, on purpose, and looked me straight in the eye after each sentence.

"My dad could never bring me anywhere so I just stayed home," Jackson's statement said. "He was always telling me I could have friends over but I didn't want anyone to see how much he drank."

A million times I sat at my desk looking at Jackson while he played video games, wondering if that's how he felt. I wanted to believe he didn't, and over the past year, it became one more thing I tried to not think about.

These were the things I wondered and worried about. These were the thoughts I tried to drink away. Now I was hearing my worst fears confirmed, in the words of my own kids, right to my face in front of fifteen other people.

"Okay," I said, as I got up to leave. "I got the point but this isn't helping me."

There was nowhere else to go, so I sat in a restroom stall and counted bathroom tiles until the group session was over. It's hard to hide out in a restroom without catching a glance of yourself in the mirror. I should know, having used countless restrooms to hide my drinking.

This was worse, because there was no escape... just a million thoughts I wanted to drink away and nothing to drink them away with.

I wasn't eating. When everyone else went to the dining hall, I stayed back in my room on the bed. At breakfast and lunch, I couldn't even stand the sight of food, much less the sight of addicts cramming it into their faces.

I couldn't sit still either. Every day, we had to endure a three-hour lecture in an auditorium filled with about a hundred patients. We weren't supposed to get up for any reason, but invariably, midway through the angsty torture, I'd get hyper agitated and start talking to myself, hoping they'd kick me out of the auditorium.

Sometimes I'd feel a mood spike percolating in the back of my head and I'd be on the verge of standing up and yelling at the speaker, "Shut the fuck up!"

You weren't supposed to do that either, so I'd stand up like making it to the bathroom was an emergency and I'd hide out there doing jumping jacks or walking in circles or flushing the urinal over and over again. I was losing it. I felt like I was on the brink of obeying my mood spikes, which meant acting on every fucked-up idea that popped into my mind.

A thirty-pack of beer would cure everything in less than two minutes, but I knew that, even if I barged out the door and off the campus, I had no way of getting my hands on one.

During the one-hour groups, I'd stare at the clock, close my eyes as long as I could, then open them up again and look at the clock to see how much time I killed. The rooms were closing in around me. I couldn't stop fidgeting and scratching my legs. I felt like I had to keep distracting myself from whoever was talking. I was constantly fighting the urge to jump up and run.

IT WAS MY TWENTIETH DAY at the Caron Foundation, and I was scheduled for a three-hour meeting in a white room staring at a giant diagram of the "relapse cycle."

Every few days, a different patient would stand in front of this circle with a big blue marker and explain, in sadistic detail, every single incident that led to their relapse.

There were twelve stages in the relapse cycle, and for three hours, the patient would write little phrases around the circle and give a little speech about each little phrase then we'd have a little discussion about where each thing should go on the relapse chart and how it pertained to one of the twelve stages.

Then a therapist would stand up there with the patient discussing each and every nuance of each and every detail of each and every phase and I felt like I was being waterboarded. I was suffocating. The horrible white walls were bulging and getting closer.

I'd already sat through two of these sessions, punching myself in the head to take my mind off the torturous repetition and that fucking circle of words, but this time the patient doing the three-hour presentation was

Kentucky Rick.

It was going to be three hours of his slow drawl talking about the events of his life and his relapse — and the facilitators had already made it clear that I wasn't allowed to make fun of him. To make matters worse, the clock on the wall was broken.

Forty-five minutes. That's how long I lasted. That's how long it took for that fucking relapse chart to drive me straight into my own relapse. I stood up and bolted from the room like I had to throw up. I hadn't planned on leaving Caron until that moment. I needed to get out of there.

I shot across the campus to my room, stuffed my suitcase and dragged it to the counselor's office. There was an assistant in there who had neither the key nor the authority to open the safe to give me my wallet. I asked for a phone book so I could call a cab. She didn't have that authority either. After a few minutes, two counselors showed up. They wanted me to sit down and talk to them.

But this mood spike had hit its mark, and now I was in a zone, like a malfunctioning drone lost in space.

"I just want my wallet and a phone book," I demanded, and I repeated the same thing every time they tried to talk to me.

There was a back and forth that went on for over an hour. Other counselors showed up, trying to get me to talk about something other than my wallet and a phone book. I blocked them out.

All I could see was a hotel room, a thirty-pack and some vodka. It felt like I was going to suffocate unless I broke free from that place. I made a conscious effort to take deep breaths, repeat my demand about leaving, and concentrate on something other than the people trying to stop me.

They made that process long and difficult. They called my mother and made me talk to her. They made me sit down with the medical doctor who had examined me three times since I'd been there.

"If you leave here right now, you'll be dead in a month," she warned. "You'll never make it in your condition, and I'm very sad about this because I really like you."

"I appreciate that but I just want my wallet and a phone book," I told her.

Then they told me I couldn't leave until I was cleared by my unit's psychologist, Mark, a condescending little prick who looked like a Jerry Garcia figurine.

"You're asking for something that is very misguided," he told me.

He spoke in a pompous, Freudian accent that was almost as pretentious as his Platonian beard and glasses. And he annoyed me enough to knock me off my script about the wallet and phone book.

"It might be misguided — by the way, don't talk down to me — but it's what I want… my wallet and a phone book," I demanded.

"Yes, they told me," he said while staring at the ceiling and sighing.

"Yes, they told you, and yet, here I am without my wallet and a phone book!"

I walked out into the hall where other thrill-seeking counselors were waiting to see what I did next.

Matt, my roommate, was also there and he looked bothered, as if he was looking for something. I didn't say anything; I just stood outside the counselor's office, hating everyone in sight. Now I was convinced that they were conspiring to keep me at Caron against my will.

Sounding like a crackhead robbing a convenience store, I yelled into the office, "Come on! It doesn't take that many of you to open a safe."

That's when Father Bill emerged from the door at the end of the long hallway. Matt stood there waiting to greet him as he got closer and closer to me and I realized they had decided to throw a Hail Mary.

The doctors and counselors and everyone else just stood all around me as the Father walked up. I tried to concentrate on my breathing and my simple demand, but I kept thinking, "Fuck, fuck, fuck, fuck, fuck!"

For a guy who never went to church, I'd had a lot of bad luck with priests.

"Son," he whispered while putting his hand on my back and escorting me back into the office. "Just give me a moment of your time."

He sat me down and then stared at me for a few seconds but it seemed like an eternity. Now I was really off my script.

"I'm sorry, Father," I pleaded. "I just can't stay here for another second and there's nothing you can say to change my mind. If I die, I die… I don't care, but I have to leave right now."

"Promise me you'll come back when you've had enough," he insisted.

"I promise. I just need my wallet and a phone book."

About an hour later, a big yellow taxi pulled up to the administration building and I wasted no time telling the driver what he needed to do. "Where's the nearest convenience store?" I asked him. "I need one quick."

I knew we were at least fifteen minutes from a traffic light. I had no idea how far we were from a thirty-pack, but my new hero, the driver, was committed to getting me there fast. As we flew past farms and cows and pastures, I concentrated on two things: my breathing and holding onto my wallet.

Finally, he pulled into a gas station and truck stop that also had a store. I was dripping with sweat when I hustled in and headed for the coolers. I couldn't find the beer section and I began sweating more and walking in circles until finally I said to the guy behind the counter, "I can't find the beer."

"Beer is only at the distributor," he said. "Where are you from?"

"What?" I shrieked. "What in the hell is a distributor? Are you saying this town is dry?"

The driver came in and tugged on the back of my shirt.

"Don't worry guy, I'll get you there. I didn't know that's what you needed. Come on with me," he said in a reassuring voice. He was gently escorting me back to the car just like the priest escorting me into the office.

My heart was racing and I couldn't stop sweating. He opened the door for me and I collapsed into the backseat. I felt like I could stop fighting now because he knew what I needed and he was going to get me there.

"Sorry, guy," he said as we drove away. "I should have known what you needed cuz of where I picked you up. We're almost there, guy. I'll even run in for you if that's what you want."

I dumped my wallet onto the front seat. "Yeah, can you please? A thirty-pack of Coors Light or Miller Lite or whatever. And get yourself something, whatever you want."

I was partially laying in the backseat wiping sweat off my face and trying to control what felt like a heart attack.

He came back with a thirty-pack of Coors Light. I opened the door, grabbed the beer and ripped open the box.

"Now listen," he said, "there's an open container law in Penns—" as I swallowed the first beer so fast it felt like I ate the can.

"Well, okay," he said. "I can see you're not worried about that."

Before I even bothered to shut the car door so we could leave, I had inhaled three beers.

"Okay," I told him. "I'm ready now. Thanks." And we drove away.

"Do you want to go to Reading?" he asked. "You don't have many choices. I saw the tag on your bag and we ain't nowhere near Albany and the Philly airport is an hour away. You look like you wanna relax, right? So how about Reading?"

I was up to five or six beers by the time he spit all that out. "Whatever you decide is fine," I told him. "I'm not in a rush any more."

"What in the hell did they do to you in that place?" he asked.

"It's what they didn't do," I said. "They didn't let me drink."

"If you don't want to stop drinking, why did you go?" he asked.

"I don't know… it's a long story," I said.

By the time we got to the Hampton Inn in Reading, the thirty-pack was half gone, so the driver stopped at another beer distributor and I bought another thirty-pack and a handful of Absolut Vodka nips.

As soon as I got to my room, I used the bedspread to cover the windows. I turned on the TV, which was the only light I wanted in the room, and sat on the bed with the remains of the thirty-pack by my side.

Out of habit, I grabbed a pen and a pad of paper. That's what I always did when I was in deep trouble. I'd make a list of things I could do to fix my situation. But this time, I knew I had thrown it all away.

I also wasn't sure how the whole thing went down. Five minutes before running across the campus demanding to be discharged, I hadn't even entertained the thought of leaving. I was just sitting in a group session listening to Kentucky Rick when, suddenly, I felt like I was suffocating and I needed to run.

Maybe now they'd know what I meant by "mood spikes."

When I got into trouble, I had to drink my way towards the solution. That's when I got to the bottom of things and fixed problems. But that wasn't working at the Hampton Inn in Reading, Pennsylvania. Not this time.

My physical crisis was over, temporarily. I wasn't suffocating and clawing at the walls any more. I stopped sweating. My heart wasn't pounding out of my chest. I was calm. I didn't feel like I was about to die.

But I was in deep, deep trouble.

Sitting there, on the edge of the bed without having to rock back and forth, no longer in a state of panic and withdrawal, I slowly began to comprehend the magnitude of what I had just done. Caron was the last stop for me, the one rehab that would help me end this unrelenting addiction to alcohol.

I thought everything was going well at Caron. The other patients had just elected me "Community President," which was something they take very seriously at Caron. It meant that, in the eyes of the other patients, I was a model of good recovery. It meant that I would represent the patients at the podium during large assemblies in Chit Chat Auditorium.

I was ready to graduate in another week and my mother was flying in from Florida to take part in the ceremony. I was actually looking forward to it.

I had no plan to get home, no cell phone, no plane ticket and no one left to call… at least no one willing and eager to help.

I started shot-gunning the beers, one after the other — hoping to drink my way to the place where none of it mattered, at least not for a few hours. I couldn't get there. I drank until I couldn't force another drop into my mouth, and it wasn't working.

I don't pray. At least, I never had. I'd never even experimented with praying because — despite all of the weird and fucked-up things I'd done — that's the only thing I couldn't do. If I tried to pray, I'd embarrass myself and start laughing and call myself a dork. I don't know why I feel that way about praying; I just always have.

But there was one time in my life when I asked a question out loud even though there was no one else there. It was in the church ten years ago, during the overdose, when I felt myself losing consciousness, and I was so confused about what I had just done to myself. Out of utter desperation, I asked, "How did I get here?"

Now, ten years later, drunk and stranded in Reading, Pennsylvania, I was desperate enough to kneel by the bed and ask whoever might be listening, "What do I do now?"

The one thing that had always worked for me wasn't working now. I was afraid to do anything. I was afraid to pick up the phone. I was afraid to see how much money was left in my bank account. I was deathly afraid to call my mom. I was drunk and afraid. That had never happened.

Until now, it was always one or the other. So I continued to force beer down my throat until every drop I poured into my mouth spilled out onto my lap.

The room phone was blinking red. The Caron Foundation had tracked me down and they were trying to get me back. My mother was working the phone even harder, trying to orchestrate a long-distance intervention with Lisa and Charles.

My mother called. "I'm sorry," I told her. "I felt like the walls were closing in all around me. I had to leave. I'm sorry about everything."

Then Lisa called. Both of them were being very careful with their words. They were talking to me like I was on a ledge.

They said everything was going to be just fine. They kept telling me I just needed to go back to Caron and finish what I started. My mother actually suggested, unconvincingly, that it was okay that I got it out of my system and now Caron was going to increase my dose of Librium to keep me more comfortable when I went back.

They never gave me Librium; they just stuck me in their white room. But I didn't say anything.

I couldn't understand why they were talking to me this way. Did they think I was crazy? I didn't care. I wasn't going back because, when I was talking to the priest, I promised myself I wouldn't forget how unbearable every minute of the day was in that asylum.

When we broke up into groups, we'd go into these horrific white rooms and sit in a circle. Everything they said in those groups reminded me of all the things I spent a lifetime drinking to forget. Then, without warning, some dark thought would race through my mind and I'd have to claw at myself to make it go away.

I promised myself not to forget what it was like and not to even entertain the thought of going back. While I was trying to get out of Caron, I told myself that it would be better to die in three months from alcoholism than to spend another day at Caron. But now I had no other options other than being on the streets of Reading Pennsylvania with no more money for beer.

Maybe this was rock bottom. I wanted my family back because I felt like I had just erased them from my life. After about forty beers, a handful of vodka nips and a lot of guilt, I broke all my promises to myself and told Caron I would go back in the morning.

Once I made that decision, I resumed drinking. This time I was able to drink myself towards the state of euphoria I was looking for because this time there was at least a glimmer of hope in my future. This time I could drink peacefully, knowing that the people who loved me were still in my corner, at least for another day. I'd worry about tomorrow, tomorrow.

I woke up about forty-five minutes before the van was supposed to pick me up. There were ten beers and three vodka nips left and I drank all of it while keeping an eye out for my ride back to hell.

When we got to Caron an hour later, they brought me straight to the building they called the "hospital." I knew they had Librium and Ativan but I also knew the lying bastards weren't going to give me any of it. The only thing waiting for me was a breathalyzer test, a vital sign check and another white room.

I laid face down on the bed and just accepted that the next twenty-four hours was going to suck. There was a window next to the bed. For about an hour I stared at the trees, pretending I was back at the lake house looking at the pine trees from my own bed, just like I did every morning before going into town for beer.

There was no clock in the room. That was going to make this detox long and hard. I still had a lot of alcohol in my system so I knew that each minute for the next twenty-four hours was going to be worse than the minute before.

Soon I would be doing "the rattle" again, sitting on the edge of the bed with my elbows on my knees rocking back and forth. I wouldn't be able to sit still or stop moving, and after that, the shakes would turn into disabling tremors.

If this were a real hospital, instead of an overpriced, overhyped, luxury piece of shit rehab, they would treat my withdrawal instead of locking me in a white room that should probably be padded.

After twenty-four hours of detox, all I wanted to do was crawl into a dark hole and plug my ears. The doctors at Caron promised that they would medicate me with Librium if I came back. They didn't. Instead, they sent me straight from the white room back to my unit.

Not surprisingly, running away from rehab is an impeachable offense and I was no longer "Community President." Mark, my Vice-Community President, took my spot.

When I returned to the unit and walked into the common area, Mark ran up to me yelling things like, "Yeah, let's hear it for John." Then he grabbed me by the shoulders and said, "We're so glad you made it back!"

"Get the fuck away from me, Mark," I said. "What the fuck is wrong with you?"

He should have known better. That's the last way to approach someone who's crawling back from a catastrophic relapse, especially because he knew I never liked him to begin with. It's a miracle I didn't hit him. As it turned out, it wouldn't have mattered if I did.

I hadn't eaten in days. The thought of food made me nauseous. I couldn't sit still or stop twitching. It felt like every breath I took had to be planned in advance. I just couldn't shake the feeling that, once again, I was being smothered and suffocated.

The breaking point, the second one in less than two days, came just a few hours after I got back. Matt and I were outside. He knew I was struggling, and in his own way, he was trying to help.

"You look like shit," he said. "Why aren't they helping you?"

That was all the prompting I needed.

"I've gotta get the hell out of here," I said. And that was it.

My suitcase was still at the counselor's station. I went through the same process of getting out as I did the day before, minus all the strong-arming lectures. They knew that if I was leaving again already, there was nothing they could do to make me stay. And they were right.

With all its pomp and circumstance and prestige and gourmet food, the Caron Foundation was nothing more than a high-priced detox unit.

My guess is that if Liza Minelli couldn't eat or if she was bouncing off the walls like a jackhammer, someone would have at least noticed.

I don't know why I went back. I had already tried and failed, which isn't to minimize the power of perseverance. But retreating back to the rehab you just ran away from because you had nowhere else to go isn't perseverance; it's just desperation.

They say if you don't know where you're going, any road will take you there. Hence, now I was in a cab heading back to Reading, a town that, if it weren't for Monopoly, I wouldn't have known existed.

In Reading, I acknowledged to myself that I was putting my poor mom, my future wife and my best friend in a three-way game of chicken. It was just a matter of who caved first by helping me get home.

My mother knew this was probably my last chance to stay alive. She was the one who would blame herself for the tragedy if I wound up dead. She knew I would regret leaving Caron, and she wanted to give me ample time to feel that regret… in Reading, Pennsylvania.

Lisa was stuck somewhere between my mother's tough love and my reassurances that everything would be fine if she'd just book me a flight home. Charles had no choice. He had to go along with whatever shitty decision I made. He was bound by our longstanding pact to lend unconditional support to the other, no matter what.

So I called Charles.

"I'm in Reading again," I told him. "I left the Caron Foundation and I'm stuck; I need to get home."

"Is that a good idea?" he asked.

I didn't know what to say. It was the closest thing to a rebuke I had ever gotten from Charles.

A good idea? No, a good idea would be taking a CPR course or volunteering at the children's hospital. Of course it's not a good idea. Since when do I call you with one of those?

"Probably not," I said. "But I was suffocating in there and I had to get out. I just need to get home."

I had spent so much money on hour-long cab fares, there was nothing left in my checking account for airfare. I couldn't book the flight myself because the process, which Lisa could easily do online while driving and talking to her children, was too confusing for me to execute from the comfort and convenience of a motel room.

After several moments of awkward and uncomfortable silence, Lisa gave me her credit card number so I could get home.

During one of those moments of silence, right before she gave me the card number, I could sense Lisa thinking to herself, *I cannot go any further with John because he doesn't want to get better. I can't leave him stranded so I will get him home but that will be the last transaction we can have together.*

She didn't say it; I just sensed it.

Charles did what he promised to do when we were at Ground Zero together on 9/11. He reluctantly booked the flight.

I went back to the room, where I would have been in heaven a few years ago, ransacking maid's carts and linen closets for towels and fancy soap. That used to be the highlight of my weekend getaways to Queensbury.

Now, I wasn't even close to having that kind of energy or spirit. I still believed, at least I think I believed, that I would feel better tomorrow. After several hours of chugging beer and vodka, I passed out on the floor.

I woke up sweating and trembling a few hours later. It was four am, and after an hour of sweating, tossing and turning, I had to drink myself back to sleep all over again.

At the Philadelphia airport the next day, I tried not to appear half as intoxicated as I definitely was. I drank all the way there — while waiting for the cab; in the cab; in the airport bar; and in the airport restroom.

I had a few more beers in my toiletry bag for the flight to Albany, but when I was in line waiting to go through security, I saw TSA agents confiscate a guy's bottle of mouthwash. I was still in a rehab state of mind so I thought they took it away because there was alcohol in it.

I panicked. I didn't want to find out if this airport had a jail too. So I wedged and weaved myself out of the line at the security gate — which freaked a lot of people out, including the TSA agent at the end of the line who checked my ticket.

"What's the problem sir?" she asked. "Where are you going?"

"I've gotta get in there," I said motioning towards the men's room, using body language that indicated I was about to have a bodily crisis.

I went into the stall, drank as much as I could in a few minutes and headed for the security gate again.

At this point, there weren't a lot of things I could do to make myself look any worse to my family, but winding up in another airport jail was at the top of the list.

I concentrated on every step I took to the plane, then balanced myself like a tightrope walker with my hands on the seat tops as I moved down the aisle, repeating my seat assignment over and over in my mind so I didn't have to keep looking down at the ticket like a confused drunk. When I got to my seat, I tried to stay alert until they shut the doors.

I woke up when the wheels hit the runway in Albany.

Charles was waiting for me at the curb. I asked him to stop at the mini-mart near the airport. I realized I was putting him in a shitty position — the reluctance was all over his face — but he honored our 9/11 agreement without raising a single objection.

I picked up plenty of beer, and there was still a whole bottle of vodka in my car, which was in Lisa's driveway. Now it was just a matter of getting back to the lake house.

I knew that whatever I said to Lisa when I got to her house would be relayed to my mother. I also knew that both of them were still stunned and confused about what happened at Caron, and that my stuttering explanations over the phone did little to help them understand.

The rehab to end all rehabs was the Caron Foundation, and I just ran away from it — twice. There was no place left to go. I wanted to think that there was still hope, that I could just go back to the lake and sit at my desk with the computer and figure this whole thing out. But I had nothing left to bluff them or myself with. I played my best hand with Caron and failed.

By the time Charles and I got to Lisa's house, I was intoxicated enough to take a stab at explaining myself. I knew I sounded like a crazy person when I talked about mood spikes and suffocating — but I didn't just make that stuff up. It was the truth. Otherwise, why would I be here? I didn't want to be here. It's not like I was going to have a party tonight. I'd get drunk, but there wasn't going to be any party. It was pure hell.

I wanted to say all that to whoever would listen, but no one asked. No one was looking for explanations about the past or reassurances about the future. At this point, why would they?

Instead, Lisa gave me a general hug, then stood with Charles and watched quietly as I moved my stuff from Charles' car to mine. I saw them talking, and I assumed they weren't talking about the weather.

Once my car was packed, I got my game face back. I acted as if

Caron was just another minor setback, and now I needed to get back to the lake house and figure the whole thing out.

Charles and Lisa just nodded slowly, looking disappointed and sad.

I was about four times the legal limit to drive so I spent the night at Lisa's. I called Mallory and Jackson that night. The three of us had lived together for a long time. There were no secrets. I told them I was sorry it was taking me so long to get better. I said I was still working on it and that I loved them.

I woke up in withdrawal at ten o'clock the next morning. The car was already packed. In a matter of minutes, Bam and I were on our way back to the lake house.

There was so much I wanted to say to Lisa, but I knew I had done serious, maybe irreparable, damage to our relationship and anything I said now might make it worse. I was so desperate to get back to the lake house, I didn't say a word about our future together. I could do that later, with a clear, intoxicated head.

It's not that I didn't care; I did. But if your parachute won't open, it doesn't make much sense to tie your shoe. Before I could do anything, I needed to get to the place I was yearning for in the white rooms.

MONTHS BEFORE I LEFT for Caron, Lisa's father and stepmother were planning a family trip to Disney. They wanted Jackson and I to join them, and I could tell that Lisa really wanted us to go. Lisa kept telling me the timing would be great because I would be fresh from a month at Caron and Disney would be a great place for early sobriety.

At the time, I agreed to go, and Jackson's mom put it on his calendar. Lisa's family paid for everything, and the tickets were non-refundable, so before they officially booked the trip, they asked Lisa one last time to confirm that Jackson and I were going.

"Yes, yes," I told her.

Almost every day after that, including over the phone when I was at Caron, Lisa anxiously asked me if I was looking forward to our Disney trip.

When I came back from Caron drunker than when I left, Lisa must have known I'd never make it to Disney, which was going to be a horrible thing to explain to her family, especially because they had already paid for it.

Lisa's demeanor signaled a certain level of acceptance but she never asked me point blank. Most likely, she didn't want to hear me make another promise she knew I couldn't keep.

For Jackson, this was just another ride to a friend's house that I couldn't give him — one more thing he could hold against me but never did.

One day, Lisa finally summoned the courage to get the bad news.

"You're not going to make it to Disney, are you?" she asked.

Disney... it barely rang a bell.

"Let's run through the details on that again," I said.

She just looked down at her hands, like she wanted to cry.

Chapter Twenty-six

"You Can't Die"

THERE WAS A CONSTANT PAIN in my stomach. When it first began a few months earlier, it was a dull ache that came and went. It started to go away while I was at Caron. Now it was back, worse than ever.

Every so often, it would pulse and throb, like it was flaring up. Sometimes it felt like a handful of nails in my stomach. Other times, the nails were railroad spikes. I worried about what it meant, but I kept telling myself it was something else, like my skid row diet.

The back deck of the lake house was packed to the rails with black trash bags filled with empty beer cans. To cut down on the amount of room the cans were taking up, I used to crush them to the size of a hockey puck with my hands before putting them in the trash. I lost the motivation, the energy and the strength to do that months ago.

These days, I was keeping the trash bag right next to the thirty-pack beside the couch. The cans never traveled more than two feet — from the thirty-pack to my mouth to the bag, usually in one continuous motion.

When the bag was full, I was usually too tired to move it fifteen feet to the deck until I'd had enough alcohol to muster the energy. Sometimes, I even started filling a second bag before moving the old one to the deck.

That and feeding Bam required a humbling amount of effort, not that anyone was watching. One would think that the most arduous part of my day was getting alcohol in town. It was, but the energy to get it done every morning came from the morbid fear of running out.

At the beginning of the summer, as I was laying on the couch drinking and watching TV, I would sporadically think about how long I had gone with exercise and I'd roll onto the floor and try doing pushups.

Before I left for Caron, I was discouraged because I could no longer do fifty. For a while I was content with forty, then thirty. When twenty became too difficult, I gave up altogether. At the beginning of the summer of 2013, I couldn't do three.

Bam never left my side. Every morning, as I knelt in front of the toilet throwing up, he hovered over me until I was done. When I passed out on the couch, he laid on the floor next to me. At night, he slept beside me on the bed. When I was struggling to get moving in the morning, he moaned and nudged me with his long German Shepherd nose.

It took at least two hours of frantic guzzling before I was relaxed enough to sit back and drink without kneeling over the thirty-pack and bottle of vodka. After that, I'd watch *Law and Order* or *NCIS* until I passed out.

When I woke up, I started the process all over again. I was living in four-hour increments. I'd drink hard for four hours so I could sleep hard for another four. I did that around-the-clock, 24/7. There was never a point in the day when I was even remotely close to sober. But there was never a point when I was as drunk as I wanted to be either.

My biggest fear of the day, aside from running out of beer, was someone showing up unannounced and disrupting the process. If the interruption was long enough, it could throw off my entire day.

The last time someone came to the door, I refused to let that happen, even though it meant being intentionally rude. It was a couple of women from town who stopped by with a trailer to pick up the cans on my deck.

I only opened the door a few inches, just enough to tell them I wasn't dressed. They could see enough of my clothed body to know I was lying, but they got the hint and took the cans without bothering me again. I stayed hidden in the bathroom with a bottle of vodka until they left.

Life wasn't great, and I didn't feel well, but at least I was in control of my freedom and fate, which was better than being trapped in an intolerable state of sobriety and having no way out.

I didn't want to kill myself, but — strange as it sounds — I needed that flexibility. I needed the peace of mind of knowing I had the option to do whatever I felt I had to do. The lake house is the only place that gave me that bare necessity of comfort: the means, the motive and the opportunity — everything but the balls.

THREE WEEKS BEFORE I LEFT CARON, my stomach pains continued to worsen. For weeks it had become harder and harder to stand up from a sitting position. Now, the throbbing pain was there even when I was laying down.

I was spending more and more of my day doubled up, waiting for the throbbing to stop so I could guzzle drinks between flare-ups. Although I had long since given up on being healthy, and I had long since abandoned the idea of going to a doctor, I needed to do something because the pain was making the drinking process harder, and at times, unbearable.

As the days wore on, I was becoming increasingly worried that the pain in my stomach was coming from my liver. I wasn't worried about having an illness that could kill me; I was worried about having an illness that would leave me strapped down in the hospital, unable to drink.

For the same reason, I needed to know what was going on in my stomach. I secured a ride to the health center in town for a midday appointment, which gave me plenty of time to get drunk first, but not enough time to pass out before I could get there.

Before I went in, I drank vanilla nut coffee mixed with Listerine strips. I didn't want the smell of alcohol on my breath to give them an obvious clue about what they should look for.

If they noticed any inebriated behavior, they must have attributed it to my stomach pain because, as part of his exam, the doctor believed the answer I gave to his routine question about drinking.

"Alcohol?" I said. "I guess I drink like everyone else."

He did some tests, drew some blood and said he'd call me. I called him first, a couple days later, praying he wouldn't say, "You've got cirrhosis" because it would force me to stop drinking when I needed to drink most: while I waited to die.

"You've got pancreatitis," he said.

All I knew about pancreatitis is that it wasn't necessarily fatal, which was everything I needed to know. As he talked about the treatment options, I took gulps of vodka, hoping to make up for the drinking time I lost while on hold.

Despite my horrific experiences with alcohol, I never stopped believing that alcohol was my perfect answer to everything and I could still make it work for me, just like it used to... a decade ago. A part of me still believed that, without me doing anything, I would wake up and everything would be fine.

Already, things were looking up. In my mind, the doctor just gave me a clean bill of health. During the five seconds I was actually listening to him, he didn't say the one word I feared: hospital.

In other words, I was as strong as an ox and I should just continue doing what I was doing.

I COULD TRICK MY MIND, but not the rest of my body. I was living like a hospice patient. I was no longer comfortable anywhere in the house except for on the couch with a thirty-pack of beer next to me. And right where my hand dangled toward the floor from the couch, there was Bam... always.

On TV, there was *Law and Order*. I watched it the same way "The Rain Man" watched "Wapner" on The People's Court. It, too, was in my comfort zone. I recognized the streets of Manhattan because I'd been drunk on a lot of them. I needed that familiarity. For some reason, it brought me serenity. When one episode ended, I closed my eyes and waited for a deep voice and the words, "In the Criminal Justice System the people are represented by two separate, yet equally important groups: The police who investigate crime and the District Attorneys who prosecute the offenders. These are their stories."

At some point in the day, I'd email Lisa and my mother. I didn't call either of them until I had been drinking for at least two hours. That was how long it took to achieve the level of intoxication where acting and faking and lying came easily.

Then it was time to pass out. The best part of my day was right before that happened.

For about a minute, just before I lost consciousness, my forehead tingled and my whole body went numb as I faded away. It was a fleeting moment of peace and contentment. And my final thought before floating away was the possibility that when I woke up this time, maybe I would feel better. I knew I wasn't going to get better; I just wanted to feel better.

For the first time since I'd overdosed on Klonopin in the church ten years earlier, I accepted death as inevitable. I wasn't scared or depressed or bitter; I was just disappointed and resigned.

When I was waiting to die in the church, I asked myself, "How did

I get here?" This time, I wasn't asking questions. I knew how I got here, yet even though I had been pushing myself to this place for over twenty years, I was still surprised it was actually happening.

I didn't want to wait for the inevitable.

At one point, I found the energy to go to the closet where I kept my guns... not to actually do it, just to act it out. But I walked to the closet anyway, thinking if there was a God and He thought it was time for me to die, I'd be stricken with the inclination to pull the trigger.

I knew I wouldn't do it because I didn't hate myself enough. Besides, I had never surrendered to God's will before and shooting myself in the head seemed like a harsh and unlikely initiation into the Hereafter.

I opened the sliding mirror door to the closet. All I could think about was Mallory and all the mornings she stood in front of the same mirror, brushing her hair before school.

"Honey, the bus is going to leave without you," I'd say, without even knowing what time it was.

"Dad, I've got another ten minutes," she'd say back, without knowing what time it was.

I stood there for a moment staring at an empty corner of the closet until I remembered that the police had come in and confiscated every gun in the house.

Bam was standing right behind me, crowding me into the corner. This was not part of my daily routine and he was uncomfortable. I kissed him on the head and we both went back to the couch.

ON THE KNOTTY PINE CEILING above my bed, three knots are arranged and shaped perfectly to look like Lisa's little dog, Molly. I woke up earlier than usual one morning and stared at it for several minutes, trying to stay still for as long as possible.

I knew that the nausea would come as soon as I moved, and on this particular morning, I wanted to delay it long enough to have a few minutes of semi-sober thinking.

As soon as my thoughts turned to something deeper than Molly's face on the ceiling, my throat began to swell and my face went numb.

The process was going to happen, with or without me so I covered my mouth, ran to the bathroom, crouched over the toilet and started heaving. Like every other morning, no food came out. It was all mucus, saliva and last night's alcohol — the combination of which left a trail of stinging, nuclear-tasting bile in my throat and a nasty film on the back of my teeth.

I could never get the hideous taste out of my mouth with a toothbrush because as soon as the brush touched my tongue, I would start heaving all over again.

The only way to stop the nausea and shaking was to somehow get some alcohol down my throat without throwing it up. I'd start by pouring a small amount of beer into my mouth while clenching my face and sometimes holding my nose.

I'd swallow hard while using the muscles in the back of my mouth to force the beer down.

The first few times, I'd puke it right back out. But I knew if I kept trying, a little alcohol would get into my system, then a little more, and eventually the nausea would go away.

Once that happened, I could drink an entire beer and some vodka, but I had trained myself to stop after a few rounds so I could maintain a reasonable blood alcohol content when I drove to the store for a thirty-pack of beer and a bottle of vodka.

Later in the day, I'd roll off the couch and lay next to Bam and just stare at his face... his short whiskers and his perfect black crouching eyebrows. He was so worried.

I hadn't been able to look at the "Me Wall" in months, maybe years. It was a wall covered with large framed pictures of me doing things with famous people like George W. Bush, Henry Kissinger, LL Cool J and a handful of elected officials.

They were all taken by the Governor's photographer, Lester Millman. They show me standing with the Governor on the stage of the 1996 Republican convention in San Diego and leaving Ground Zero on 9/11.

I'm drunk or hungover in every one of the photos, except the ones taken on 9/11. In those, I'm in full-blown alcohol withdrawal, and you can tell. You can tell I'm drunk in the photo with Bush and you can see me trying to conceal a vodka nip while talking to Kissinger.

Especially since I left Caron, I couldn't look at that corner of the room because it had defeated its own purpose. Now it was proof that, all along, I was wrong. And I got it wrong at the worst possible time: at the beginning.

Things were not going to get better, and now I knew it.

MY MOTHER WAS SCHEDULED to take a trip to China at the end of the summer. I knew she was worried about not being able to reach me so I tried to put her mind at ease with a series of surprisingly lucid, albeit untruthful, emails.

MOM: Hi, email me and let me know how you are doing.

ME: Don't worry. I'm doing surprisingly well. I'm fine... hope you're having fun!

MOM: Email me and tell me the truth about how you are doing. Would you like to come to Florida when I get back?

ME: I'm doing okay. I'm struggling a bit, but I'm making a little progress.

MOM: I was thinking about how close you and Jackson are and how he loved being with you. Please think about what it would be like for him if anything happened to you. None of us can even bear the idea of not having you around. You can't die. Please, please accept some help. We love you.

I looked at the corkboard by my desk. There were pictures of Mallory and Jackson playing with Bam and a few picture strips of Mallory and Jackson making goofy faces in a photo booth.

There were class portraits of both of them, of course, but my two favorite pictures were Jackson with his guitar and Mallory with her varsity cross-country team.

I did my best to hide most of what was going on from both kids. I purposely hadn't seen them in months. When I got out of Caron, I told their mother I was having a hard time and I needed to get better before they came back to the lake house.

Lisa came over on the weekends, but aside from keeping my mother apprised, she didn't know what to do. Or maybe she knew what to do but also knew that if she took too firm of a stand with me, I'd just tell her to leave and not come back.

Sadly, that's probably exactly what I would have done. In her mind, it was best to make sure I didn't die before my mother got back from China so everyone could figure out what to do.

One night, Lisa mentioned something about my family coming, but I didn't think anything of it until I had no choice.

Chapter Twenty-seven

Last Prayer for St. Mary's

EVEN BEFORE MY EYES OPENED the next morning, I was in a panic. I didn't know if it was a nightmare or if it was really scheduled to happen; I just remembered Lisa's comment the night before and I woke up thinking something bad was happening today.

I went straight to the fridge. There were only five beers left, which meant there were only three because the first two would go straight from my mouth into the toilet.

Only once had I been desperate enough to use a bowl to re-drink the beers I had thrown up. This might be the second time. My heart was beating out of my chest and I was shaking so much I had to plant my elbow on the sink to steady my hand so I could get the first beer to my mouth.

I poured as much as I could into my mouth and held it for a few seconds while concentrating on not throwing it up. The sink drain was closed so I could scoop it back up and drink it again if I had to, which is exactly what happened.

For the first time ever, I actually managed to get the first two beers into my system by saving the regurgitated beer in the sink and drinking it again. Things were looking up again. I was solving problems.

Those five beers were enough to control the shaking so I could make it into town. It was 7:50 am and I sat in my car counting down the seconds to eight, when it was legal to buy alcohol. As usual, I grabbed a thirty-pack of Coors Light and a forty-ounce bottle of Budweiser for the ride to the liquor store.

I finished the forty-ouncer on the dirt road to the lake house then went in and called Lisa.

I didn't want her to know how clueless I was about what was supposed to happen that day. I tried to be clever about coaxing information out of her without actually asking any questions.

"Today's the big day, huh?"

"I hope so," she said.

"How do you think it'll play out?" I asked.

"Only you know the answer to that."

After a few seconds, I realized I wasn't going to be able to figure it out.

"Okay, what's happening today?" I asked. "I don't remember."

"Your mom and aunt and uncle are on the way there," she explained.

Fuck. I knew I needed a plan, a plan that would undoubtedly entail running away, but first, I had to get drunk — drunker than ever — so I'd have the balls to carry out the plan before they got there. It may sound confusing but to me it made perfect sense.

By happenstance, Part One of the plan worked so well there was never any need for a Part Two. I have no way of knowing if I managed to get drunker than ever, but clearly, I came within spitting distance.

My mom and my aunt came through the door around five pm. They said I was lying on the floor moaning about how I was going to die. Apparently, Bam was hovering above me, licking my face and I said, "Even Bam knows I'm going to die." I don't remember any of that.

I refused to go to the hospital; I do remember that.

I was adamant about staying right where I was. The thought of leaving my couch, my dog, my house, my fridge… it was like asking me to jump off a ten-story building.

I was petrified to take a single step in that direction. And I remembered the white room at Caron where I cursed and hated myself for getting too drunk and too weak to stand up for myself and winding up shaking on the edge of a bed. I swore I'd never let it happen again.

I fought them off with everything I had. I used my strongest words and arguments. I threw my arsenal at them. I asserted every right I knew I had — civil, state, federal and God-given. I cited the Bill of Rights, I quoted Paine, Jefferson, Scalia and Reagan.

But my mother — the strongest and most influential person in my life — the one constant through every ebb and flow of every day of my life — brought her A Game. She stood there like an iron statue and deflected every word of it.

Even in my rock-bottom, disastrous state, I was awed by the strength of their determination.

My aunt stood her ground, right next to my mother, who was locked in on the single purpose of getting me in the car and to the hospital. But I knew that once I got in the car, I'd want to jump out. I knew that as soon as the alcohol starting wearing off, I'd want, and maybe try, to kill myself. I kept remembering those white rooms, those torture chambers. I wasn't going.

I disappeared into the bathroom for a few minutes, caught another glimpse of myself in the mirror, then walked out and said, "Okay, let's go."

IT TAKES OVER an hour to get from Chestertown to St Mary's Hospital in Troy, New York. One thing I remember vividly, for some reason, is collapsing into the backseat and landing in an awkward, uncomfortable position, then staying frozen in that same position for the rest of the trip.

For about two minutes, I was drunk and content and resigned back there. But as soon as we turned off my dirt road, my heart started pounding. It pounded harder when the car headed for the Adirondack Northway instead of turning right into town, like I did every day when I went to get beer and vodka.

Once we actually got on the Northway heading south to Albany, I had panicked myself sober, even though my blood alcohol content was at least four times the legal limit to drive.

I couldn't even open my mouth to say anything to my mom and aunt. I didn't know what to say. I wanted to open the door and jump out. And once again, I was cursing myself — hard — for making the same mistake — again.

I told myself in that white room at Caron that I would never do this to myself again, and here I was, in the backseat of a car, doing it again and hating myself more than ever.

The self-loathing got worse the further we drove, especially when my aunt, thinking I had a beer in my hand, turned around and asked, "How many of those did you bring?" They must have assumed I'd have alcohol with me when I got into the car. Apparently, that would have been okay, and for some baffling reason, I didn't take advantage of it. Maybe I wasn't an alcoholic after all. I mean, what alcoholic in his maladjusted mind would forget to bring beer on a road trip?

Even though it would have only prolonged the inevitable misery of withdrawal, I considered asking them to stop at a convenience store so I could go to the bathroom, but neither one of them was that stupid.

I began blacking out about halfway there, then passed out as soon as we got to the Emergency Room. When I woke up and felt the IVs in my arm, I knew I wasn't going anywhere soon. I didn't even know where I was. When you're staring up from a gurney bed, which was a regular occurrence for me, all hospitals look and smell the same.

With narcotics running through my veins, I wasn't putting up much of a fight to go anywhere. I stayed in the ER for two days due to severe dehydration and high blood pressure, then moved to the intensive care unit for an additional six days of treatment for elevated liver enzymes and pancreatitis. They kept me agreeable with a narcotic drip of Ativan.

This time, especially for my mother, it was just a depressing formality, one step above scattering your son's ashes.

The highest expectation of me this time was simply living for another month without breaking through a window and climbing down the fire escape. At best, it would give my mother and my fiancée a few days of peace of mind until I was sober enough to assert my rights and leave.

Still, they knew that, at least for seventy-two hours, I probably wouldn't die, although the doctors at St. Mary's weren't even promising that much.

Mallory, Jackson and my ex-wife came to see me, but I was in and out of consciousness most of the time. I don't remember seeing them or what, if anything, I said to them.

After several days in Intensive Care, the nurses began prepping me to move up to the rehab unit. The first order of business was going to be the worst: pulling the plug on the comfort drugs. This was when I expected to turn back into my own worst enemy, with cravings and mood spikes calling the shots.

But this time, I was too weak to mount much of an offense. I slept right through the process, and stayed asleep for my first twelve hours without narcotic assistance. When I woke up, they brought me up to the rehabilitation unit — and I immediately fell asleep again.

They woke me up for dinner, and I shuffled down the hall to eat without talking to anybody, then shuffled right back to my bed. I sat on the edge of the bed for an hour rocking back and forth before laying down and counting sheep and other shit.

Every twenty minutes, I ran to the bathroom to deal with fluid draining from the wrong parts of my body. Each time, I was fine one second and the next second it was an emergency. Up until now, it was just my brain that was prone to mood spikes; now my body was having them too.

After about five trips to the toilet, I decided I could sleep through the next emergency and everything would be fine. I was wrong. Withdrawal isn't pretty and neither was my first night in the rehab.

OF ALL THE REHABS I had been to, this one, on paper, should have been the one I hated most. For starters, it wasn't really a rehab; it was a hospital unit, a long white hallway with a meeting room on one end, a nurse's station in the middle and an alarm on anything with hinges.

I was at the end of the hall, in the detox area, where no one is faking their misery. Everyone is in withdrawal — except, ironically, heroin addicts, who can be annoyingly high-spirited. They have a shitty withdrawal, but they also get the best drugs, like Suboxone and Methadone, which are as good or better than what they were using on the street.

I was hoping there wouldn't be too many of them on the rehab side of the hall. I had nothing against them as a group, but their meds made them too happy, and who in the hell wants to be around that while detoxing?

They'd get on their pink clouds and start acting like life coaches. At breakfast one morning, one of them was talking about how unhealthy bacon is.

I snapped at him: "This from someone with track marks?"

After a couple of days, they moved me out of the detox area and put me with the rest of the rehab patients. My first roommate was a quiet, black guy about my age. He looked like Scottie Pippen of the Chicago Bulls, and he was about the same height.

I couldn't tell if he was still in withdrawal or if he just had something really heavy on his mind. Whatever it was, it had to be bad because he was breaking in a new Bible with a fancy bookmark, ribbon reminders, a highlighter and everything else you need when you're in deep shit.

Finally, I got bored and restless enough to ask, "Why are you here?"

"Same as you, alcohol," he replied.

"Oh."

"Why 'Oh'?" he asked.

"Everyone else is on heroin and meth," I grumbled. "Settle down."

"Doesn't matter," he said. "I think they're going to kick me out."

His insurance company was questioning whether or not he really needed to be there and the hospital wasn't making a strong enough case for him. Turns out, due to some bureaucratic stupidity, the insurance company wouldn't approve his full stay unless the hospital could justify keeping him for another twenty-four hours.

"The lady here said they needed a reason to hold me for another day but I didn't understand what I'm supposed to do," he complained.

"Say you're going to kill yourself," I told him.

"I'd never do that," he insisted.

"You don't have to *do* it. Just say you *feel* like doing it."

He sat there without saying anything for a minute, holding on to that damn Bible.

"How about you say something along those lines for me?" he proposed.

I should have kept my mouth shut. I didn't feel like doing anything, much less this. A couple hours later, I dragged myself out of bed and went to the head nurse.

"You might want to talk to my roommate. He's talking to his Bible."

"It's called praying," she squawked.

"He's praying to die. You might want to check it out."

I shuffled back to the room and told him, "When they ask you what's going on, just look at your Bible and don't say anything."

I collapsed on the bed, exhausted from all the talking and shuffling.

A few minutes later, a different nurse than the one I talked to poked her head in our room. "Robert, we just need to go over a few things with you, okay?"

The two of them disappeared down the hall and he didn't come back for almost an hour. This was more activity than I was in the mood for. The withdrawal was coming back, so I rocked back and forth on the bed until he came back an hour later.

He had the guilty look of victory on his face. "They made me sign an agreement not to leave in the next seventy-two hours, which means I can stay the full twenty-one days," he reported. "Thanks, man."

"No problem," I said. "I hope they let you move back here when you return."

"They're not *moving* me," he said.

"Oh, I bet they are," I laughed. "You're suicidal." And that's the last time I saw him. Apparently, his insurance company moved him to a better facility. Whatever facility it was, I'd probably been there myself a few times.

AS A NURSE WAS GOING over my chart with me, I realized that I'd been to two different rehabs named St. Mary's. Actually, I didn't realize it on my own; she took the time to point it out to me.

It annoyed the shit out of me, but since everything was going to annoy me for the rest of my life, I needed to practice keeping my mouth shut.

"So," she said while looking in the very thick folder with my name on it. "You've certainly made the rounds."

"Yes," I sarcastically agreed. "I've certainly made the rounds. Are those my medical records."

"Uh huh," she sighed. "You went to Conifer Park in 2003 and you were at Four Winds in 2004 and 2011, then again just recently?"

"Yes," I said.

"And you had a whole bunch of visits to the detox St. Peter's Hospital?"

"Yeah, I mean, those are my records so if something's in there it's probably true because…"

"Then you were at the other St. Mary's in Troy in 2012," she interrupted. "Oh, and you went to the Caron Foundation earlier this year... how was that?"

"I didn't like it very much."

As I sat there playing Truth or False with this nurse, I didn't have the same physical energy I had four months earlier when I sprinted across the Caron campus demanding to be released. Otherwise, I'd have busted out of that hospital the moment the ativan stopped dripping.

My escape from Caron... that was me in my prime, for lack of a more arrogant way to describe an angry and defiant alcoholic prick in denial. And although I didn't know how my stint at St. Mary's was going to end, I knew it wasn't going to end the way it had at Caron and everywhere else I'd been to. I was too weak, too broken. My days of making demands from the gutter were over. I wasn't going anywhere.

By the time my mom and aunt brought me to St. Mary's, I'd already hit rock bottom. Dying was the only way to go lower. If I drank when I got out this time, it would just be long enough to put the period at the end of the sentence. I'd live longer juggling dirty needles.

Despite myself, I had to stay at St. Mary's, no matter what — not because I wanted to but because I had no other choice. I was too sick and tired to bushwhack my way through the red tape that comes with leaving against medical advice.

The hardest part of staying here was going to be enduring the long withdrawal process without doing something that could derail my progress, like killing someone.

Withdrawal made me hate everyone, even people I'd normally like, so you can imagine how it made me feel about the people I'd normally hate, like Devon — a loud, cowboy-boot-wearing wife-beater and meth head from... wherever his trailer was double parked.

Fortunately, the black patients hated him even more than I did, and I was content to wait for them to kill him so I didn't have to.

I was one of only three people who wasn't in serious legal trouble. Most of them still had charges pending — and those were the ones I couldn't stand to be around, not because of the crimes they committed, but because of their self-righteous posturing for the counselors.

They wanted to get high marks in the program to impress a probation officer or judge. They knew exactly what the counselors wanted to hear, and they said it repeatedly, verbatim, ad nauseam.

Even their casual conversations with counselors were packed with recovery jargon, AA slogans and hackneyed, cringy motivational quotes. Invariably, they all found God the moment they foolishly believed that doing so would dazzle the people trying to put them in prison. Some said they found their higher power in the rehab bathroom or in the back of a squad car. Others were somehow able to make *Footprints In the Sand* even drippier by changing a few words and passing it off as their own. When I say I couldn't stand listening to it, I don't mean I disliked it; I mean I physically couldn't be in the same room.

If there was a trigger for the mood spikes that got me in so much trouble over the years, this was definitely one of them. At Caron, when Kentucky Rick was waxing intellectual (which was impossible with his drawl) about every little incident that led to his catastrophic relapse, I ran for my life and didn't stop until I got to the lake house.

His counterpart at St. Mary's was Chase, a coke addict and con-man from Albany who looked like a perfectly coiffed TV evangelist who didn't have time to clean his ears.

Every day, Chase repeated a sermon packed with psychiatric pontificating, syrupy observations about his life, and dollar store self-help slogans.

One day, I was sweating through one of his longer sermons, counting down the seconds and massaging my temples while staring at the floor.

"All I need to be is better than the man I was yesterday," he told the group.

"That shouldn't be hard," I added.

"What?" he screamed.

A counselor jumped up, thinking Chase was going to come after me. "Whoa, whoa, John," the counselor yelled. "You know better than to cross-talk. Feedback must be solution-oriented, not snarky."

"Sorry, I just don't want life tips from someone who was robbing old ladies for crack money last week."

Chase was so pissed off he couldn't get a word out of his mouth. The counselors gave me another pass on the cross-talking infraction and told me to "pay attention to [my] tone."

But here's the thing: I felt better after saying it, If I had similarly liberated myself at Caron when Kentucky Rick was droning on, I might have stayed there and completed the program.

Or maybe I would have been thrown out.

Part of my recovery, I suppose, meant finding a different way to liberate myself. It's hard, because even outside of rehab, I couldn't stand people turning their shitty behavior into a virtue, like the interviewee who says her worst flaw is that she's a perfectionist.

I was an alcoholic; at least I put it out there loudly and owned it.

One morning, a twenty-eight-year-old mother who put Xanax in her baby's formula so he'd stay asleep in the car while she made a drug run was telling the group about her "asshole husband."

"I devoted all of my time and emotional energy to my kids," she lied, "and at the end of the day, no one was there for me and I would fill the void with drugs."

"Oh Jesus," I griped. "Can I plug my ears?"

Later that day, one of the counselors pulled me aside and stated the obvious. "When you think someone else is deflecting their problems like that," she said, "the best thing to do is examine some of your own thoughts to make sure you're not doing the same thing."

"Yep," I said. "You're right."

I was hoping she'd leave it at that, but I knew my big mouth had left me wide open for scrutiny.

"You're very good about one thing," she told me. "You don't blame your drinking on anyone but yourself. You don't blame it on bad genes or bad luck. The problem is, you don't attribute it to anything. You just say, 'That's just the way it is.'

"It's a convenient way to take responsibility without having to do anything to change," she said. "What about the people who have to suffer while watching you kill yourself?"

"Okay, no more cross-talk," I promised. I couldn't think of anything better to say.

My whole shtick on drinking took a royal beating that day. There is zero virtue, I guess, in being honest and forthright about your shortcomings unless you're serious about fixing them.

The thing I hated most in other people — playing the victim — was essentially what I had been doing all along. I wasn't whining or looking for sympathy in the process.

Instead, I was trying to drink with impunity by treating my alcoholism like an incurable disease. It would have been a tough pill to swallow if it hadn't been crammed down my throat. It's probably the most important thing I learned about myself at St. Mary's, or anywhere else.

It didn't change the fact that I couldn't live with alcohol; it just changed my perspective about it.

IT HAD BEEN THREE WEEKS since I entered the hospital and I was still in protracted alcohol withdrawal. The medications they were giving me at night were helping me sleep, but at certain times of the day, I was still sweating and shaking. And somewhere along the line, I picked up a stutter.

The neurologist was called in because the nurses were concerned about the severity of my tremors and the possibility of seizures. He asked me to draw a circle and a square, then sign my name a few times. When I was done, the circle looked like a saw wheel and the square looked like something you'd find on the wall of a cave in Egypt.

He prescribed Phenobarbital on an "as needed" basis but I never asked for it, for three reasons.

First, it wasn't beer or vodka. Anything else was just prolonging the inevitable withdrawal.

Second, I asked him for Ativan and he said, "No way. That would be like giving you a case of beer," from which I concluded Phenobarbital sucked.

And third, I thought I should at least try to be as courageous as the only guy in there who was in rougher shape than me.

His name was Dave and he was only thirty-eight years old. He had cirrhosis of the liver and about a fifty-percent chance of living long enough to get a new liver. Just to get on the liver transplant list, he had to be sober for at least one year.

So when I was with him, he was battling alcohol addiction while simultaneously enduring the daily pain of an untreated liver that was getting worse every day.

His plan was to fight. Under the same circumstances, my plan was to expedite the dying process by doing all the drugs I was always afraid to experiment with when I was drinking. Despite Dave's courage, I still liked my plan better.

He reminded me of Kentucky Rick at Caron. They both had southern accents that I mocked loudly and relentlessly and they both took the ribbing like southern gentlemen. And both were into sports — star athletes in high school and loyal fans as adults.

The most striking similarity between them was their "aw shucks" attitude about their drinking. Dave used to mock his own obliviousness: "I was just drinking beer with the boys one summer and fifteen years later I was sneaking Southern Comfort in the closet."

Dave was living my worst nightmare and he was doing it with a lot more honor and courage than my best thinking was able to muster. If there is a God, and He was willing to give me one chance to defeat alcohol, He must have wanted me to have some humility first, so He put Dave in my path to recovery.

Perhaps as a test, He also arranged for me to cross paths with Ramon. I was just starting to feel confident about completing the program without bolting or getting thrown out. The tremors, sweating and mood changes were still there, but overall, I was a little less miserable and more even-tempered. The stuttering was becoming an issue. The doctor said stuttering was common for chronic alcoholics in early recovery.

"It will go away, gradually," he promised. "Talking is overrated anyway."

"Maybe it's a good thing," I said. "It'll help me keep my mouth shut."

It didn't.

Ramon was a mouthy, gangbanging felon from the Bronx. He had an arrogant Bronx-Puerto Rican accent, and a pissed-off demeanor that was clearly meant to be intimidating.

He thought he deserved instant respect from everybody, and he tried to scare others by hanging his head in his hoodie while staring at them sideways with a snarl on his face.

During a group session, the sign-in sheet was going around. After I signed in, I tried handing the clipboard to him. He wouldn't take it from me. He just looked at it like I was handing him a dead kitten.

So I tried to hand him the pen and he didn't take that either.

I thought maybe he just didn't know what to do so I said, "You just have to write your name down so they know you were here."

"Who the fuck is you, motherfucker?" he yelled.

"I'm trying to help you, you stupid fuck!" I yelled back.

He jumped to his feet and screamed, "White boy is talking to me?"

That's the kind of thing punks say to take the pressure off themselves by dragging bystanders into their battles. It didn't work, because as soon as he said it, the black and Hispanic patients immediately heckled him with a loud, droning "Noooo!" I just stayed on the couch and glared at him to see what he was going to think up next.

"You're just a punk," I said. "But I don't want to get thrown out so sit down."

He stood in front of me doing that thing where you trash someone while looking at someone else. He left the whole left side of his face wide open, and my first instinct was to take the shot and end it quickly.

"Listen, little Ricky Martin," I laughed. "If I have to stand up, you'll never walk out of this hospital."

"White punk-ass bitch," he bit back.

I wasn't biting. I knew if I stood up, I'd be tossed out of St. Mary's immediately and drunk by the end of the day.

"Let's be friends, Ricky," I mused, and that pissed him off even more.

They tossed him out of the program an hour later, probably because he continued to talk smack to the counselor who escorted him out of the room.

The counselor later told me why they tossed him out of the program instead of me.

"The two of you could never be in the same room again so someone had to go," he explained. "It was him only because he stood up [from the couch] first. Plus, he was being racial and threatening whereas you were being mostly obnoxious."

I had a different theory about why they tossed him instead of me: For the first time ever, I didn't do anything.

RIGHT BEFORE MY FATHER left for treatment in 1987, he opened up to me a little about his alcoholism.

"I have to drink for an hour or two just to feel the way normal people feel all the time."

That was his assessment of himself at his worst. He drank to be his sober self. I drank for *fear* of my sober self. He drank alcoholically, but manageably. I drank cataclysmically. There was no way to manage what I was doing. I drank more in one night than he drank in a week.

If you've been to rehab, if you've been mandated to a mental facility, if you watch a lot of *Law and Order* — or if you're like me and you've done all three — you know what happens when someone with a mental illness stops taking their medicine. They go crazy and get into some kind of trouble.

For the past twenty-five years, my medicine was alcohol and in the past, only bad things happened when I was off my medicine.

Of course, being sober in the controlled setting of a hospital rehab, especially when you're being medicated, isn't an indication of how you'll act when you walk out the door.

I thought about this stuff repeatedly while lying in bed at night, waiting for the Trazadone they gave me for sleep — which worked about as well as a Five-Hour Energy drink — to do its job so I could close my eyes and go to bed.

For hours every night, I wondered how long it would take for me to feel the "normal" my dad was talking about. It only took him two or three months, but I drank so much more than him.

My father and grandfather were doctors and they were both incredibly smart but they were so antisocial and weird. I wondered if, in addition to alcoholism, I had inherited something else from my dad's side of the family. They could recognize their own symptoms and prescribe stuff to themselves. What was I supposed to do?

The incident with Ramon was almost too good to be true. *"There's no way,"* I wrote in my (mandatory) journal that night, *"that the real me, the sober guy I rejected and laid to rest in the church, is that calm, cool and collected. He couldn't be, or I wouldn't have felt the need to control his behavior with booze in the first place."*

Days before I was scheduled to leave St. Mary's, my counselor asked me, one last time, what I was going to do after I was discharged. Both her and my mother wanted me to continue treatment in a three-month inpatient program, then move to a six-month program in a halfway house.

Lisa's loyalty, as usual, was evenly split between what I wanted and what was best for me, which were rarely the same thing.

At St. Mary's, I was safe from my greatest threat: me. If I learned anything at St. Mary's, it's that I was my own worst enabler, agitator and saboteur. I didn't trust myself to stay in the right frame of mind once I walked out of St. Mary's. I was afraid to leave but I was also afraid to go into a three-month program because I didn't trust myself to stay there that long.

And I was afraid to go to a halfway house because I knew that, in my world, a semi-controlled setting means all rules are optional. Mostly, I was afraid of getting back the freedom I had spent my whole life trying to protect. I didn't trust myself sober. I didn't even *know* myself sober.

I didn't tell my counselor any of this because I don't tell people things. I dropped a hint about it, though. When she asked me if I was ready to leave St. Mary's, I said, "I don't know. I think I've begun to identify with my captors."

Chapter Twenty-eight

"What Do I Do Now?"

WHEN I WALKED OUT of Conifer Park ten years earlier, I was under a microscope. My family and friends were watching closely to see if my personality changed while I was in rehab. Charles told me that some of the troopers asked him if I was still funny. I also knew that several people in the Governor's Office, maybe even the Governor himself, were wondering if I'd still be able to write.

It was different when I came back from St. Mary's.

There were only a handful of people who even knew I was there, and once I was out, they weren't watching with hope as much as they were wincing with fear. They knew that if I drank again, there would be nothing they could do. It would simply be a matter of whether I shot myself or waited a few months for alcohol to finish the job — and consistent with the progression of my drinking, it wouldn't have been any longer than that.

It wasn't until I walked out of St. Mary's that I finally realized what all the doctors and counselors in my life meant when they said my drinking was progressive. I always thought it meant that the more I drank, the more I'd need. It does mean that, but I should have waited around to hear the rest.

From the time I stepped onto a wrestling mat drunk in college right up to the time I was wheeled into the ICU at St. Mary's, I swore I could make drinking work.

Even when my drinking started to cause problems, I thought I could go to rehab and get all the alcohol out of my system, then start over again — as good as new — when I got out.

Not only did that not work, it did the opposite of working. Each time I walked out of rehab and began drinking again, I wound up drinking even more than I did a month earlier when I walked in. When I left Caron in the spring of 2013, I didn't have any further to fall.

At this stage of my progression, there's no such thing as a single slip. Any amount of alcohol in my bloodstream might as well be cyanide. Either way, it would be impossible to recover.

My track record wasn't good. Time and again, I baffled myself by going against my own wishes and doing the opposite of what I wanted to do. One minute, I'd pledge allegiance to Plan A. The next minute, I would move full steam ahead with Plan B. The minute after that, I'd hate myself for defying Plan A.

I worried about what it all meant. I worried, especially, that alcohol might not be my only problem. Even if I could live without alcohol — and I still wasn't sure if I could — would I just be an unhappy sober person fighting a different disease... the one that alcohol was covering up?

Would I be calling Charles every day after attacking lawyers and bus drivers and overdosing in churches?

Wouldn't it be better to do what I was doing — drinking quietly on my way to an unglamorous but predictable end? To me, that was better than Mallory and Jackson having to tell their children that Grandpa's little choo-choo went chugging around the bend.

I never talked about this with anyone in rehab or anywhere else. The last thing I wanted to do was plant that seed in anybody's head. Then one day my mom gave me some closure on the whole issue.

I don't know how the subject came up, but I was telling her about some of the research on alcoholism they were doing at the Caron Foundation.

I asked her what she knew about alcoholism and mental illness. I told her that research at Caron showed that alcoholism often masks an underlying mental illness. According to the study, when these alcoholics stopped drinking, the mental illnesses rose to the surface.

"What do you think about that?" she asked me.

I knew what I thought about it, but I wasn't sure what to say.

Finally, I said, "Well, that's fine. What did grandma always say... Que Sera, Sera?"

"Yep," she replied. "That's all."

I'D SLEPT AT LISA'S HOUSE dozens of times, but when I woke up there the morning after leaving St. Mary's, I was as oblivious as the day I emerged from life support ten years earlier.

My eyes opened and I was staring at a white ceiling — not the beer-colored knotty pine ceiling at the lake house, but an institutional pitch-white ceiling, just like the ones in airport jails and rehabs and hospitals.

I had no idea where I was. And just like the times I woke up confused in those other places, I stared at the white ceiling for a while, racking my brain to figure out where I was before daring to look around for the answer.

Once I realized I was at Lisa's house, I stayed on the bed and tried to remember everything else. *Where is Jackson, Mallory, Lisa, Bam, my car?* It took me about an hour to get it straight in my mind. I'd never been in Lisa's house this way before — sober, that is. I was always either drunk or sneaking around *trying* to get drunk.

Bam's big head appeared out of nowhere. He nudged me, so I rolled on to the floor and I laid next to him, clutching his paw like I had done so many times during the rough nights at the lake house. He was probably wondering why I wasn't in the bathroom with my head in the toilet.

I put my nose up to his and popped the big question.

"What in the hell are we supposed to do now?"

His eyebrows furrowed and seemed to say, "Let's take it slow."

I didn't leave the house that day. At one point, I opened the garage door and looked around for the blue Dodge Charger. That's the kind of car I used to own before buying the white Chevy Impala that was parked in the driveway. In other words, the rewards of sobriety don't come overnight — at least not on the first night. But for the first time in a long time, maybe in decades, I believed that time was on my side, that I was going to get better with each passing hour, not worse. Of course, there were bound to be peaks and valleys.

The next morning, I woke up sweating and terrified, convinced that I'd gotten drunk the night before. It was just the first of the many "drunk dreams" I'd have in early recovery. Some people call them "freebies" because you get to be drunk without actually relapsing. I can't imagine how that could ever be a good thing. Drunk dreams are an absolute nightmare for those who know their next drink will kill them.

Fortunately, there was an Alcoholics Anonymous meeting right down the road that morning. It was at St. Michael's Church in South Glens Falls. My hands were shaking as I sat in my car watching people go in. About five minutes before the meeting, I forced myself out of the car and dragged my feet into the church, wishing I was dead every step of the way.

There was a group of ancient, John McCain-looking AA dudes in the corner of the room. I didn't feel like talking to them, or anyone, so I pretended to read a newspaper that was on the table.

I wasn't really reading; I was eavesdropping, just to get a sense of what the Buick crowd talks about when their life is over because they can't drink any more.

I assumed they'd be talking about upcoming sober sock hops, the weather and their colons.

That's what scared me about AA and sobriety — boredom. I wasn't sure where I wanted to be in twenty or thirty years, but I *knew* I didn't want to be in a corner talking about my prostate. I don't even know where my prostate is.

I kept eyeballing the door, praying someone would barge in and scream, "The church is on fire! Get out of here and go home!"

As I was slowly flipping the newspaper pages, I saw the words, "Whitney Houston's estate." At first, I thought it was a reference to her mansion, but then I glanced at it a second time and saw something about her kids.

"Wait a minute," I gasped out loud. "Is Whitney Houston dead?"

The coffin-dodgers looked over at me, giggling like eight-year-old girls. The oldest one in the group hacked out an answer.

"She's been dead for two years."

Another scrotum-faced retro piled on. "And so is Michael Jackson… and Buddy Holly."

They continued to chuckle or cackle or whatever you call it when a bunch of crotchety alcoholics laugh at themselves.

I wanted to yell "Boo!" and send all of them into cardiac arrest.

Right about then, a banging gavel rang out and scared the crap out of me. That's when I closed my eyes, tuned out everything around me, and experienced my first-ever sober blackout. It lasted for exactly one hour. That's when everyone joined hands and started praying and I made a break for the door.

The church parking lot was jammed. There were cars scattered all over the place. It looked like God took a handful of cars and threw them down like grass seed onto the parking lot. Apparently, someone died on a day that was inconvenient for me — that's how I perceived it at the time — and now they were going to further inconvenience me by lining up for a funeral procession. Bastards!

It was the kind of scene you would expect to see when two hundred people over the age of eighty put on their little tweed driving hats, ease themselves into their cars and drive with their turn signals on all the way to the church.

The real chaos comes when all those Oldsmobiles and Buicks, with their AAA Motor Club stickers, converge on one parking lot at the same time.

There was no way to get to the exits, so I drove behind the church. You'd have to see the layout of the parking lot to appreciate what a stupid idea that was. It's like waiting in line at the front door, then running around the building and getting back in the same line.

Suddenly, a guy in a black suit started waving me into a lane of traffic cones. At first, I thought he was trying to expedite the flow of traffic out of the parking lot.

Then I realized that I was the fifth car in a growing line of vehicles with their headlights on. At the front of the line there were two hearses.

Not only was I in a funeral procession, I was at the front of it with the deceased's family members. I couldn't escape. The guy in the black suit had me packed in there nice and tight, bumper to bumper, with traffic cones on both sides.

After a few minutes, there were at least thirty cars lined up behind me. A whistle blew and two guys in black suits began waving the hearses and the rest of the procession forward to Route 9.

The hearses were turning left, and I figured that would be my opportunity to break free from the procession by turning right. Nope.

The motorcycle cop with the puffy equestrian pants and the whistle wasn't going to let it happen. He had his motorcycle parked in the middle of the road so the old people in the procession couldn't screw up and turn right. He had us marching in formation like penguins. I was going left, whether I liked it or not.

Out of respect, I turned on my headlights.

We drove about twenty-five miles per hour up Route 9, from South Glens Falls to Glens Falls, and eventually, to Queensbury. I was going to the gym in Queensbury anyway, so I just stayed in line with my lights on and let the motorcycle cop wave me through the red lights.

Onlookers from cars going in the other direction gave us sympathetic smiles, especially those of us at the front of the procession who were grieving the most.

We passed Crandall Park on the left, then wound our way into the commercial district of Queensbury where Route 9 turns into two lanes.

I knew it was time to say goodbye.

THE ONLY REASON I found St. Michael's that morning is because there was no way not to. There was no traffic, no turns and no way to miss the sign. It would have been a bad time to get confused, sweaty and pissed off because, along the way, I passed five convenience stores and two liquor stores. I could have cleared up my confusion at any one of them in about five minutes.

I wasn't worried about the inconvenience or embarrassment of being confused; I just didn't want my confusion to erupt into something truly inconvenient and embarrassing, like another overdose with a complimentary stay at a mental hospital, followed by ten years of drunken chaos.

I didn't want to tell Lisa how much trouble I was having, but I wanted her help so I casually mentioned it at the end of a phone conversation, like it was no big deal.

"Oh, uh… one more thing," I said. "Sometimes in the morning I can't remember important stuff, like my name. How about we talk every morning for a while."

There wasn't the slightest pause.

"I'll call every morning at nine-thirty, and we'll talk about everything that's going on."

"Thanks, honey. What time?"

It was going to be a slow recovery.

THERE WAS A THURSDAY NIGHT meeting at a halfway house on Crandall Street in Glens Falls, but I was nervous about driving at night. I could see myself getting lost, confused, mad, drunk — in that order — then driving back up to the lake house.

I printed out a map and directions from MapQuest. (It was 2013 and I hadn't even heard about GPS yet. Apparently, I wasn't too far removed from the old people in the funeral procession.) Anyway, according to my compass, the latest land data and the coordinates I ascertained from MapQuest, Crandall Street was four miles away — a straight line for three miles, through a roundabout, then another straight line right to the meeting. Lisa and MapQuest said it would take me about fifteen minutes, so I left an hour early.

About five minutes into the first straight line, I started wondering if a roundabout was the same thing as a turnabout and if either of those things was the same thing as a rotary. After a minute of doing that, I convinced myself that I didn't know what I was looking for and I had gone too far.

There was a Cumberland Farms so, even though I had two very specific maps, I stopped to ask where Crandall Street was. I figured I'd get a coffee while I was there, but there was no coffee area. Everywhere I looked, there was just beer — domestic beer, imported beer, kegged beer.

Was this the prelude to some sort of weird relapse where everything looked like beer? Maybe I was looking at golden Twinkies, but my brain processed it as Corona.

"Help ya find something?" asked the guy behind the counter.

"I was just gonna grab some coffee."

"No coffee here," he replied.

"Okay... um, is Crandall... Street close by?"

"Keep going north on Route 9, through the rotary, and you'll run right into it. There's a pond on the left. You can't miss it."

Of course I can, I thought, watch me.

"Thanks. Oh, and is it a *rotary* or a roundabout?"

"It's a circle. You can call it whatever you want."

I walked out totally baffled. How can a Cumberland Farms have no coffee but plenty of Japanese Beer? Or maybe the store *used* to be a Cumberland Farms but never painted over the blue and orange Cumby colors.

When I got to the car, I compared the guy's directions to my maps. There was a discrepancy about exactly what to do at the roundabout. I decided to iron that out when I got there, but it didn't really matter because once I got to the roundabout and started driving in a circle, I lost my bearings and all four turn offs looked equally wrong.

So I took a wild guess, and that brought me right to the pond the Japanese beer guy was talking about.

I assumed the road next to the pond was Crandall Street, so I turned onto it and started looking for a church or a school. But now it was pitch black because there were no streetlights, and with the Supreme Being as my witness, I was suddenly caught up in a cacophony of quacking.

Now that I was officially lost and confused, I got mad, which is Step Two in a sequence that never ends well for me. Getting drunk was on deck. I banged on the steering wheel until my hands and the car windows fogged up. I had a choice to make. I had no idea how to get to the meeting; I *kind of* knew how to get home. And I *definitely* knew how to get the Sapporo beer. Instead of doing any of that, I turned into a Dunkin Donuts and stayed there for forty-five minutes studying my maps, then made my way home where I lied to Lisa about how great the meeting was.

The next morning, I retraced my steps on Google Maps. The quacks I heard were the ducks in the pond at Crandall *Park*, which is nowhere near Crandall *Street*. I would have known that if I had trusted the straight lines on my maps.

The rehab people told me this was going to happen, but I just shrugged it off. As soon as I got out of St. Mary's, my own doctor gave it to me straight. He said I would just have to accept that life was going to be like this for a while, probably for at least a year.

"Twenty-eight days isn't long enough to erase nearly three decades of alcoholic thinking and programming," he explained. "It's going to take some time before you feel normal."

"It would be nice if I could have one normal, clear day *now*," I told him. "I'd settle for an hour. At least then I'd know what I'm struggling towards, because right now, it's just not worth it."

"There's not a pill for that," he said. "So, 'no' is the answer to whatever else you were about to ask me."

Chapter Twenty-nine

In Sickness and Health?

IF IT WEREN'T FOR MY MOTHER, I never would have gone to St. Mary's. If it weren't for Lisa, I wouldn't have stayed there. A golden rule of recovery is, "Don't get into any relationships and don't make any drastic decisions during your first year of sobriety."

In my mind, marrying Lisa wasn't a drastic decision. Not marrying the woman who helped lead me away from drinking would have put a far bigger strain on my recovery.

Most women won't roll the dice on a man who's "in between jobs," much less a man who's "in between rehabs." I had all the markings of a guy whose best days were behind him and whose subsequent days were numbered — but we needed each other. It was obvious why I needed her. Why she needed me is less clear. From the start, we just loved being with each other.

About a month after I left St. Mary's, my brother, whose sentimental side is as refined as a grenade, said, "You know she saved your life, right?"

On May 10th, 2014, seven months after I left St. Mary's, Lisa and I got married in a stone chapel along the shores of Lake George in Silver Bay, New York. We invited seventy close friends and family members.

Some came from as far away as Virginia and Colorado — and of course, my mom and stepfather flew in from Florida. Mallory, Jackson and Lisa's children, Michael and Rachel, all took part in the ceremony. I had two best men: Charles and Jackson.

For some, the wedding may have seemed more fantasy than fairy tale. The last time Charles and I were in a church together, I was dead. Both he and my mother — and even Lisa — had every reason to temper their celebrations with an asterisk — not because my love for Lisa wouldn't last, but because my sobriety might not.

The only one with nothing to prove was Lisa. When it came time to part of the vows that read, "I promise to be true in good times and bad and in sickness and health," Lisa had earned the right to say, "Yeah... I already did that."

I could tell that Charles put a lot of time and thought into the toast. He quoted large portions of a speech I wrote on the evening of September 11, 2001. When I wrote it thirteen years earlier, eleven hours after the attacks, Charles was literally reading over my shoulder, and as soon as I typed the last word, we started our long walk back to Lower Manhattan.

So, it was altogether fitting that Charles held on to the speech all this time, waiting thirteen years for the right occasion to read it his own way.

It was a new beginning in more ways than one. I've heard people compare being sober for the first time in their life to being born again. That's exactly what it is, but only because I felt as clueless as an infant. For me, it was literally like being reborn, which is to say, coming out of the womb and having to learn everything all over again, from the beginning.

I was lucky to find a woman willing, for reasons only she could know, to help me grow up all over again. It was a responsibility that couldn't have been too difficult to wrestle away from my mom, who would have been justified in saying, "Go ahead and open the jar; it'll be easy now that I loosened it for you."

Chapter Thirty

A Day of Clarity

THERE'S A SAYING in recovery that goes, "You can get a drunken horse thief sober, but then you're left with a sober horse thief." Marrying Lisa wasn't going to speed up my recovery. Even after eleven agitated, sweaty, dysfunctional months, alcohol still had a grip on me. I was stuck in a hangover-ish fog — and yes, I wanted to drink because I knew, or thought, that getting drunk would clear up my confusion and return me to the state of existence to which I was accustomed. I fully expected to be a new person after a few months, but it almost felt like I was getting worse. It was as if my body and my mind were rejecting my sobriety, the same way bodies sometimes reject donated hearts and livers. Or maybe my doctor was right when he said it would take a while to feel normal, and by "a while" he meant a year. Either way, I was getting tired of waiting.

The Ides of August brought one long, unbearable day after another. One morning, I woke up in a panic to the sound of sirens in the distance. It made me think about all the police cars and ambulances that raced to the lake house over the years. Bam never let them anywhere near the front door, which always gave me a chance to move a few things around before letting anyone in. I cringed when I thought about the brawl at the Panther Mountain Inn. I cringed harder when I thought about telling Mallory to kill the house lights when the cops showed up.

It was just one of a hundred other thoughts that tormented me eleven months after leaving St. Mary's. I couldn't muster a single happy memory. All I could think about was the nosedive my life had taken after my pitiful mental prostration in the church. The most lucid memories I had were the ones I was desperately trying to forget, like Ground Zero and the endless eulogies of 9/11. I agonized over what may or may not have happened during my thousands of blackouts. The second I sat still, my mind raced with visions of my decline at the lake house. The thoughts were like nasty black flies, pecking away at my brain, beating me down, piling regret on confusion.

I was still a kid when I walked onto that wrestling mat drunk, trying to prove a point. That's when the blackouts began. Now I was middle-aged (and that's putting it charitably), struggling to piece it all back together and figure out what happened to the twenty-six years I barely remember. And it's not like my brain simply blocked all the *bad* things. The good things were gone too, lost forever. It was all gone, wasted.

Then one day, one ordinary random day, everything changed. I was driving down Route 9 on my way home from an appointment. As usual, I was agitated and confused. My forehead was dripping with sweat, my heart was racing, and I was getting pelted by those sudden, horrifying thoughts that came out of nowhere and pierced my brain like poison-tipped arrows.

My mind went back to the church ten years earlier. I thought about what the guy at the AA meeting said that night — that he'd rather be dead than endure another day of sobriety. Then I started believing that he was right. An alcoholic without alcohol is destined for a life of misery.

I tried thinking of good things, but each thought quickly led someplace else and turned negative, dark, even fatalistic. Just like it's always been with me, I didn't know what popped into my mind or why my mood turned so ugly so quickly.

I remember having the thought; I just couldn't remember what it was. It just came and went, like a nightmare without the memory, leaving behind just enough of an aftermath to know it was too dreadful to keep.

Whatever it was, I was immediately compelled to drown it with thirty cans of beer and a fifth of vodka, a compulsion hit me the instant I saw the sign for Cumberland Farms. Everything after that was like a reflex. I pulled into the lot and made a beeline for the beer coolers.

I don't know how long I stood there, motionless, staring at the shelves of thirty-packs, but it was long enough to get the attention of the store clerk.

"Everything okay over there?" he yelled from the front counter.

Without thinking, I spun around and yelled right back at him.

"Where's the bread?"

I didn't wait for his answer because it was right in front of me, so I grabbed a loaf, paid for it and drove across the street to a small parking area inside Crandall Park, the same park I got lost in months earlier while looking for an AA meeting.

This park had what I needed: a pond, lots of ducks and what Mallory describes as, "The smell of the lake house, the smell of pine, moss, lake and dirt."

It's the soothing aroma of the Adirondacks, from Loon Lake to the summer camp where I spent my summers as a ten-year-old boy, long before I knew what it was like to need a drink.

I distanced myself from the car — just as I should have distanced myself from the black Crown Vic with Klonopin in it ten years earlier — and walked to a footbridge that crossed a narrow section of the pond. I stood there for a while, leaning over the rail, staring down at the sunfish basking in the warm water close to the shore.

There was a giant pine tree towering above a little lagoon along a narrow bend in the pond, surrounded by a thick bed of pine needles. I lay down in the middle of it and did something I'd never done before, which was to follow the suggestions of the people in AA who tried to help me.

I closed my eyes, focused carefully on the sounds around me and tried to paint a mental picture of what I was hearing.

For about a half hour, the only sounds I could hear were the annoying ones, like traffic moaning in the distance. But after a while, I could tune those sounds out. Every minute or so, about twenty feet away, there was a distinct splash, a *kerplunk*, like a stone hitting the water, probably a small bass jumping for insects on the surface of the water. At least that's how I imagined it.

Coming from the other side of the lake, I heard two boys, about ten or eleven years old, yelling for their father in unison.

"Look, Dad, look! Come here!"

My eyes were still closed but I could tell they both got a bite on their fishing poles at the same time. As they reeled in their lines, it became a competition to see who'd get their fish onto the shore first.

The boys had to be twins. At one point, their simultaneous yelping almost sounded like the Everly Brothers. After a minute or two, the competition was over. It sounded like the fish battle ended in a tie. They were laughing hysterically and yelling to their father.

"We got trout! We both got a trout!"

Their screams roused the ducks, touching off a chorus of quacking across the pond, then a triumphant muttering from a second congregation of ducks on the far shore, as they floated on with their bread, not a care in the world, but still a safe distance from the chaos.

When the commotion subsided, I opened my eyes and saw all of it, as clear as day, just the way I imagined it would be.

I felt better, but I decided to lie back down for a while, just to be sure. I tried to remember what I was thinking about before turning into the park. But now all I could think about was ripping up the maps and finding my way back home.

That was nine years ago. Looking back on it now, in 2022, with the hindsight of nine years and the perspective of thousands of meetings, it's hard to know if my experience at Crandall Park was something divine or just the euphoria of suddenly feeling normal again.

People ask me if it was a miracle. There are *miracles* and then there are miracles. There are miracles of God, miracles of science, miracles of nature and Miracles on Ice. There's even a Miracle Ear. For some of us, there's a miracle drug. It's just a matter of, well, miracles — and perspective.

The miracle isn't what happened in the park. The miracle is that I never drank again.

Newcomers to AA are always asking me how I did it. I certainly didn't do it the *right* way. I got sober by hitting rock bottom and almost dying.

"You are in a meeting," I tell them. "*That's* how I got sober. I went to a meeting every day. Everything fell into place after that."

IT'S HARD TO LIVE TWENTY-FIVE YEARS of your life under the influence of alcohol without being haunted by your past. Once you're sober, it all comes back to you slowly, one regrettable memory at a time, flashing into your mind at various times without warning. Sometimes, when these vague recollections pop into your head, a guilty conscience will complete the memory with worst-case assumptions, and the result can either kill you or save your life. I had it both ways.

The lake house reminded me of how far I had fallen, especially during my final year there. When Lisa and I first went back a few weeks after I got out of St. Mary's, no one had stepped foot in the house since my mom and my aunt escorted me out the front door.

My last beer was still on the floor, next to an empty thirty-pack container and a plastic bag of empties. I was stunned by the stillness and silence. The air was dead. The living room had the aura of a museum display or a crime scene, like there should be a body on the floor. I could see myself as that body, right where they found me, in the middle of the living room floor under the ceiling fan with Bam at my side.

This was the place of my dreams as a kid. It's where I found serenity after 9/11. It's where I came to live after things went wrong in the church. It's where I brought Mallory and Jackson, hoping to give them the best part of my childhood, and it's where a piece of me died when they were no longer there. It's where I lived a million moments I will never remember, and a million more I'll die trying to forget.

As I was leaving St. Mary's, my brother said the first thing I should do is "burn the fucking place to the ground." That's what I wanted to do in the summer of 2013, with me in it — not out of disdain for the house, but to eliminate any remnants or remembrances of my downfall.

By 2020, I realized that the lake house — as much as it meant to me — would always remind me of things I was working to forget, so I sold it and never went back to Chestertown or Loon Lake again.

Two years later, in 2022, Bam went to Rainbow Bridge. It happened a few months before his thirteenth birthday, peacefully, on the floor of our kitchen. A veterinarian came to the house when Bam was no longer able to get to his feet. Lisa was there, hovering over me and Bam, pacing inconsolably. I was right where I was supposed to be — laying beside him, on the floor, holding his paw one last time to comfort the beautiful soul who had done the same for me during the worst days of my life.

According to the song, Mr Bojangles was still mourning the loss of his dog twenty years later. That'll be me, for sure. (Only through the process of writing this book did I discover — and own — my myriad of propinquities to the homeless street performer from Tennessee.)

I've heard people in AA talk about the "gift of alcoholism" and express gratitude for being born an alcoholic. "Otherwise," they say, "we wouldn't know the glory of recovery."

I don't know about all that. Personally, I'd rather enjoy the glory of recovery without having to inaugurate it with the agony of addiction. And I would gladly surrender the glory of recovery to give my kids the glory of a life without it.

I'm one of the few people who wasn't shocked when Robin Williams suddenly hung himself from a closet door in the summer of 2014. At the time, Lisa was saying, "It makes no sense." It did to me. He had been living sober for years, but in the months before his suicide, he talked about going back to rehab "for a tune-up."

Sobriety is a dangerous state of mind for those of us who've spent so little of our lifetimes there. After twenty-five years of living on the outskirts of reality, you don't just walk out of rehab and fling yourself back into life.

You have to start all over again, which means repeating your life-long understanding of trial and error. Along the way, it's easy to mistake your past for your future, and that's when you start envisioning your worst fears of going backwards again. That's when you lose hope.

One of the most important lessons I've learned over the years is this: Everything that crosses your mind isn't true. It's one thing to have the thought. But once you believe it, the thought becomes a curse. I now know that the "mood spikes" I always attributed to alcohol withdrawal really had nothing to do with alcohol. They were still there long after the alcohol was gone.

The more I drank, the less I remembered; the less I remembered, the more I feared. The mood spikes were just bits of information trying to get through.

Like I told my mom, once you remove all that alcohol, God only knows what's hiding underneath. You must be prepared to see what's there and accept it, but only for what it was, not what you feared it was.

You can't escape your past, but you can eclipse it. There's no such thing as wasted time. Nothing is wasted. I'm no longer haunted by things that never happened. I just keep moving forward. Sometimes I stumble, but I never look back, and it feels good to be that free.

-The End-